NATURAL
COMPANIONS

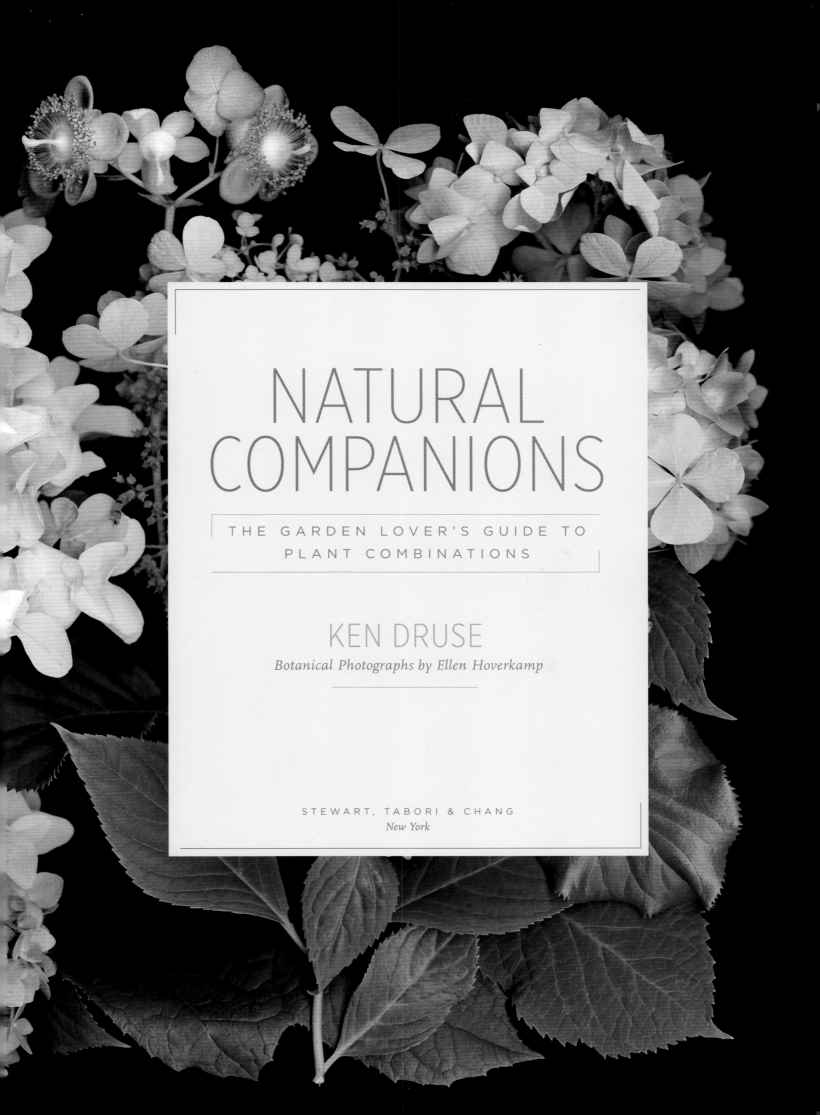

NATURAL
COMPANIONS

THE GARDEN LOVER'S GUIDE TO PLANT COMBINATIONS

KEN DRUSE

Botanical Photographs by Ellen Hoverkamp

STEWART, TABORI & CHANG
New York

Published in 2012 by Stewart, Tabori & Chang
An imprint of ABRAMS

Library of Congress Cataloging-in-Publication Data:
Druse, Kenneth.
Natural companions : the garden lover's guide to plant combinations / Ken Druse
with Ellen Hoverkamp.
  p. cm.
 ISBN 978-1-58479-901-6
1. Companion planting. 2. Plants, Ornamental. 3. Gardens—Design. I. Hoverkamp, Ellen. II. Title.
 SB453.6.D78 2012
 635—dc23

                        2011036180

Editor: Dervla Kelly
Designer: Anna Christian
Production Manager: Jacquie Poirier

The text of this book was composed in Scala and Gotham.

Printed and bound in China.

10 9 8 7 6 5 4 3

Stewart, Tabori & Chang books are available at special discounts when purchased in quantity
for premiums and promotions as well as fundraising or educational use. Special editions
can also be created to specification. For details, contact specialsales@abramsbooks.com
or the address below.

115 West 18th Street
New York, NY 10011
www.abramsbooks.com

Dedication

Louis Bauer

Timothy King Jr.

Contents

8 PREFACE

10 INTRODUCTION

22 **SEASONS**

56 **FAMILIES**

92 **FORM FOLLOWS FUNCTION**

128 **COLOR**

156 **SPIRIT OF PLACE**

188 **THEMES**

236 AFTERWORD

238 APPENDIX

244 ACKNOWLEDGMENTS

246 INDEX

Preface

I met Ellen Hoverkamp several years ago, when she was exhibiting her work at a gardening symposium. Ellen creates unparalleled images of plants—photographs—on the oversize, twelve-by-seventeen-inch surface of a flatbed scanner. Her art is unrivaled, and yet harkens to traditions of botanical illustration and flower photography—kind of Imogen Cunningham meets Mrs. Delany, the botanical collage artist from the 1780s.

I was immediately struck by the depth, beauty, and personality of Ellen's arrangements. As a gardener, I realized that the images represented plants captured at moments in time. It occurred to me that Ellen's work could demonstrate potential flower and foliage schemes and thus serve as a novel and inspiring guide to share with other gardeners and designers. And that's what we have produced here with more than 200 images.

Ellen has been immortalizing the plants grown by her neighbors and gardener friends since 1997. She travels in a minivan with a large cooler in the back filled with glass jars, water, and a bag of ice to transport specimens safely from their gardens to her studio.

"I'm in awe of what gardeners do," says Ellen. "And they let me have cuttings, which is like giving me their treasures. I've found a way to make a souvenir, a lasting memory of how my friends nurture nature. I want to show other people what gardeners know about the beauty of plants."

For our collaboration, I knew we had to offer more than pretty plants. I made lists of themes and subjects such as plant families, palettes, and other reasons to bring plants together. I grew many of the plants for our project in my garden, and Ellen went to her gardening friends, lists in hand, for more. We called in plants from friends in the Southeast and Southwest, on the West Coast, and at other locales around the country to be sure to touch on as many regions as possible. Then Ellen had to scan them.

Back in her darkened studio, she arranged flowers and plants facedown on the glass surface of the scanner. So they were not crushed, Ellen suspended some of the stems from wires. Following several trial passes, she created the final versions of the works you see in the book.

During the hot summer, Ellen set up a work space in the basement of my house in the northwest corner of New Jersey.

I picked; she scanned. In many of the arrangements, we tried to present a hierarchy as it might appear in a planting: from the low ground cover in the foreground, medium-size samples in the middle, and finally the tallest constituents at the top. The results in this book are slices of planting schemes, as if you could isolate a pie wedge from a bed or border to create an exhibition with samples plucked from the garden.

OPPOSITE Blossoms of night-blooming cereus (*Epiphyllum oxypetalum*) open for one night in late summer. The large, fragrant flowers co-evolved with bat pollinators in their native habitat. ABOVE Flower form and leaf texture in (top to bottom) *Acer japonicum* 'Aconitifolium', *Deutzia* 'Magicien', crab apple (probably *Malus* 'Prairie Fire'), and *Syneilesis aconitifolia*.

Introduction
THE TIME OF THEIR LIVES

The Edwardian garden designer Gertrude Jekyll is often credited with having invented the perennial border, but her artistic contributions go well beyond that significant accomplishment. She recognized the ephemeral nature of flowers, the persistent role of foliage, and that the most successful compositions combine texture, scale, and color from bulbs, annuals, perennials, shrubs, and trees. To create some of her plantings, Jekyll would wander through landscapes plucking blossoms and leafy branches to bring together, compare, and combine. I also gather flowers and foliage from my garden when I want to visualize a future planting, or if I need to find something to tweak an existing arrangement, I'll carry a flower from one place to the next, seeking new combinations.

The components of Jekyll's gatherings and mine have things in common; we both selected cuttings that either work together or present contrasts in form. The plants would need to have similar requirements of light and moisture, and peak at the same moment in the garden. Later, Jekyll might have placed her cuttings in vases to decorate her home or to portray in a watercolor still life. For several months, I brought my samples to Ellen Hoverkamp to construct her stunning arrangements. Our goal was to share suggestions for perfect plant pairings through her images of diverse species harvested and shown in their prime.

For example, at the end of summer when the garden really needed a boost, I picked a cobalt blue flowering spike from the gold-leafed bluebeard shrub (*Caryopteris* x *clandonensis* 'Worcester Gold'). I like to put lemon yellow with blues as a bright accent to make the subdued shades appear more vibrant. So, I cut a few branched flowering stems from a sunflower (*Helianthus* 'Lemon Queen'). The colors looked good. Also, the vertical spike of the medium-size bluebeard contrasted with the round, daisy-like sunflowers from that towering herbaceous perennial. Both plants have slender leaves, so I thought I should introduce something to add contrasting volume. I brought in a fluffy hydrangea known for its green-tinged flowers (*H. paniculata* 'Limelight'). I needed a

lower-growing plant with a different scale for the bottom of my conceptual arrangement, so I picked a leaf of a Russian comfrey known for its variegated foliage—in willow green and butter-cream—*Symphytum* x *uplandicum* 'Axminster Gold'. Next spring, I'll move these plants together.

When I buy a blooming plant from the nursery in a container, I carry it or just a stem of it around the garden. For the most part, however, I move plants that are already growing in the soil of the garden. New gardeners may not realize that plants are transportable. It takes a bit of confidence to dig up and transplant a prized perennial. But as gardening experience grows, one discovers that most plants—including small trees—can be moved.

We also learn that many plants *have* to be moved. As most herbaceous perennials age, their stems and roots become congested, and they stop blooming. These plants require renewal and rejuvenation: uprooting, splitting, and replanting. Not only do the plants become more vigorous after being divided, there will be more of each, thus enlarging the troupe and offering opportunities for developing the drifts and sweeps of color and texture that were the hallmarks of Jekyll's compositions.

You can record these bits and pieces for potential plantings in your garden journal, a useful tool for noting which plants to move in the spring. *Natural Companions* serves a similar purpose, but we bring the samples to you, and we present an extremely varied palette of plants to acquire. If you are composing a new planting, that's all the better. Find some of the plants you see in the photographs in this book to combine at the outset. Make lists to take to your garden center—like swatches to the fabric store—and develop confident arrangements with plants that hit their high points simultaneously.

THE PLANTS

The joy of getting a wonderful plant cutting from a fellow gardening friend has been an inspiration for this book, as well. To put forward a wide-ranging survey, we have gathered plants from colder and warmer climates than where I garden in New Jersey, USDA Zone 6, where temperatures dip to around 10 degrees below zero F. We asked gardeners to send

OPPOSITE (left to right) *Symphytum* x *uplandicum* 'Variegatum', *Helianthus* 'Lemon Queen', *Caryopteris* x *clandonensis*, and *Hydrangea paniculata* 'Limelight' inspire a future scheme.

us lists of their favorite combinations, and in many cases, we went to sample their gardens. (Ellen jokingly called these visits "raids.") A few gardeners from other parts of the country actually picked for us and sent their clippings when weather permitted. Louise Wrinkle provided us with a FedEx box filled with plants from her late winter garden in Birmingham, Alabama. Grant Meyer sent us samples from his Flagstaff, Arizona, garden. Ellen's plant patron Sandi Blaze invited her to raid her Connecticut gardens, as she has for years. When Ellen and I look at the final images of our friends' plants, memories of these people and the days we spent in their gardens pop into our minds.

When I visit a public or private garden for inspiration, I usually jot down the plant names (if I can find them), or take a snapshot of a section of a planting including the ground covers in front, the plants of the middle ground, and the taller ones at the back. In most cases, the plants are arranged in the scans to approximate their positions in the garden, from ground up—bottom to top. The low, creeping ground covers are usually placed to form the base of the composition, pieces

of tall plants or trees can be seen at the top, and medium-size plants in the middle. The plants in each scan also bloom at the same time and, therefore, may be planted together for a companion effect.

I do not pick from the gardens I visit, of course, unless I have been given permission. And if a gardener is open to the idea of trading plant cuttings to propagate, I am certainly up for that—at the right time of year. Plants in flower rarely make good candidates for propagation. The hardest time for us to reproduce a plant asexually or vegetatively from a cutting is when it is blooming and has put its energy into making fruits and seeds, rather than into producing new, young growth like shoots and roots. Then again, with a good deal of care and a bit of luck, there is a chance that a cutting might just take root.

Propagation is one of my passions. Years ago, I was giving a lecture at Mohonk Mountain House, a nineteenth-century resort near New Paltz, New York. A lovely bouquet had been placed in my room starring a hydrangea with a huge panicle of pure white flowers. I plucked one blossoming stem

from the arrangement, cut off the flower, wrapped the cut end in moist tissue, and slipped it into a plastic bag. Today, an eight-foot-tall shrub grown from this source blooms in my garden. Whenever I look at this shrub, I remember that beautiful bouquet and one wonderful weekend of an upstate New York summer.

In general, soft immature tissue roots fastest. That might be the stem of a woody deciduous shrub in spring when it is still new and has not hardened to take on the character of its mature state—green versus brown. Some plants, such as tropical ones, may retain their soft tissue throughout their entire life: Picture a begonia houseplant, for example, or a coleus. Outdoor, hardy herbaceous perennials, those that die back to the ground in winter and return with new growth in the spring, have their times in the season when they are easiest and often fastest to propagate, as well. In this case, too, the cuttings to root are taken from new soft tissue in mid-spring.

We only show pieces of plants in the images. Besides aesthetic concerns, we considered similar needs for sunlight, moisture, and soil conditions.

Another task is to decide how much of each plant is needed for the look you hope to achieve. Some will be planted singly, for instance a specimen tree. An arrangement of two is customary when formality is desired, perhaps two boxwood shrubs flanking the gateway to a garden. Planting in odd numbers—three, five, or more—always looks natural and well integrated.

To establish rhythm, you'll need repetition. Repeat the same variety of plant, or ones in similar colors and scale, throughout the planting. Heighten drama with contrast by juxtaposing textures, scale, and form.

To create a lush display, you will need plenty of plants. When I hit the nursery or garden center, I tend to go crazy and want to buy one of everything. It is much more effective, however, to buy several of one kind of plant than a lot of different varieties, which results in a polka-dot planting that will not hold together. The most eye-catching and pleasing presentations come from using enough individuals of the same plant—think of those sweeps and drifts of color. Use masses of one type of plant or another for the middle area, and for foreground ground covers. Consult mail-order catalogs and plant reference books to discover the ultimate height and width of a given plant, and estimate the number of each you will need—information that is not always easy to find.

You may not have to buy all the plants you need, since you can propagate your own, from seeds, for instance, or buy one or two of the desired variety, and make more by dividing those and taking cuttings.

Bring along your plant wish list when you go shopping, and also note one or two substitutes—either similar varieties or genera. Perhaps catmint (*Nepeta* 'Walker's Low') will work if lavender isn't available.

In order to make the best impression, you will want to have your plantings show up and show off by planning for a background foil. You may be lucky enough to have a low stone wall or be able to build one. Even a simple split-rail fence can work, and certainly a dark evergreen hedge is always becoming.

When planning a bed or border, decide which plants you want to form the structural skeleton of the planting. Generally this framework will be created by shrubs, but they might be subshrubs in a small garden or trees in a large one. These more permanent woody plants set the stage for the various shapes of herbaceous foliage and colors of flowers for the middle and foreground. Remember to leave extra space for young shrubs to grow. The area may look empty in the beginning, but patience will pay off when you find you do not have to dig up and transplant shrubs that are

OPPOSITE From Grant Meyer's Southwest garden in winter: A *Euphorbia rigida*; B *Aloe* 'Blue Elf'; C *Lachenalia aloides*; D *Opuntia engelmanii*; E *Bryophyllum daigremontianum*; F *Cassia didymabotrya*; G *Agave americana* 'Variegata'; H *Citrofortunella mitis* 'Variegata'. ABOVE Repetition of color, texture, and scale create a rhythm through a planting in Kingston, Washington, by the founders of Heronswood Nursery, Dan Hinkley and Robert Jones.

outgrowing their allotted place. If you cannot bear the sight of naked soil or mulch, consider planting annuals or even perennials for a season or two.

SEASONS

Dates on the calendar are not major markers for gardens. The calendar says the New Year begins on January 1. To a student in North America, the year seems to begin in early September with the advent of school. Imagine the first day of our summer, and then picture a sweltering Christmas Day in Australia when some poor guy has to don a beard and a Santa suit.

The gardener's year begins when the growing season commences. Perhaps that time we call spring begins when bulbs first appear or when we sow vegetable seeds indoors under lights or in a sunny window. In USDA Zones 2–8, we don't start seeds on a certain date, like March 15, but instead, six to eight weeks before the last frost is likely to hit in our gardens. After all danger of a killing frost has passed, we can begin to harden off our seedlings for planting outdoors. We take them outdoors for an hour the first day, two the next, and so on; move them to a cold frame; or place them in a sheltered, bright, and wind-free spot for a while.

Spring in the frost-free areas of the California or Florida coast could be said to begin with the end of the rainy season. All plants have a dormant period in their growing cycle, which is usually followed by a burst of new growth and often flowers. We think of dormancy in the northern states as beginning in the fall with shortening hours of daylight and impending cold weather, but dormancy is often a function of available moisture. In dry climates, plants like tulips lose their leaves and retreat to their underground moisture and nutrient storage facilities—bulbs—in summer. When cold weather comes to New England, deciduous trees lose their leaves. Like the dormant tulips, these trees will lack moisture—not because of heat and drought, but since the moisture is locked up in the form of ice and snow.

In this book, we show combinations of plants captured at a particular moment in the garden. However, everyone has to figure out when his or her own season occurs. In a climate where flowering bulbs flourish, the first open blossom

OPPOSITE Late May in central New Jersey (top to bottom): rare bulb *Nectoscordum tripedale*; *Paeonia lactiflora* 'Pink Dawn'; *Viburnum plicatum* 'Rosace' (the large shrub's pink flowers fade to white through the month). ABOVE John Bierne's *Cercis canadensis* varieties: light red 'Tennessee Pink'; palest 'Rubye Atkinson'; purple 'Oklahoma'; light purple species; dark pink 'Appalachian Red'.

on a vernal crocus (*Crocus chrysanthus* varieties) could mark the arrival of spring. That moment in Alabama may be in January. In Connecticut, it may be in April. The commencement of a new season is relative depending on where you happen to live.

The incredible dream of having every part of a garden appear at the pinnacle of perfection all through the growing season is just that: a fantasy. Even with a staff of professional gardeners, it would be next to impossible to achieve such success. In most of North America, flowering plants look good for days, not weeks or months as they might in places with moderate climates and cool growing seasons like Great Britain, New Zealand, or our own Pacific Northwest coast. Even in the most garden-friendly locations, however, there might be surprises: drought, flood, heat, cold. After years of synchronous blooming, some plants might suddenly stagger their flowering cycles and throw off the timing. Just as often, accidental associations could turn out to be quite wonderful.

When I give friends tours of my garden, I bring them to the places where the action is, and we turn our backs on those spots that are resting. There are usually several places to visit that are reaching their crescendos. Meander: Why race along the arc of the rainbow to reach the pot of gold at the end? Take time to enjoy the journey, and stop along the way.

Time is the common element in every garden, and in every image in this book. But as you'll see, we've arranged our plants to tell many other stories.

FAMILIES

If a plant is doing well for me, I hope to find other species and varieties in the genus to acquire. That is certainly the case with hydrangeas, and especially the cold-hardy and easy-to-grow *H. paniculata* varieties, of which I have about a dozen.

Which plant is related to another? Recognizing plant families may hint at individual requirements. For instance, most of the hydrangeas and their relatives like acidic soil. It's fun and fascinating to deduce which family a plant belongs to, but these days, learning a basket full of familial relationships is pretty tough.

It wasn't always that hard. There were thought to be fewer families even as recently as the turn of the last century. Taxonomists made generalizations based on physical characteristics. Pines are evergreens with long needles; single roses have five petals and so do many of their cousins; mints have square stems, so plants with square stems were considered members of the mint family; and so on. Modern techniques have made more detailed investigations possible. Now scientists use DNA analysis to confirm genetic relationships. The poor lily was once the patriarch of a giant family. Now it is lonely with only a handful of cousins.

The largest of all the families—Asteraceae, the daisies—maintains its standing, despite having had a member genus like *Chrysanthemum* split into a half dozen or so new genera like *Leucanthemum* and *Tanacetum*. These plants still have flowers that typify the daisy family with a central button of tiny fertile flowers surrounded by a ruff of sterile ray florets—the sun-ray petals of black-eyed Susan (*Rudbeckia*), coneflower (*Echinacea*), and sunflowers (*Helianthus*) are among the 1,600 or so other genera. Anomalies abound: Thistles like the artichoke are rayless members of the family.

Plant collectors sometimes fall in love with one genus or another and decide to collect as many species and varieties as possible. Think of the begonia collector, the daylily enthusiast, or the daffodil lover. Assembling such groupings drives the direction of combinations in some collectors' gardens. At the very least, accumulating more and more relatives simplifies the placement of the latest acquisition. (The new daylily goes in the daylily bed.)

Do these family matters matter to a gardener who is interested primarily in aesthetics? Well, we are all interested in why plants look the way they do and curious about genealogy and relationships. In this book we are looking at combinations and companions—associations. When it comes to associations, perhaps everything is relative.

FORM FOLLOWS FUNCTION

Simply put, morphology is the branch of biology that deals with the way plants look. Physiology covers how these physical developments function. In many cases, we gardeners are most interested in plant appearance. Nearly everyone puts fragrance high on his or her list too. Sight-impaired gardeners may find touch most important and like the way plants feel; the glassy surface of one leaf and the velvety texture of another offer an opportunity to contrast characteristics.

The shape of leaves and flowers is important. We appreciate the needle leaves that are the province of most coniferous plants—trees and shrubs that produce cones. The broad leaves of plants like hostas provide a soothing mass of green or, if they have variegation, excitement in a planting. The broad-leafed plants evolved to gather as much light as possible, and this suggests them as candidates for a shady corner of the landscape.

The more variety we bring to a planting, the more interest there will be, especially in the details. In designing a bed or border, however, we might be drawn by the form of a shrub with a bushy, mounding habit of growth. On the other hand, we can capitalize on the spire-like stature of another as punctuation—exclamation points for our compositions. We need to know how tall the trees may grow, and how short the ground covers might be.

Think about the stature and structure of flowers. The flowering stem of a plant or the aggregate of flowers on a blooming stalk is a plant's inflorescence. Some plants, like alliums, have hemispheric umbels, similar in form to an umbrella, with a multitude of flowers. There are plants like *Thalictrum rochebrunianum* with many small pale purple, white, and yellow blossoms in their inflorescence that appear like fluttering butterflies atop eight-foot-tall stems. Wisteria flowers are attached to a long stem or raceme, and lilac shrubs bear an accumulation of flowers on a panicle—a branched cluster of blooms. Many plants like camellias, single roses, and the relatives of the asters have simple, wide-open daisy blossoms.

When it comes to living things, flowers in this case, everything is about coevolution. A flat flower provides a bee landing pad for these pollinators and often includes a visual guidance system, for instance, a bull's-eye in wavelengths of light we cannot see but the bees can. The tubular flower might attract a hummingbird or moth with the corresponding long tongue or unfurled proboscis for sipping nectar and pollinating the blossom in the bargain.

The night-blooming cereus (*Epiphyllum oxypetalum*), also called queen of the night, blooms only once a year during the hours of darkness and then fades. The flower is huge—at least eight inches across. This Central and South American plant evolved along with its pollinator—a nectar-seeking bat that is attracted by its intense fragrance reminiscent of

wintergreen, anise, and honey. Most important for the nocturnal bat, the blossom is bright white to reflect moonlight in the dark jungle understory. Color is usually the most striking aspect of morphology.

COLOR

Aesthetic relationships encompass shape, stature, and scale, but perhaps color most of all. The way color is perceived is not just subjective, or sociological, but scientifically personal; we all see color a bit differently. Humans perceive color as light striking and reflecting off of objects. Each hue, or pure color, has its own electromagnetic energy visible to the rods and cones in our retinas. The rods are much more numerous, however, it is the cones that interpret shades and tints, hues and tones.

I've often said that I know what good taste is. It's no secret: Good taste is *my* taste; good taste is *your* taste. The way we "feel" color is also subjective. Colors may have meanings and associations. Black signifies death to some people; others might think it chic. There are cultural influences, as well. Yellow, for example, may stand for cowardice in our society,

but it means courage in Japan, nourishment in China, and mourning in Egypt.

Putting colors together is part of our art. You don't have to know a lot about color theory to make a pretty planting, but I find that what I've learned about color helps me adjust the picture even before I plant. For instance, I know how to make one hue pop or another recede.

The section on color will show many bright examples for inspiration. However, our examination includes green: the color we humans may find has the most visible variation. For the sake of a garden and its plants, green is often considered neutral, a foil for other colors and infrequently used as a major player. But when shades of green lean toward chartreuse, silver, or gold, or leaves are dappled and splashed with yellow or white variegations, they can attract a lot of attention on their own.

Ellen and I have assembled stems, leaves, and flowers to illustrate elements of color theory such as analogous,

complementary, and triadic combinations. But putting that all aside, I recommend finding inspiration anywhere you can. Perhaps a room with a window that looks out on the garden could inspire a composition to fill that view. Maybe a flower bed could echo a favorite bedspread or the muted shades of an antique Persian carpet.

It would be fun to interpret a favorite painting with plants using the colors or forms of its elements. It has been said that the paintings of the British master J.M.W. Turner inspired Jekyll. The sky's the limit for inspiration: Think azure blue and white with sunset pink and orange.

PLACES

Many of the plants pictured in this book will thrive in the most populated parts of the United States and places where gardening is especially popular. There are also many regional garden styles that may inspire planting designs. We have created a few images with plants for a California garden. We offer representations of Chinese and Japanese designs, and there is an image that features species like those from the rocky sunbaked countries of the Mediterranean region.

If pressed, I would have to say the noblest resource is nearby nature itself. Consider the small bits of almost wild areas that may be growing near your home. There are very few wild areas left in the United States, but there may be preserves and restorations that can serve as living catalogs of the plants that grew hundreds or thousands of years ago.

I garden on an island in a river. When I first came to this place in 1995, there was a tiny remnant of the plant community that had probably existed here for a thousand years. This "useless" niche had been saved because it wasn't worth developing. It was on the side of a large rock outcropping right against the river. It didn't have large trees to cut and couldn't be cleared for farming or pasture. So it was left alone.

Sadly, this patch of natives is gone now, having been overtaken by weed species that have crept into my county over the last decade and a widely planted invasive ground cover from Europe known well as vinca or periwinkle (*Vinca minor*), which spread onto the rock from a conventional planted landscape next door.

I put together samples from various plant communities around the country for Ellen to scan featuring indigenous plants. For example, we scanned plants from the tallgrass prairies of the upper Midwest, the forest understory of the Appalachian Mountains, a pond community in the Northeast, and a Mid-Atlantic meadow.

Although I admire the discipline it would take to establish an all-native landscape, I love too many plants to make that stringent a limitation. However, I did create a woodland garden on my property where I grow plants that are or were native to a ten-mile radius of the site—what I call "local species." I never collect plants from the wild, but grow some nursery-propagated individuals of the same species I first observed there. I gathered flowers from some of those plants for a woodland understory image (page 158).

I also have a planting in which I have included cultivated varieties (cultivars) of those natives, as well. For example, a ruby selection of the local bleeding heart (*Dicentra eximia*) that I culled from seedlings myself. I also have a white form of the Virginia bluebells (*Mertensia virginica* 'Alba') and white-flowered redbud (*Cercis canadensis* 'Alba'). Oxymoronic names aside, these variations should be kept from escaping into wild areas like alien plants, for sometimes cultivars and hybrids are more vigorous than wild species and could take over local populations.

If you live near the woods, a meadow, or a prairie, you owe it to nature to keep your exotic, fancy ornamental plants close to the house and encourage local plants around the edges of your property. Perhaps the most important thing for a gardener *not* to do is plant potentially invasive species.

In *Natural Companions*, we decided not to include known invasive exotic plants—vines like Hall's honeysuckle (*Lonicera japonica* 'Halliana') and the five-leaf akebia (*Akebia quinata*). We did not scan chameleon plant (*Houttuynia cordata* 'Variegata') or goutweed (*Aegopodium podagraria*)—monsters that spread any way they can and, once planted, will most likely outlive the gardener. We didn't even show the ubiquitous *Vinca minor*. All of these plants are sold at nurseries and garden centers and through Internet mail-order sources: It is a shame.

Some plants are harmless in one area and downright thugs in another. For example, some Asian ornamental grasses self-sow in warm climates and have invaded meadows and lawns. These same grasses would not be a problem in my garden because my season is too short for their flowers and seeds to ripen. The few *Miscanthus* species I have do not always bloom, and if they do, it is shortly before the first killing frost, which in some years hits in the middle of September. In any event, I keep an eagle eye on them.

As for a handful of these questionable varieties, I've noted them in captions with an asterisk after their names, indicating their invasive potential. These are plants to learn about or keep an eye on and, if they begin to appear where you did not plant them or spread a little too fast, to dispatch (in the trash, not the compost pile) and seek alternatives. If you think I'm being overly dramatic, just imagine if you had

to devote a good deal of the precious time you have for our beloved pastime constantly digging out a weed that you yourself brought to the garden.

I do not have plantings inspired by a lot of places due to the limitations of my garden's mostly shaded valley. I do have a Mediterranean-inspired planting in one of the sunnier spots. I love the plants my friends in Northern California can grow like *Phormium, Elegia, Farfugium, Passiflora, Furcraea, Citrus, Aloe,* and *Abutilon.* I have species in these genera that form a summer container garden and, in the fall, retreat to the cool sunroom.

THEMES

Ellen and I have also gathered plants to tell stories. Perhaps you would like to create a planting for fragrance. Or you might like a butterfly planting that attracts these lovely insects (and their larva). It might be nice to note some of the plants mentioned in the works of William Shakespeare. We have also found inspiration from gardens designed by contemporary landscape architects and by some famous garden artists from the past. We have tried to honor the late English writer and designer Rosemary Verey with an arrangement featuring plants from one of her best-known creations, the Laburnum Walk at Barnsley House in Gloucestershire in the Cotswolds. One caveat: People who live in the United States do not live in the United Kingdom. That qualification sounds obvious, but I state it here because there are photographs in some books and magazines of perennials and shrubs growing together in gardens that are absolutely irresistible. However, in most parts of the United States, with the possible exception of the Pacific Northwest, flowers do not last as long as they do in the remarkable climate of England. There, lilacs may bloom with roses since the cooler days allow the blossoms to last for weeks and overlap the blooming season of others. On the other hand, in 2010, "lilac time" in my garden seemed like one Tuesday in April. We simply have hotter days. In some cases, this heat has an advantage. Daylilies do very well in America, as do other plants that need the heat of summer to mature.

One of our themes could be said to have been inspired by 1930s English novels. We have a few presentations dealing with medicinal plants, but one garden's collection of

OPPOSITE *Eustoma*, often called *Lisianthus*, is an annual herbaceous member of the gentian family native from the American Southwest to South America. Hybrids of *E. russeliana*, which may be pink, violet, white, striped, single or double, are popular to grow as long-lasting cut flowers.

ABOVE Garden design for kids? How about a circular pizza garden with plum tomatoes, basil, and garlic in wedge-shaped beds?

beneficial species may be another's group of toxic denizens. Very often, these plants are the same—the critical difference being the dosage. A *little* bit of something could cure, a *lot* might kill. The foxglove, for example, is the source of the heart medication digitalis, but in higher concentrations, it is the means of dispatching a character in a murder mystery.

To take the storytelling idea a bit further, we have featured a secret garden with subtle plants for a shady oasis. In an even more literal way, we have let the plants tell the story when we feature the Victorian "language of flowers." There was a time when most plants were assigned a meaning, and people could communicate ideas through them that might not have been proper to say directly. In those days, a young man might pledge his devotion to a young lady by offering her a meaningful bouquet (perhaps along with a language of flowers dictionary). In return, the young lady might have expressed her acceptance, rejection, or indifference with the flowers she gave her suitor in return.

The Victorians also conveyed condolences through flowers. Many people still plan memorial gardens. Using flowers that signify sympathy might be appropriate. Ellen has made an image she calls "Heartsease" (another name for pansies) with comforting plants that have that meaning. We discuss plants for making a sophisticated cutting garden; another image features "farm stand" flowers. We talk about plants appealing to children.

Ellen's images and the accompanying garden photos are filled with ideas for combinations for various conditions. There are arrangements for shade, partial shade, full sun, and moist or dry locations. There are more combinations for several different climate zones and seasons. You may want to put a few of these companions together for a design in your garden, or you may use this book as a guide for creating floral arrangements with plants gathered from your garden or from your florist shop. Then again, you may just want to scan the pages with your eyes and enjoy the remarkably vivid, deep, and rich pictures.

This book may be just the thing to review when you want to take a break from spring's hectic gardening schedule and recharge your green fingers. Or on ice-cold evenings in winter, curl up by the fire and dream about future planting combinations with a pile of mail-order nursery catalogs and this book open by your side.

I'm sure you've heard at least one gardener lament: "If only you could have been here yesterday!" I know from experience that many things only last a day. The fleeting bloom of a daylily is a good example—here today and gone tomorrow. But rather than a particular flower, it's those perfect, ephemeral moments of just being in the garden that I most miss when they go by.

I don't want to freeze these occasions. I want instead to be truly present, and all too often, I am not. Traveling away from the garden makes being there all the more precious. (I'm writing this in winter, when thankfully, the memory of noxious weeds has faded, and I've recovered enough from the tough tasks to be thinking again of plants and next year's garden. In a month, I'll be champing at the bit to get back out there.)

There will be a day in early spring when the breeze blowing across my face feels warm for the first time. There will be the summer days when combinations, planned for years, finally click and come together. There will be the crescendo of autumn colors. And yes, there will also be the first snowfall with flakes as big as postage stamps or as fine as dust, coating the earth and turning the messy tangle of faded perennials angel white.

Author Allen Lacy wrote in his 1992 book, *The Gardener's Eye*, "Gardeners, like everyone else, live second by second and minute by minute. What we see at one particular moment is then and there before us. But there is a second way of seeing. Seeing with the eye of memory, not the eye of our anatomy, calls up days and seasons past and years gone by."

It's funny to admit in a book like this with its feasts for the eyes, that *all* of my senses are delighted by the garden. The sensations that summon the dearest recollections are often smells. There are the sweet perfumes of summer roses and autumn aromas like the caramel and toast of the weeping katsura tree's turning leaves (*Cercidiphyllum japonicum* 'Pendula'). Perhaps the smell that conjures the strongest memories for me is the earth as it begins to thaw: The plants stir and come back to life in nature's first season—spring.

Thankfully, Ellen's scans capture something about these moments—forever.

OPPOSITE In early March, Louise Wrinkle's Birmingham, Alabama, garden is already colorful with pink and white flowering quinces (*Chaenomeles speciosa* varieties), double pink *Camellia japonica* 'Debutante', and the white-edged dark green leaves of fragrant *Daphne odorata* 'Variegata'.

SIGNS OF SPRING

According to the calendar, the New Year begins on January 1, but nature's New Year begins in spring. When does spring start in your climate? The sight of the first robin used to be a sure sign of winter's end, but according to Ohio wildlife expert Jim McCormac, you're apt to see robins year-round now since their migration patterns began changing in the 1990s. If we are judging by the earth and sun, winter ends on March 20, the equinox when darkness and daylight both last for the same number of hours. That date is pretty much in line with the earliest things in my garden—crocus, *Eranthis, Iris reticulata*—but the saucer magnolias in my friend Tom Koster's neighborhood in Oakland, California, are already in full bloom by then.

When Louise Wrinkle's garden in Birmingham, Alabama, presents a surprise every single day, the calendar claims it's still winter. By March 21, her camellias have been blooming for months, the buds of the flowering quince (*Chaenomeles* varieties) are opening, and *Daphne odora* 'Variegata' fills the air with its spicy fragrance. The plants were scanned in February.

At least I can count on daffodils to herald spring—early spring—the first one to bloom in my Brooklyn garden, a *cyclamineus* type, opens in January. The daffs continue to flower by variety, through 'Toy Boat' and 'Irish Coffee' to ivory 'Thalia' until the very last one fades—in early July. Spring daffodils pay no attention to what month it is.

Most people think of daffodils as being yellow with trumpets and collars (corona and perianth), but there are, depending on whom you consult, between 20 and 50 *Narcissus* species, and over 25,000 named and registered hybrids and cultivars in 13 divisions of the official classification system.

A few times when I was giving lectures, I took an informal, unscientific poll of my gardening audience, and asked them in what month they were born. The response was surprising. Many gardeners were born in the spring. The number one month was April. March and May were close seconds: Aries and Taurus for those of you into astrology (I'm not). Perhaps people associate their birthday celebrations with the coming of the new growing season, specks of green leaves on twigs, the first flowers. I told my findings to a friend, and he said that was ridiculous. His mother was the best gardener he ever knew, and she was born in November. After further discussion, I discovered she was born in the Southern Hemisphere. Go figure.

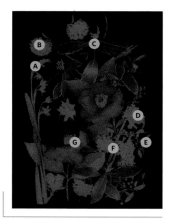

OPPOSITE Mid-March, Alabama: A *Leucojum vernum*; B *Edgeworthia chrysantha* flowers; C *Daphne odorata* 'Variegata'; D split-cup double yellow daffodil; E *Ilex vomitoria* (yaupon holly); F *Edgeworthia chrysantha*; G *Camellia japonica*.
ABOVE Many varieties of early May "daffs" in Sandi Blaze's Connecticut garden.

FRESH START

Allen Haskell, the late landscape designer, once said, "Anyone can do spring." He was dismissing proud homeowners' achievements with a flippant remark. I know what he meant. You can drive around old neighborhoods in March, April, or May depending on where you live, and see the riotous colors of evergreen Kurume azaleas—hot orange, magenta, and violet. And how about those spring-flowering bulbs that come with the blossom already formed and stored in the center of their onion-like layers. What do you have to do to get color from these plants? Stick 'em in the ground and forget 'em.

Nature's on the gardener's side.

The alpine plant authority Geoffrey Charlesworth wrote something nicer: "Spring makes its own statement, so loud and clear that the gardener seems to be only one of the instruments, not the composer."

Anyone can do spring, but not everyone takes advantage of nature's more subtle gifts. *Salix chaenomeloides* is a pussy willow that begins its display of silvery catkins every February in my Zone 6 garden—more than a month before *S. caprea*, the variety usually seen in public and private gardens, or sold as cut branches. The large shrub also bears handsome matte gray-green leaves.

There are even more surprises that appear weeks before the flaming azaleas. For instance, plants' newly emerging leaves and shoots—"pubescent growth." The flower buds on the wild red maple (*Acer rubrum*) trees swell, and the highway near my New Jersey garden appears as if a pale crimson fog has settled in the hollows between the hills.

The gold-leaved *Spiraea japonica* varieties have amber new growth that lasts for months before its leaves attain their mature chartreuse color. I've planted the early tulip 'Orange

Emperor' and later 'Prinses Irene' next to *S.* 'Magic Carpet' for a color echo. The flowering quince variety 'Cameo' blossoms in the background to continue the color scheme.

Baptisia species, herbaceous perennial members of the pea family, look like asparagus when they begin to emerge. The shoots on the cultivar 'Purple Smoke' are nearly black. Beneath these perennials, small, early "minor bulbs" bloom, including the pale pink glory-of-the-snow (*Chionodoxa forbesii* 'Pink Giant'), white *Puschkinia scilloides* 'Alba', and an understated baby pink grape hyacinth (*Muscari* 'Pink Sunrise').

Sure, yellow daffodils and red tulips and, forgive me, those garish azaleas pack a punch. Yet, there are so many other, more restrained plants that personalize the vernal performance. By selecting the most interesting plants and putting them together thoughtfully and beautifully, you can be the conductor of your own spring symphony.

OPPOSITE Late April, northwest New Jersey. (Left to right) New growth on Japanese maple 'Butterflies'; tulip 'Orange Emperor'; double-flowered quince *Chaenomeles speciosa* 'Cameo'; tulip 'Prinses Irene'; reddish new growth on *Spiraea x bumalda* 'Magic Carpet'; *Geum rivale* bud. RIGHT Early April, central New Jersey: (left to right) *Scilla bifolia* 'Rosea'; *Chinodoxa forbesii* 'Pink Giant'; *Stachyurus praecox* 'Rubriflora'; *Magnolia stellata*; *Muscari* 'Pink Sunrise'; *Puschkinia scilloides* 'Alba'.

COMEBACK

t is said that tulips aren't perennial. The recommendation for planting tulips is that you buy new ones to replace last year's every fall. The fancy tall bedding tulips with the largest flowers do not always come back, and certainly not with flowers like they had their first spring. Those bulbs have been grown in fields for up to seven years, and have had their flowers snipped off before they fully developed so that the energy built up by the green leaves went into making buds for super flowers. Once they have bloomed, it will take years to get them back, if they return at all. You would need to feed them and pinch out any flower buds for several years, not to mention simulating the conditions of their homeland of Central Asia.

The most reliable rebloomers are the wild or species tulips and heirloom selections. Some species produce multiple flowers, and many increase in numbers like daffodils. Most are four to eight inches tall with bowl- and star-shaped

blossoms, two to six inches wide. Most are red, but some are yellow. A few of these perfect rock garden plants have striped foliage, and several are fragrant. *Tulipa bakeri, T. batalinii, T. eichleri, T. humilis, T. kaufmanniana* (the waterlily tulip), and *T. turkestanica* bloom early. *T. linifolia, T. neustruevae, T. sprengeri,* and *T. vvedenskyi* bloom late.

My favorites are foot-tall versions of *Tulipa clusiana.* Their pointed buds are cerise and white, and open in sunlight into stars, closing each night for a week or more. When you go to buy these, you might find varieties like the white and dark pink 'Lady Jane' or others in cream or yellow and pink. Purists disparage these, but I say buy them all.

I grow a few heirloom varieties with "broken" colors— blooms with contrasting color stripes and flares. The original broken tulips led to the collapse of the Dutch economy in 1637, when tulip futures were traded on the stock market. One bulb back then was equal in value to a town house in Amsterdam, twelve acres of quality farmland, or twenty-four tons of butter.

A virus caused the variegated colors, and today, in order to protect the industry from infected stock, they cannot be sold. However, there are similarly colored tulips that mimic the antiques without disease. One heirloom is 'Insulinde' from 1914. This tulip blooms every year for me, and one season each flower lasted for more than two weeks.

OPPOSITE May, northwest New Jersey: (top to bottom) *Cornus* x *rutgersensis* 'Stellar Pink', a hybrid between North American and Asian flowering dogwood trees, tends to bloom heavily every other year. Pointed *Tulipa clusiana* varieties (cerise and yellow 'Cynthia', dark pink and white 'Lady Jane'); greenish yellow *Weigela subsessilis* 'Canary' flowers; yellow-green fuzzy foliage of *Stachys byzantina* "Primrose Heron'. LEFT (Counterclockwise from top left) *Corylus maxima* 'Purpurea'; white *Viburnum macrocephalum*; double lilac (*Syringa vulgaris* 'Charles Joly'); white bleeding heart (*Dicentra* [syn. *Lamprocapnos*] *spectabilis* 'Alba'); antique tulip *T.* 'Insulinda'.

The successful split-complementary color combination (page 151) can be seen in my gravel garden in late spring from hybrid Dutch iris, *I.* x *hollandica* 'Oriental Beauty', and purple spheres of *Allium aflatunense*.

COOL GREEN

Many of the "vegetables" we grow in our gardens are actually fruits—parts of plants containing seeds like tomatoes, squash, corn, beans, and peas. Then there are the true vegetables, of course, that offer edible roots, tubers, stems, and leaves. Some vegetable plants are perennials that will be in the garden for decades. Fiddlehead ferns, asparagus, and rhubarb have to be harvested early in spring either before the fern crosiers develop, their shoots reach ten inches, or the rhubarb bolts—sending up its flower spike. There are also annual vegetables to sow and harvest in spring.

Leaf lettuces do not travel well, and although greens are available at most supermarkets, homegrown is a treat—from garden to table in minutes. It is also quite inexpensive to grow your own leaf lettuce, and unlike the head-forming kinds (cos or romaine, butterhead and crisphead, or iceberg types), you pick leaves without harvesting the entire plant.

Lettuce is a cool-season crop to grow outdoors, but the seeds germinate best at 70 degrees F indoors in flats with individual cells filled with sowing-medium (plugs) so they can be removed with minimal root disturbance. The seeds need light to germinate and should be sown on the surface and just barely pressed into the medium or sprinkled atop a thin layer of fine grit or coarse sand. Successive crops should be sown every seven days (indoors until the weather warms a bit, and then directly outdoors for a few more weeks) to provide a few months of harvestable leaves.

The seedlings appear quickly, and when roots show at the outer edge of a soil plug, they are ready to transplant to the garden rows. If your soil is good—enriched with compost or well-rotted and composted manure, the lettuce will not need fertilizing.

Be sure the plants get enough water. Their roots are shallow: Too much sunlight or heat will toast the leaves. On the other hand, if the soil surface stays too wet, or if too thickly mulched, slugs may attack.

Leaf lettuce comes in several colors and many shapes. These plants may be used to decorate spring containers outdoors. You can also make a leaf lettuce border for a formal spring planting of tulips and violas, for example. Some popular varieties of leaf lettuce include 'Oakleaf' (shade-tolerant), 'Green Ice', 'Red Sails' (ruffled red), 'Salad Bowl' (lime green), 'Red Fire', 'Grand Rapids' (curled leaves), 'Black Seeded Simpson' (frilly, juicy, quick), 'Slobolt', 'Lollo Rosso' (pink-bronze edges), 'Ruby', and 'Rossimo' (fringed, bright red, puckered).

OPPOSITE Mid-May in the northeastern United States:
A *Primula veris*; B *Brunnera macrophylla* 'Hadspen Cream';
C *Tiarella cordifolia*; D *Antennaria neglecta*; E *Houstonia caerulea*; F *Brunnera macrophylla* 'Hadspen Cream' (leaves);
G *Viola sororia*. ABOVE Cool spring leaf lettuces come in many colors. Leaves may be harvested until hot weather ends their season. Seeds can be sown in late summer for an autumn crop.

IN THE PINK

The first rose blossoms herald the last days of spring and hint of summer ahead. One of my dreams has always been to grow roses as if they were regular garden shrubs among other plants instead of the "isolation wards" you often find them in. That idea came about first so that people visiting a place with old roses (for example, Empress Josephine's Malmaison), could delight in the magnificent blossoms during the four- to six-week annual bloom and compare their fragrance, shapes, and colors.

The introduction of the "blood" from Chinese roses for breeding brought about varieties that bloom more than once. The longest-blooming, repeat-flowering bushes are the hybrid teas. But those plants are notoriously disease-prone. That's the other reason for rose ICUs. By the 1950s, when

"better gardening through chemistry" was the mantra of the home gardener, it was normal for devotees (or their husbands) to don HAZMAT suits (or not) for the weekly spraying of the roses with fungicides and insecticides. Putting all the plants together made that task easier. You can visit rose gardens and see plants in naked beds with mulch to keep water from splashing on the leaves. Today, roses are being bred to be disease resistant, ever-blooming, and easy. There have been successes, but these roses are not fragrant. If there is a solution, the discovery of the perfect rose, it lies in the future.

I grow some English shrub roses bred by David Austin. They are fragrant and some of them are fairly disease resistant. But I try to grow all of the roses in my garden with other plants with varying success. If there is any one tip to overcoming diseases without chemicals, it is to provide excellent air circulation if you can. Healthy roses resist disease. Place three new plants of each variety in a large hole in soil enriched with both drainage material and nutritious compost. Water the rose soil (not the leaves) weekly in summer with the equivalent of two inches of rainwater and feed them regularly. If the spot you hope to grow roses receives less than eight hours of direct sunlight in summer, move them.

My favorite companions for roses include catmint, colorful-leaved plants like the chartreuse shrub bluebeard (*Caryopteris* 'Worcester Gold'), purple smoke bush, and small trees planted to the north, like the red-leaved peach (*Prunus persica* varieties) and Chinese dogwood (*Cornus kousa*). Ground covers may be planted in front of, but not touching, the roses' woody stems.

OPPOSITE (Clockwise from top left) At the end of the third month of spring, peach pink yarrow blooms with roses: small single 'Ballerina'; large double 'Evelyn'; semi-double 'Mortimer Slacker'. LEFT (Clockwise from top left) Red-leafed peach tree; royal fern (*Osmunda regalis*); a young leaf of *Ligularia* 'Britt Marie Crawford'; red *Rosa* 'Dr. Huey' (in various stages); *Rosa* 'Abraham Darby'.

SUDDENLY SUMMER

It seems that the transition from spring to summer in my garden happens in minutes, rather than days or weeks. One day it's not, and the next day it's hot. The woodland wildflowers are fading, like the lady's slipper orchids (*Cypripedium* species) that grow along the path of a bed that mimics the forest floor. The small *C. pubescens* has a yellow version of the pouch that gives the plant its common name, while the largest of these orchids, *C. kentuckience*, has a pouch the size and color of a hen's egg.

Memorial Day, the last Monday in May, is the unofficial start of the summer season, and in my garden as well, as roses begin to bloom. In a quieter spot that basks in equal hours of sun and

shade, colorful foliage lights the shadows. On the northeast side of the stone wall around my gravel garden, one last *Cypripedium* is in full bloom: the showy lady slipper, *C. reginae*. Unlike most, this native orchid is not an acid lover, but grows in neutral to alkaline soil and does well in a normal garden setting. Every year, the number of flowers doubles, and the clump has become a destination for early summer garden visitors. They come to pay homage to such a spectacular example of nature's work. Lucky for us, some intrepid nurseries are growing these plants, and they are available to us through the mail.

A grapevine (*Vitis vinifera* 'Incana') crawls along the top of the wall, with gray-green leaves that are pure silver underneath. Nearby, a golden *Filipendula ulmaria* 'Aurea' is forming buds for its fuzzy cream flowers.

There is a three- to four-foot-tall shrub growing in a sunnier spot across the garden, and as spring turns to summer, the 'Ballerina' rose is covered with clusters of little single blossoms—pale pink on the edges, near white inside. The rose is perfectly underplanted with one of the best perennial partners for these shrubs—catmint (*nepeta* varieties). The wands of catmint are covered with hairs that repel water, so it does not encourage the diseases that might also attack the rose—unless, that is, it is growing in a wet, shaded spot with poor air circulation. If a bad location was chosen, both the catmint and the rose would be under attack.

Some years I cut the catmint back early so that it will grow shorter and not flop over when shaded by the rose, but then the blossoming does not coincide with the rose's. So, I've taken to poking nearly a dozen stakes into the ground that stick up 12 inches or so, and I zigzag jute twine between them. The catmint grows up through this cat's-cradle frame.

OPPOSITE (Clockwise from top) *Vitis vinifera* 'Argentea' is an ornamental grape with silver beneath its leaves; *Campanula garantica* 'Dickson's Gold' (blue flowers); *Sedum rupestre* 'Angelique'; the showy orchid *Cypripedium reginae*; and chartreuse *Filipendula ulmaria* 'Aurea'. **ABOVE** What to plant with roses, to hide their knobby knees? Drought-tolerant sub-shrubs like chartreuse-leaved *Caryopteris* x *clandonensis* 'Worcester Gold' (top), and catmint (*Nepeta* varieties) with a pink rose (R. 'Ballerina').

IT'S ALL GREEK TO ME

Jerusalem sage (*Phlomis russeliana*) originated in the Middle East. *Digitalis grandiflora* (syn. *D. ambigua*) comes from the mountainous regions of Europe and parts of Asia. This creamy-yellow foxglove is one true perennial in a genus that features mostly biennial species. Shade-tolerant Japanese Hakone grass (*Hakonechloa macra*) obviously comes from that country. For decades the very slow-growing variegated variety 'Aureola' was the most popular garden selection, but in the first decade of the twenty-first century, several cultivars have gained in popularity. These versions grow faster, including 'All Gold', which is a stunning yellow grass.

Greek valerian is the common name for a plant that hails from the eastern half of the United States. Also called Jacob's ladder, one selection is *Polemonium reptans* 'Stairway to Heaven' found by Bill Cullina—the best of the variegated forms, others of which may be lax or barely perennial. *Reptans* means creeping (perhaps a reference to something underground), but this one grows to two feet and is topped by blue-violet flowers from late spring into early summer.

All of these plants are lovely together in a very cosmopolitan yellow planting scheme along with a touch of that color's complement: violet blue.

Hydrangeas are not Greek. The genus is practically circum-global with species originating in Asia and North and South America, and cousins like *Deutzia* and mock orange (*Philadelphus*). The blooming season lasts most of the summer. Most scientific names for plants are Latin in origin, but not the hydrangea's. The name means water vessel in Greek, and it describes the plants' seed capsule. (The origin of the name of another cousin, *Kirengeshoma*, is Japanese.)

There are many good reasons to learn plants' real, scientific names, be they Latin, Greek, or of any other origin. If you are hoping to find out about a plant, the scientific name is the way to go, since it is universal. *Hydrangea* bears the same name in Topeka, Kansas, and Tokyo, Japan—this plant's country of origin. Few people refer to *Hydrangea macrophylla* by the common names mophead or Hortensia. We call them hydrangea. Learning the actual names helps each type to stand out and, therefore, receive the fine-tuned care it needs. If you think you will never be able to learn the names of the plants, consider how many you already know: hydrangea, rhododendron, chrysanthemum, philodendron, begonia, and so on!

OPPOSITE With the most hours of daylight, some flowers in my garden synchronize. A color scheme of yellow with a touch of blue growing in light shade. (Left to right) Hakone, or Japanese forest grass (*Hakonechloa macra* 'All Gold'); variegated Jacob's ladder (*Polemonium reptans* 'Stairway to Heaven'); the yellow flowered Jerusalem sage (*Phlomis russeliana*); violet *Polemonium* flowers; perennial foxglove (*Digitalis grandiflora*); and variegated *Lysimachia punctata* 'Alexander'. ABOVE Pure summer: a collection of single and double varieties of *Hydrangea macrophylla*. *Hydrangea* is Greek derived from the words describing the shape of the fruit or capsule—water (*hydro*) and jar (*aggeion*).

FRESH
FROM THE GARDEN

Summer garden flowers, especially annuals from seed, beg to be cut for the house. There are ways to make flowers last as long as possible. Cut early in the morning when the blossoms are full of moisture and the air is cool. Some flowers cut in bud will open; others will not. Roses, irises, gladiolas, and daffodils can be cut in bud (give daffs their own vase; they shorten the lives of other flowers). Lilacs should be cut when half of the buds have opened. Marigolds, delphiniums, dianthus, and zinnias should be cut when they are completely open. Try to collect zinnias when the ray florets (the sterile flowers around the outside) are unfurled, but the tiny fertile ray florets (at the center of the flower) are just beginning to bloom.

Carry a bucket of water, and a very sharp knife. Immediately plunge the cut stems in deep water. Bring the flowers into a cool place. The stems may be left submerged for hours.

You should always recut the stems before you use them and, if possible, underwater. Air bubbles can get into the soda-straw-like tubes within the stems and seal them—trapping some water in the stem, but also keeping more water out.

A few exceptions are plants like poppies, which have sap in their stems. Those plants should be recut, and the tip of the stem held over a flame until it blackens. Woody plants like shrubs should have their ends smashed with a hammer, slit a few times about two inches up the stem lengthwise, and/or have the bark scraped from the bottom few inches to expose the most area to water.

Store-bought packets of preservative work, or you can make your own. Mix one part naturally sweetened citric soda like 7Up to three parts water for a bacteria-deterring, nutritional solution. Other home remedies also have some value. A penny in the water may help reduce fungus. Aspirin is acidic and prevents bacteria growth just like the citric acid, as does a quarter teaspoon of bleach per quart of water.

Flowers will last longest if kept cool—even in cold storage, down to 38 degrees F. Keep flowers in the house out of direct sun and do not put arrangements near fruit, which gives off ethylene gas, shortening their life. Most important: recut the stems and change the water every day. I use warm water, except for bulbs. Sometimes, warm or even hot water may revive a wilted flower.

OPPOSITE In high summer, the annuals grown from seeds sown at the end of last winter are in bloom, for example cheerful zinnias. These flowers are ready to cut when the fertile florets at the center of the blossom (the disc) are just beginning to open. LEFT Non-invasive annual white Queen Anne's lace–like *Ammi majus*, dark pink dahlias, chartreuse *Nicotiana* 'Lime Green', and orange-red *Gomphrena* 'Strawberry Fields' (globe amaranth).

AUTUMN IN NEW YORK

Every fall, Wave Hill, the public garden in the Bronx, holds their Gardener's Picnic. It is a very popular event for people interested in horticulture (and plant sales). The big draw is Wave Hill's incredible gardens, which look great throughout the year (even in winter), but most of all in autumn. Of course, the backdrop of New Jersey's Palisades—cliffs across the Hudson River—and sunsets beyond the George Washington Bridge don't hurt.

Marco Polo Stufano, the former director of horticulture at Wave Hill, is one of the few people in the United States who gets to introduce unusual plants to gardeners. When I've met up with him at lectures touting "new" plants, he often scoffs, "We grew that at Wave Hill twenty years ago," or "We threw that on the compost at Wave Hill twenty years ago." I admire his ability to toss a less-than-stellar plant and move on to brighter things. I've coddled sickly plants for decades until they finally gave up the ghost.

A trip to Wave Hill's gardens, now directed by Scott Canning, is like delving into the pages of a living catalog of must-have treasures. On a recent trip, I met a purple-leafed form of the ground cover *Salvia lyrata*, a variegated nettle (*Boehmeria nipononivea* 'Kogane Mushi'), a short yellow-flowered *Crocosmia*, and the hardy autumn shrub *Loropetalum chinensis* 'Rubrum' with magenta ribbon flowers growing in a pot in the sunny herb garden.

In the fall, the Wild Garden blooms with discoveries. And the planted containers around the twenty-eight-acre property, filled with tropicals, are equally enlightening. Fortunately, labels accompany most specimens. There are selections that were found and introduced at Wave Hill, like *Boltonia asteroides* 'Nally's Lime Dots', a rayless daisy family member that sports chartreuse pompoms atop five-foot-tall stems in the fall.

Wave Hill is famous for its containers, many of which are planted as late as July 4 to look perfect for the September picnic. Autumn is peak time for the tropical plants—just before frost when they are to be brought indoors, used for cuttings, or struck down by cold. Great containers can also be found in the Scott Arboretum at Swarthmore College in Pennsylvania under the direction of Andrew Bunting; in Steve Silk's Connecticut backyard—photographed to illustrate his articles and books; and planted by Dan Benarcik in the entry garden of Chanticleer in Wayne, PA—one of the most innovative gardens in the East today.

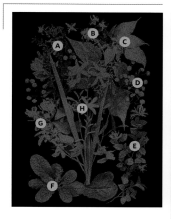

OPPOSITE Plants for sun in early autumn at "The Wild Garden" of Wave Hill: A *Salvia coccinea* 'Forest Fire'; B *Clematis terniflora*; C *Boehmeria nipononivea* 'Kogane Mushi'; D *Boltonia asteroides* 'Nally's Lime Dots'; E *Loropetalum chinensis* var. *rubrum*; F *Salvia lyrata* 'Purple Knockout'; G *Euphorbia marginata*; H *Crocosmia* 'George Davidson'. ABOVE In the shortening days of September, a perennial goldenrod combines beautifully with its partner, a refined hybrid of the annual *Salvia splendens*.

MADE IN THE SHADE

No plant can grow in the dark, and only a few will thrive if no direct sun ever strikes their leaves—even if the light from the open sky is bright. I wish I had more sun. It would be nice to be able to grow more tomatoes and have perennials that do not lean toward the light. I suppose I should be careful what I wish for. When the temperature approaches 100 degrees F, the last thing I would want to do is weed a sunny border.

Shade provides shelter and psychological comfort. In the shady places like a woodland, for instance, there is a quiet peace that encourages primordial reflection. One reason for this reminder to renew our connection to the natural world is that plants in the shady garden have to be viewed up close and personal, for a beetle's-eye view of the delicate flowers and often elegant foliage.

There are shady spots in most gardens. Buildings may block the sun, and there isn't much you can do about that, although painting a structure white will amplify the reflected light. Most shade comes from trees, above. Trees with tiny leaves like honey locust may produce dappled shade, with patches of sunlight that are always moving.

Many of the plants that bloom in the shade come from the forests of the world. These may be spring bulbs and woodland ephemerals, which are pollinated, develop fruit and seed, replenish themselves through photosynthesis, and sometimes become dormant by the time the leaves on the trees have fully expanded and cast the forest understory in shadow for the summer.

Perhaps the greatest challenge to the shade gardener is dry soil when tree roots are competing for moisture. A few choices could include *Epimedium* species and hybrids, *Kirengeshoma koreana* and *K. palmata*, *Begonia grandis* and *Tricyrtis* varieties. Bulbs and corms that bloom in early fall act a bit like spring flowers, only backward. Fall crocus and colchicum bloom late, but without leaves (those appear in spring). *Lycoris* and *Amaryllis* (not the tropical indoor plant, *Hippeastrum*), with common names like surprise lily and naked ladies, also bloom without foliage. Many hardy cyclamen blossom in late summer and their flowers are followed by leaves that remain evergreen through the winter, even under the snow, to absorb light and replenish their underground bulb-like corms for next year's flowering.

OPPOSITE Fall flowers in a shady part of the Wild Garden at Wave Hill: A *Begonia grandis* 'Alba'; B *Keringoshima koreana*; C *Tricyrtis hirta*; D *Strobilanthes attenuata* (flower bud); E *Cyclamen hederifolium*; F *Colchicum speciosum* 'Album'; G *Colchicum autumnale*. LEFT Double-flowered *Colchicum* 'Water Lily' is called autumn crocus or meadow saffron. Place where there will be space for the foliage that appears in spring sunlight.

MUM'S THE WORD
(AND ASTER)

The gardening season in the Southeast used to last two weeks in April when the azaleas bloomed—followed by a bolt indoors to escape the heat. In the 1980s, Southern gardeners discovered that autumn was a comfortable, lingering season of opportunity. A few astute hort-heads noticed that tropical plants like bananas and even houseplants like coleus, which grew as large as hydrangea shrubs, lasted until frost in December.

To some people up north, the gardening season ends when the fall mums appear at the supermarket. Although I like most plants (as long as they are not invasive), supermarket mums leave me cold. Chrysanthemums in the garden are supposed to be pinched back weekly until July Fourth to make them branchy and compact. Most years, I'm too busy to do that. Anyway, I prefer my mums kind of floppy—natural. Favorites include the warm pink Korean hybrids (*Chrysanthemum koreanum*, syn. *Dendranthemum koreanum*)—like 'Franz', 'Sheffield Pink', and 'Korean Apricot'.

In autumn, I can find wild New York and New England asters in meadows and at the edge of the woods. There is the five- to six-foot-tall *Aster tataricus* from Siberia and the reliable space-filling varieties of *Kalimeris* spp.

This is a time to look at berries and colorful leaves. I try to be conscientious with my berry plantings since birds and other animals might eat them and transport their seeds to unexposed territory. The solution is to seek out local plants, or ones that have little to offer wildlife. The fruits of the winterberry holly last into winter, when birds settle for carbohydrates. Varieties bear pale gold through orange to scarlet berries. You'll need to tuck in a male plant for fruit. For example, if you grow *I. v.* 'Scarlett O'Hara', you'll need 'Rhett Butler'.

Autumn of course is when leaves turn. Maple leaves are famous for their striking color, and I've brought many *Acer* varieties to the garden, like the cut-leaf Japanese selections. But plants not famous for their autumn color could be, if given the chance, and that's why I grow yellowroot (*Xanthorhiza simplicissima*) and the Chinese quince (*Pseudocydonia sinensis*), a tree with colorful leaves and fruits and patchy exfoliating bark that looks like camouflage.

OPPOSITE Mid-to-late October: A *Anemone japonica* (after petal fall); B Peacock maple (*Acer japonicum* 'Aconitifolium'); C *Lindera glauca*; D *Chrysanthemum* x *koreana* 'Single Apricot'; E faded hydrangea blossom; F royal fern (*Osmunda regalis*); G *Sedum spectabile* 'Atropurpureum'; H *Mahonia repens* (leaves turn burgundy in winter); I fruit of hardy trifoliate orange (*Poncirus trifoliata*); J *Pyracantha* 'Gold Rush'. RIGHT Creamsicle-orange *Ilex verticilata* 'Aurantiaca; bluish New York aster; dark brown leaves of yellowroot (*Xanthorhiza simpliccima*); curly lion's head maple (*Acer palmatum* 'Shishiagashira'); oval leaves of Chinese quince (*Pseudocydonia sinensis*); and Japanese aster (*Kalimeris yomena* 'Fuji Snow').

One of the best herbaceous perennials for autumn color is *Amsonia hubrichtii*. Green plumes appear in early spring, grow to two feet, bloom with blue stars, and as the growing season comes to a close, turn pink, orange, and yellow.

IT AIN'T OVER 'TIL IT'S OVER

Frost occurs when the moisture in cold air drops from the sky and goes straight from a gas (water vapor) to a solid (ice crystals) that coats our plants, letting us know the growing season is pretty much over. But the garden isn't. Hardy evergreens have their ways of dealing with cold, whether they are pines or hellebores. After the colorful leaves of autumn have fallen, the garden is as subtle as it is in late winter—you just have to look for seasonal attractions. *Amsonia hubrichtii* has just about the best fall color of any herbaceous plant. However nipped by the frost, the color drains away, and if the weather stays dry, the needlelike foliage will persist pale yellow and then beige. Another plant with sensational autumn leaves is the willow-leaved spicebush, *Lindera glauca* var. *salicifolia*. Its autumn colors like lacquer red, burnt orange, coral, and yellow glow until the killing frost turns them all to fawn. The tan leaves persist until they are pushed off by new growth in spring. Brown is a lovely color, too.

The undersides of southern *Magnolia grandiflora* leaves bear a fuzzy covering of hairs or bristles called an *indumentum*. These evergreen trees appear to have sienna felt beneath their shiny leaves. One I grow with success is 'Edith Bogue', which tolerates cold and even salt where several were planted as a screen along the road. Unfortunately, 'Edith Bogue' does not have much to look at beneath her leaves. 'Bracken's Brown Beauty' is hardy, and the undersides of the smaller leaves are completely flocked. Large lemon-scented summer flowers are a bonus, as are the red seeds in dry fruits that follow them. When ripe, the seeds are released from the fruits but dangle—suspended on slender threads.

A few plants from the vegetable garden may still be colorful, like the bright purple pods of *Dolichos lablab* (syn. *Lablab purpureus*), the hyacinth bean. Fruits grown for ornament, like gourds, are other pleasures of the late autumn garden. The Chinese quince tree (*Pseudocydonia sinensis*) has hard yellow fruits. Although pretty much inedible, their perfume is strong enough to scent a room indoors for about a month. The hardy trifoliate orange (*Poncirus trifoliata*) bears attractive golf-ball-sized fuzzy yellow fruits.

Late autumn's fallen leaves, bleached native grasses, nuts, berries, and cones may not stop the show like summer's colors, but they are certainly worth a second glance.

OPPOSITE After the frost, bits of bark still provide garden interest along with a super-hardy variety of evergreen Southern magnolia (*M. grandiflora*) 'Edith Bogue', feathery herbaceous perennial *Amsonia hubrichtii*, the yellow fruit of the Chinese quince (*Pseudocydonia sinensis*), and magnolia fruits filled with scarlet seeds. ABOVE "Flower" arrangements can be made at any time of the year, even in November for the Thanksgiving table—just scoop up all you can find in the garden—the last purple lablab beans and ornamental black corn from the vegetable patch, evergreen sprigs, *Nandina domestica* berries*, and any interesting fallen tree leaves.

*potentially invasive in some climates

SLEEPING BEAUTY

There are camellias that bloom in the late fall (*C. sasanqua* varieties) and many more that flower in winter (including *C. japonica* varieties). Shrub dogwoods and certain willows are grown for their winter twigs. These are pruned hard in late winter to force colorful new shoots. *Cornus stolonifera* 'Flavarima' has yellow twigs; *C. alba* 'Argenteo-marginata' or 'Elegantissima' is a variegated selection with red twigs. *C. sanguinea* 'Midwinter Fire' displays apricot, coral, and orange on the same stems. Plant these so their south-facing sides—where the color is brightest—will be in view. Cut the three-year-old stems down to two inches.

Some of the colorful willows are red-orange *Salix alba* 'Britzensis', yellow to red 'Chermesina', and bright yellow 'Vitellina'. Hybrid *S.* x 'Flame' is red and orange. *S. fragilis* 'Belgian Red' is almost maroon. *S. purpurea* 'Eugenii' has purple stems. These willows can be cut back nearly to the ground every year, which will result in growth that is, depending on variety, four to ten feet tall.

There are surprising evergreen subshrubs like the variegated yuccas for winter in all but the coldest climates. Other early blooming genera include wintersweet (*Chimonanthus praecox*), Cornelian cherry (*Cornus mas*), winterhazel (*Corylopsis* spp.), spring heath (*Erica carnea*), winter jasmine (*Jasminum nudiflorum*), winter honeysuckle

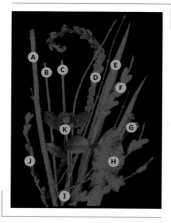

(*Lonicera fragrantissima*), *Stachyurus praecox*, 'Dawn' Viburnum (*Viburnum* x *bodnantense* 'Dawn'), and the most welcome winter shrubs—witch hazels with tiny ribbon flowers. *Hamamelis vernalis*, which grows naturally from Missouri down to Louisiana, blooms with yellow to orange fragrant flowers even before the vernal season—the source of its specific epithet. There are a few new *H. vernalis* with purple to reddish flowers, like the varieties 'Amethyst' and 'Purpurea'. (*H. virginiana* is a hefty North American shrub with yellow flowers in fall.)

The winter witch hazel stars are often hybrids listed as *Hamamelis* x *intermedia*. Most are fragrant, either up close, cut and brought inside, or sampled on the breeze. 'Rochester' has the strongest perfume. Popular varieties include bright yellow and red 'Arnold Promise', clay red 'Diane', copper 'Jelena', bright yellow 'Primavera', and soft yellow, lightly-scented 'Westerstede'.

The witch hazels want sun and moist soil, and for best effect, should be sited in front of evergreens and where the low rays of the winter sun can ignite the flowers. In leaf, these shrubs are somewhat coarse, and should be planted where they can recede into the background come summer. Some have good fall color.

OPPOSITE In the depth of winter in Zone 6, color comes from: A ghost bramble (*Rubus thibetanus*), silver coating has worn off; B *Salix alba* subsp. *vitellina* 'Britzensis'; C yellow twig dogwood *Cornus sericea* 'Silver and Gold'; D fishtail willow (*Salix sachalinensis* 'Sekka'); E variegated evergreen *Yucca filamentosa* 'Color Guard'; F early giant pussy willow (*Salix chaenomeloides*); G buds of *Viburnum farreri*; H leaf of *Arum italicum*; I coral-bark maple (*Acer palmatum* 'Sango Kaku'); J common pussy willow *Salix caprea*; K early red *Camellia japonica* 'Adeyaka'. ABOVE Late winter witch hazel varieties of *Hamamelis* x *intermedia* (clockwise from bottom left): 'Nina', 'Jelena', 'Arnold Promise', 'Sunburst', 'Diane', 'Strawberries and Cream', 'James Wells'.

AWAKENINGS

Although they often bloom in winter, as early as January, snowdrops are often thought of as the first flowers of spring. To most of us gardeners, the snowdrop is *Galanthus nivalis*, a slow-spreading bulb with strappy green leaves and nodding white flowers. A few years ago, I was given a clump of *G. elwesii*. That species has gray-green leaves, the color of leeks, and is not shy in increasing numbers.

To my surprise, a cult of snowdrops has arisen in England. Collectors wriggle on their bellies to examine the minute variations in flowers. Galanthophiles "ooh" and "ah" over slight variations in the blossoms: a spot of green at the tips, or no green at all, stripes, double flowers, cream-colored ones, or even yellow blooms. At Greenwood Gardens in Short Hills, New Jersey, they were planted behind a chest-high retaining wall to view without back or belly injury.

There are 19 species and some 1,500 varieties of this little flower. On January 31, 2011, one bulb of *Galanthus plicatus* (folded or pleated petals) 'E.A. Bowles', named for the gardener who discovered it, sold on eBay for £357. Variations may turn up anywhere, so keep your eye out for them.

While down on your stomach, catch the winter aconites, *Eranthis hyemalis*—buttercup cousins that open on sunny winter days, even in snow. They can survive subzero temperatures and bloom at below 32 degrees F. Proteins and sugars in the cells may thwart the damage from freezing.

The flowers we probably know best for blooming in winter are hellebores. *Helleborus niger* is the first to bloom. Called the Christmas rose, the plants rarely flower in December, but certainly do later. More common are the so-called Oriental hybrids—*H. orientalis* or *H. x hybridus*. These plants bear white to pale pink long-lasting sepals that ripen green. Competition has lowered prices and initiated a race to breed ever-more intricate hybrids with double or frilly sepals, and colors including apricot pink, daffodil yellow, and slate gray.

Though considered evergreen, one-year-old leaves should be cut off before new growth begins in winter. Be very careful not to damage flower buds or emerging new leaves.

OPPOSITE In late winter, *Galanthus* (snow drops) varieties hint of spring: **A** *G.* 'Atkinsii'; **B** *G. elwesii*; **C** *G. nivalis* 'Lady Elphinstone'; **D** *Eranthis hyemalis*; **E** *Sedum album* 'Coral Carpet'; **F** *Ajuga reptans* 'Bronze Beauty'; **G** *Hedera helix* 'Blue Moon'; **H** *Mahonia repens*; **I** *G.* 'Ophelia'; **J** *G.* 'Sherlock'. **ABOVE** Late winter in USDA Zone 8 is highlighted by flowers, clockwise from bottom center: *Trillium decumbens*; single white *Chaenomeles* x *superba* 'Jet Trails'; Japanese Andromeda *Pieris japonica* with lily-of-the-valley-like–flowers; white *Leucojum vernum*; green flowers of *Helleborus foetidus*.

Part Two

FAMILIES

Of the hundreds of thousands of plants on earth, gardeners are concerned with those in cultivation—either as ornamental or edible crops. Most of the plants in this book are considered ornamental, even if they have uses other than feeding our souls, such as herbs for culinary or medicinal purposes. We grow these plants, or hope to, in our gardens.

Plants are classified in a system of scientific categories, the first being class, and all with the most general characteristics in common are sorted together. There are two classes—plants with seeds inside fruit and those with naked seeds. Then there are the subclass, superorder, order, and next comes family. Family is where we begin to recognize our garden plants and where we can distinguish which ones are related. The number of plant families varies depending on whose organizational structure you are following—after all, these things change over time as new details are uncovered. There may be 150 to 300 families (we are showing some popular ones), followed by subfamilies that further distinguish the plants by common traits. Then there are the tribes, subtribes, genera, species, varieties, forms, and cultivars. *Cultivar* (cv.) is a contraction of the words "cultivated" and "variety" and refers to plants selected by horticulturists and introduced to the trade. So, you might grow a cultivar named *Kalmia latifolia* 'Snowdrift': a white mountain laurel in the genus *Kalmia*, of the species *latifolia*, and the Cv. 'Snowdrift'.

What's with all of this Latin? The problem with common names is that they may be regional or local, and not universally consistent. Imagine if a third-grade teacher called all of her students "kid." She might use a more descriptive name like "third-row boy." If the child got lost, and she stopped a police officer to ask for help, she might be out of luck. The officer knows that youngster by a different name: "redhead." But if everyone were searching for Jason Quimbly, they would have a better chance of finding him.

There are other reasons to know Jason Quimbly's actual name. For instance, when the teacher knows her students as specific individuals, she can better provide for their needs. (Jason Quimbly loves ice cream.)

The same is true in the garden. When you learn the scientific name of a plant, you will be better able to care for it: That's one of the best tips for successful gardening.

OPPOSITE Ericaceae members (top to bottom) *Enkianthus campanulatus* var. *sikkokianus*; pink *Rhododendron amagianum*; a pink Robin Hill rhododendron hybrid; red-orange azalea *R. kaempferi tachisene*; and white *Eubotrys racemosa*.

ALL IN THE FAMILY

t is unlikely that you would or could grow the wild white parasitic Indian pipe (*Monotropa uniflora*), which does not use chlorophyll to produce its food, feeding instead on a subterranean fungus associated with coniferous and hardwood forests across North America. Still, it turns out that the Indian pipe has some rather unexpected relatives along with other acid-loving genera from *Andromeda* to *Zenobia*, including rhododendron, blueberry, enkianthus, mountain laurel, heath, and heather: The family is Ericaceae.

Taxonomy is the area of botany that deals with naming, classifying, and sorting plants. Within the families there are the genera, and within those, species. With tongue firmly in cheek, horticulturists sometimes refer to taxonomists as either "lumpers"—those who want to group plants into large families—or "splitters"—the scientists who try to divide them into smaller groups. At one time the lily family (Liliaceae) was huge. But in recent times, former members like succulent yuccas, hostas, daylilies, and asparagus have been plucked from the lily ranks to join other families. At least a rose is still a rose (and in the family Rosaceae).

Family names are capitalized, and end in a-c-e-a-e. As for pronunciation, that's another issue. I've heard *a-see-ee*, *a-see-a*, a somewhat classical *a-see-ee-eye*, and other ways. (Who can correct our Latin? The Romans are long gone.)

But how does a plant like Indian pipe end up in the same family as the Japanese andromeda (*Pieris*

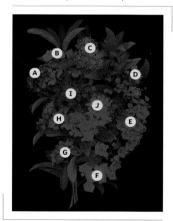

japonica)? If you look very closely, you might see some physical similarities between the little bell-shaped flowers of blueberries and those of the Indian pipe. DNA analysis confirms the relationship. In a way, it even seems odd that broadleaf evergreen rhododendrons and deciduous azaleas are in the same genus. (Although that may even have changed by the time you are reading this book.)

Rhododendrons, especially the broadleaf evergreen types, seem to have more lovers and haters than most plants. I can see this polarization coming from the overuse of a few varieties, and out of bloom, some may look like Volkswagen Beetles parked in front of suburban picture windows. But this is prejudice, plain and simple. Meeting more rhodies and discovering that there are glorious deciduous fragrant native plants and Asian species with chamois felt under their leaves will enchant the uninitiated.

OPPOSITE Nurseryman Dick Jayne's mountain laurel (Kalmia latifolia) varieties: A 'Bullseye'; B 'Snow Drift'; C 'Carousel'; D 'Olympic Wedding'; E 'Freckles'; F 'Snowdrift'; G 'Minuet'; H 'Hoffman's Pink'; I 'Kaleidoscope'; J 'Shooting Star'. RIGHT If you are lucky, and cast an eagle eye along the floor of an evergreen forest, you might encounter the ghostly white Indian pipe. Surprisingly, this parasitic plant without chlorophyll is related to rhododendrons—in the family Ericaceae.

Late winter at Middleton Place in Charleston, South Carolina, the oldest landscaped gardens in America, begun in 1741. The Rice Mill Pond, created by damming a creek to power the 1851 mill, features colorful *Rhododendron indicum* hybrids.

SOW AND SEEK

A cultivated variety, or cultivar (cv.), is a version of a species that someone has discovered, propagated, and put into production. The variety may be found by accident—when something special just happens to pop up in the garden—or intentionally by looking at a lot of plants from a mass sowing to see if there is one with a quirk worth noting, like variegated leaves or double flowers. Dan Heims of Terra Nova Nurseries, who has introduced more than 600 cultivars, says he often roams the benches of growers looking at thousands of individual plants hoping to discover a "sport"— a mutation that makes a plant unique. The cultivar name follows the standard binomial of genus and species, begins with capital letters, and is placed in single quotes, for example, *Echinacea purpurea* 'Green Envy', discovered by and in the garden of amateur Mark Veeder.

Cultivar names are not supposed to be Latinized. For example, *Cercis canadensis* 'Silver Cloud' has a modern name, while *C. c.* 'Alba' with its white flowers has an old-fashioned identifier: *alba* is Latin for white. It has also gone out of style to name a plant after a person, for instance, the hybrid *Clematis* 'Betty Corning'. (Naming a plant after a living person is still done, but if you're thinking of doing so, be sure to get permission, or just name the discovery after yourself or your favorite garden writer!)

The current trend is to use descriptive "fancy names." I'll make one up: a cultivar with pointed, compact red flower buds could be called 'Lil' Lipstick'.

Growers who discover a new variety and hope to make money on its introduction often apply for a patent. A patented plant is protected and cannot be legally propagated until the patent expires. There are companies that apply a trademark name to a plant after securing permission from the patent holder. The idea is to have the public associate the plant with the trademarked name, so that they will still ask for it by this registered name after the patent expires. In other situations, a trademark name is applied to a cultivar that has not been patented and may be propagated by anyone. If the name catches on, the plant can be mass-produced and the price increased. Whether this is legal or not, it seems a bit dodgy to me.

The bottom line: Become a "sport fisherman" like Heims, and look for happy accidents.

OPPOSITE When scores of plants grow from seeds, a random and interesting anomaly may appear. For instance, a green-tipped purple, daisy-like flower of the species *Echincaea purpurea* appeared as an odd offspring. Gardener Mark Veeder vegetatively propagated the plant and introduced it to horticulture. The cultivated variety, or cultivar (cv.), was named 'Green Envy'. Similar things occurred in finding the double-flowered *Hydrangea quercifolia* 'Snowflake' and the variegated redbud *Cercis canadensis* 'Silver Cloud'. LEFT A white selection of the North American hardy terrestrial showy lady's slipper orchid *Cypripedium reginae* var. *albolabium*.

X MARKS THE SPOT

Every offspring that results from the mingling of male and female genes is a hybrid. Most often, the parents are two individuals in a single species (called *intraspecific*), but we commonly reserve the term *hybrid* for the offspring of less similar plants, for instance, the progeny that result from the unexpected mingling of genes from two closely related species (known as *interspecific*), or Mr. Burpee's crossing of varieties: tomato to tomato, marigold to marigold. Seeds of annuals resulting from the cross of two varieties are often called F1 hybrids—first generation.

Crosses among species occur in nature all the time, but those involving more elaborate parentage are rare. A plant hybridizer intervenes to bring the pollen from one particular species, variety, or hybrid with certain desirable characteristics to another in search of cultivating features such as stature, vigor, flower color, and form.

Perennial hybrids are usually identified with the genus name followed by a proper name in single quotes, for instance, the deciduous azalea *Rhododendron* 'Viscosepala', which could also be listed as *Rhododendron molle* x *R. viscosum*. "X" indicates hybridization.

An even more challenging hybrid would be a cross between two very closely related genera from the same family. *Mahonia* (grape holly) was crossed with *Berberis* (barberry)—both in the family Berberidaceae—and thus, the intergeneric hybrid was named x *Mahoberberis*. This plant "mule" is the botanical equivalent of something like a zorse, the cross between a zebra and a horse. A similar process led to x *Sinocalycanthus*.

Carolina sweetshrub (*Calycanthus floridus*) is a big, sturdy, and reliable shrub for the outer edge of the landscape. In spring to summer, deep red flowers are borne that have a haunting fragrance described variably by visitors to my garden as green apple, whiskey barrel, bubble gum, melon, or lacquer thinner. In the 1960s, a closely related, unscented Chinese genus was discovered: *Sinocalycanthus chinensis*.

The Chinese sweetshrub has lovely white with yellow blossoms and pink centers that are larger than the Carolina sweetshrub's, but not fragrant. One hybrid came to be known as *Sinocalycanthus* 'Venus', with large white fragrant flowers. (Now known as *calycalycanthus* x *raulstonii* 'Venus',

the variety was a complex mix of *Sinocalycanthus chinensis* and *Calycanthus floridus* crossed with *C. occidentalis*, the California sweetshrub.) In the end, taxonomists decided that *Sinocalycanthus* wasn't really its own species after all. So, the allegedly complex intergeneric hybrid turned out to be the mingling of physically distant, but genetically closer cousins.

OPPOSITE The intentional crosses of species within one genus or closely related genera may produce interesting new plants. Various *Calycanthus* species have given us hybrids like white C. 'Venus' and the large red C. x *raulstonii* 'Hartlage Wine' with one of their parents—the small, intensely fragrant red flowered C. *floridus* (Carolina sweetshrub). ABOVE 'Athens' is a light green selection of the native C. *florida*, which smells variably like green apples or cantaloupe. A hybrid *Clematis* x *triternata* 'Rubromarginata' threads up through this sweetshrub.

IN THE HOOD

Besides the two classes, there are two divisions of plants with seeds—monocotyledons and dicotyledons. The former sprouts from a seed with a single leaf, while the latter sends up a two-parted leaf. Next botany lesson: Some genera have male and female flowers on separate individuals; most have both sexes in the same flower, but avoid self-pollination, perhaps by releasing male pollen when the female flowers are no longer receptive. None of that is weird, but one thing about the best-known cold-hardy members of the Araceae family is odd. The *Arisaema*, Jack-in-the-pulpits, can change genders from year to year depending on environmental conditions. After a season with good moisture and sunlight, the plant will be female, and following a lean season, male.

Plants in the family Araceae are typified by an inflorescence that has a hooded spathe enfolding a flower-covered spadix. These plants are collectively known as aroids. There are two North American *Arisaema* species, *A. triphyllum* and *A. dracontium* (green dragon), and perhaps 100 Asian species—we don't know for sure.

Some of the best-known tropical aroids are also ornamental houseplants like philodendron, peace lily (*Spathiphyllum*), arrowhead vines (*Syngonium podophyllum* varieties), *Anthurium* spp., *Aglaonema* (Chinese evergreen), and dumb cane (*Dieffenbachia*). For outdoor summer gardens, there are calla lilies, many tuberous-rooted caladiums, and elephant ears (*Alocasia* spp., *Xanthosoma* spp. and *Colocasia* spp.).

True taro (*Colocasia esculenta*), native to Southeast Asia, is an important and ancient food source, also known as dasheen, elephant yam, and as the source of Hawaiian poi. Eating *Colocasia* seems a bit startling once you learn that taro and just about all of the aroids contain poisonous calcium oxalate crystals. Dumb cane got its name for the near-paralyzing effect it has on one's vocal cords if ingested. Fortunately, the toxins in taro can be destroyed through elaborate preparation. I can't imagine how people discovered this cooking process.

Many of the cold-hardy plants in the family have "thermogenic" properties: They can raise the temperature within the spathe to attract pollinators (usually beetles) by offering them a warm shelter. Our eastern skunk cabbage (*Symplocarpus foetidus*) does this in late winter within its wine and mustard-colored spathe. The yellow western North American skunk cabbage and its white Japanese counterpart (*Lysichiton americanum, L. camtschatcensis*) also bloom in late winter before nearly any other plants. These arguably more ornamental species can be grown to highlight the emerging leaves of other moisture-loving plants like red maple with its colorful flowers and leaf buds.

OPPOSITE Araceae cousins are typified by a flower-covered spadix shrouded by a hooded spathe. Hardy and tropical aroid leaves and flowers in early summer from left to right: Call lily (*Zantedeschia* 'Crystal Blush'); *Arisaema fargesii* inflorescence (beneath *Alocasia* leaf); nearly white *Caladium* x *hortulanum* 'Candidum' leaf; three colorful small *Syngonium* 'Strawberry Cream' leaves; dwarf *Alocasia amazonica* 'Polly' with metallic veins; and a matte gray-green *Colocascia esculenta* 'Fontanesii' leaf. ABOVE Common swamp-dwelling skunk cabbage (*Symplocarpus foetidus*, bottom left and far right) blooms beneath flowering red maple trees. The Western U.S. skunk cabbage (*Lysichiton americanus*) has a yellow spathe, and its Japanese counterpart *L. camtschatcensis* (shown) is white.

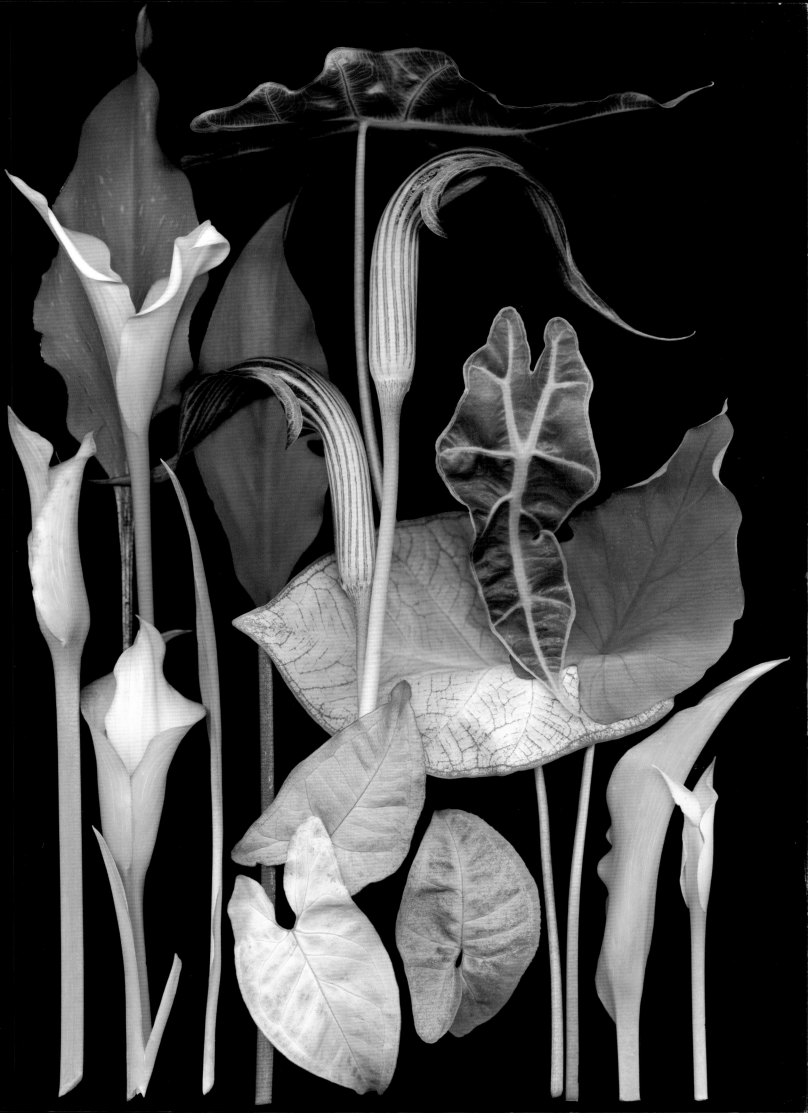

SUNNY DISPOSITIONS

The largest of all the families is the one that is probably the easiest to recognize. Nearly 10 percent of all flowering plants have blooms that look like daisies with a button at the center known as the disk, surrounded by the colorful parts, known as rays. These are the "loves-me, loves-me-not" petals that tell of the intentions of a hoped-for beloved. The tiny fertile flowers sprout on the disk; the sterile petals attract potential pollinators and give them a place to land. The combination of the disk and rays gave the family its former moniker, Compositae. Now the entire family has been renamed for one of its most populous constituents, the asters: Asteraceae.

There are some relatives that have given up their sterile ray florets. Thistles, like the artichoke, for example, only bear disk florets. Other rayless flowers include Joe Pye weed, globe thistle (*Echinops* spp.), and sea holly (*Eryngium* spp.). A further anomaly can be found in the dandelion, which has ray florets and no disk.

There are nearly 23,000 species growing in a wide band around the globe in all but the coldest climates, on every continent but Antarctica. Among these are some very familiar garden plants, like dahlias, chrysanthemums, black-eyed Susan, coneflower, cornflower, and cosmos. Succulent ice plants (*Mesembryanthemum* spp.) have daisy-like flowers. If you've ever seen lettuce bolt and flower, or chicory (endive) blooming with blue daisy flowers by the roadside, then you know those plants are also part of the family.

Many relatives have agricultural value, from the oil and seeds of the sunflower to the artichoke bud, or the tea made from chamomile. Many, like the dandelion, are weeds.

The name of the genus *Aster* comes from the ancient Greek word for star, and there are numerous species—if far fewer than there once were. After morphological and molecular research, taxonomists decided to split the group, and renamed the North American species *Symphyotrichum*. Gardeners are resistant to change, though, and many of us insist on our New England asters being *Aster novae-angliae*, rather than the newer *Symphyotrichum novae-angliae*.

Perhaps with all of the name changes, we should just stick with "daisy"?

OPPOSITE In summer: A *Ligularia japonica*; B *Coreopsis* 'Sienna Sunset'; C *Tanacetum parthenium*; D *Eryngium planum*; E *Achillea sibirica* var. *kamtschatica*; F *Coreopsis* 'Red Shift'; G *Silphium laciniata*; H *Centaurea cyanus*; I *Coreopsis grandiflora* 'Sunray'; J *Eryngium yuccafolium*; K *Anthemis tinctoria* 'Sauce Hollandaise'; L *Achillea millefolium* 'Terra Cotta'; M *Rudbeckia hirta* 'Prairie Sun'. RIGHT Wispy white *Boltonia asteroids* 'Snowbank; tiny *lateriflorus* 'Lady in Black'; pale pink *Boltonia asteroides* 'Pink'; dark pink *Symphyotrichum* 'Raspberry Swirl'; bluish *S. oblongifolius* 'Raydon's Favorite'; pink *S. nova-angliae* 'Honeysong Pink' (bottom).

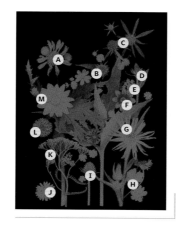

PEAS ON EARTH

Legumes include some of the most nutritious plants on earth and some of the most toxic. In this family can be found vines, herbs, shrubs, annuals, perennials, and trees. The family now called Fabaceae is the third largest behind asters and orchids. Most plant families can be recognized by the organs in their flowers. The pea family might be more familiar for the appearance of its fruits. Like a pea pod, the fruits have seams on both sides of the pods, one usually acting as a hinge while the opposite seam splits open when ripe and dries to let the seeds fall out.

Perhaps the weirdest example of a legume pod is the peanut's. Its flowering stem bends down to the earth and drives into the soil where the pod develops.

Soil is important in the development of legumes, not for what it gives the plants, but more perhaps for what the plants help to give back. The roots have a symbiotic relationship with *rhizobia* bacteria that can take nitrogen gas out of the air and make it available in a useful form to the plants themselves and others nearby in a process called nitrogen fixation. That soil-enriching benefit is one reason Fabaceae members like alfalfa are such popular cover crops grown to be turned under the soil and to enrich it.

Most of the pea family plants have compound leaves—pinnate or bipinnate like feathers or fern fronds. The finely divided leaves of many species appear to "pray" as they close up at night or on cloudy days. *Mimosa pudica*, called the sensitive plant, thrills children, closing instantly at the slightest touch or breath, and bowing when stroked. *Mimosa* has lent its scientific name as a common moniker to other species with similar feathery pinnate leaves and spherical powderpuff flowers.

In northern gardens, *Albizia julibrissin* (called mimosa) is a wide-spreading tree that can become a weed. In tropical climates, *Acacia* species (also called mimosa) are important trees everywhere they grow, as cut flowers, back-scratchers for elephants, the source of gum arabic, or harvested for expensive perfume.

Most Fabaceae flowers, however, are recognizable for resembling those of the sweet pea and grow either individually or together on upright stems like those of lupines, or in dangling racemes like wisteria vines. Redbud trees (*Cercis canadensis*) have tiny pea flowers that sprout right out of the woody branches of old growth.

OPPOSITE Ornamental relatives of the pea in the family Fabaceae, left to right: *Indigofera psuedotinctoria* 'Rose Carpet'; hybrid *Baptisia* 'Chocolate Chip'; violet and pink *Lupinus* hybrids. ABOVE Yellow false indigo, *Baptisia* 'Carolina Moonlight', with a background of the spring-flowering, gold-leaved shrub *Spiraea thunbergii* 'Ogon'.

A ROSE BY ANY NAME

A rose is not always a rose—it might be a flowering quince, a hawthorn, mountain ash, cotoneaster, or a host of evergreen or deciduous shrubs, trees, and herbaceous perennials. Many members of the family Rosaceae have showy flowers, and of course, there are some famous edibles like plum, pear, and almond.

It is at once possible and difficult to generalize about the family. The flowers nearly always have five petals. (Cut an apple in half around its middle, and you'll see a five-pointed star, a vestige of the flower's ovary.) Yet, the diversity of fruits is boggling. A peach is called a stone fruit or drupe, having one seed encased in a hard pit surrounded by juicy flesh. The almond is like the peach, only we eat the dry seed inside the pit—a true nut. A raspberry isn't a berry but an aggregate or assemblage of individual drupelets. The strawberry fruit is even weirder with its seeds on the outside.

Rosaceae family flowers are nearly as diverse in size and color. Deciduous flowering shrubs including *Spiraea prunifolia* 'Flore Pleno' have thousands of tiny double "roses," while *S. thunbergii* and the golden version *S. t.* 'Ogon' showcase thousands of single white flowers cascading along weeping stems. *S. japonica* varieties are known for early summer deep pink flowers and varieties with lime green to gold foliage. Ninebark (*Physocarpus opulifolius*) is a large, incredibly cold-hardy North American shrub that was long overlooked until varieties with gold, bronze, or even chocolate-colored foliage came on the market.

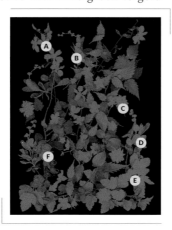

Herbaceous rose family flowers include avens, more commonly known as *Geum*. From a design standpoint, herbaceous lady's mantle, or alchemilla (*A. mollis*) as a frothy filler for the foreground, and filipendula species like queen of the prairie (*Filipendula rubra*) with tall pink plumes in summer make fine additions to a garden. There are soft-tissue and woody species even in the same genus *Potentilla*—called cinquefoil for their five leaves.

Many trees in the family are known for their beautiful blossoms. Think of the early-flowering apricot, *Prunus mume*, and Japanese cherry varieties. *Amelanchier* is also known as shadblow (for its coincidence with the shad fish run) and serviceberry. Plant lore holds that graves could not be dug for people who died when the ground was frozen, so the bodies were kept until the ground thawed, so clusters of the five-petaled white *Amelanchier alnifolia* flowers blooming at that time were used for the funeral service.

OPPOSITE Rose family shrubs include: A *Kerria japonica* 'Picta'; B *K. j.* 'Alba'; C *K. j.* 'Flora Pleno'; D *Exochorda racemosa* 'The Pearl'; E *Physocarpus opulifolius* 'Dart's Gold'; F *Chaenomeles* x *superba*. ABOVE Lavender flowered catmint, *Nepeta* spp., are perfect companions to plant in front of rosebushes.

HEAD OF THE CLASS

There are some 100 species in the genus *Rosa* in the family Rosaceae. They have existed for millennia and grow around the world, including a handful of North American species found in places like the tallgrass prairies of the Midwest, the West Coast, and in the East. I grow near-white *Rosa carolina* (Carolina rose) and pink *R. palustris* (the swamp rose), which I believe I saw growing in a drainage ditch near my garden in northwest New Jersey. The ubiquitous "wild" beach rose (*R. rugosa*) is a species that originated in Japan and Korea and came to U.S. shores in the 1850s. This salt- and wind-tolerant rose with crinkled leaves is considered an invasive exotic in many places where it has pushed out local species.

Natural, pre-hybridized species are considered one class of roses. Then there are old garden roses (those in cultivation before 1847 when the first hybrid tea 'La France' was introduced), and there are several classes among the modern roses that followed. Hybrid tea roses are the most popular of the modern rose classes, with pointed buds on long stems and thirty to forty angular petals on flowers with high centers. Hybrid teas are generally susceptible to disease, but these vase-shaped bushes bloom on and off through the season. Floribunda roses are useful landscape shrubs to four feet that are easier to care for, with flowers resembling hybrid teas born in trusses with multiple blossoms open at a time. One standby is white-flowered 'Iceberg'. Longer-stemmed grandiflora roses are larger shrubs that originated as crosses between hybrid tea and floribunda varieties, first introduced in 1954 with 'Queen Elizabeth'. Polyantha roses are twiggy, thorny short plants with large clusters of small flowers and are often repeat bloomers.

Miniature rose plants are like hybrid teas and floribundas, but the flowers are much smaller and on plants only fifteen to twenty inches tall. Mini-flora, or patio roses fall between miniature and floribunda roses in size. The classification of "shrub rose" comprises a variety of plants including hybrid *kordesii*, hybrid *moyesii*, hybrid musk, hybrid rugosa, and hybridizer David Austin's English roses.

Large-flowered climbing roses have long arching canes that need supports to lean on. Ramblers, or hybrid Wichuraiana roses, are not always considered a class. They are once-blooming sprawling plants that cover the ground or, like my monster 'American Pillar', arch from fence post to fence posts. The bloom time is late, but flowers continue for four weeks in summer.

OPPOSITE Types of roses are categorized by class: A hybrid tea 'Sunset Celebration'; B tall modern shrub rose, hybrid musk 'Sally Homes'; C miniature 'Constellation'; D shrub (English rose) 'Royal Wedding'; E shrub (English rose) 'English Garden'; F shrub rose 'Distant Drums'. ABOVE The first David Austin introduction was 'Constance Spry' in 1960.

LITTLE FROGS

Do you remember when your childhood playmates held buttercups beneath each other's chins? If the flower reflected yellow, and it always did, you loved butter. That shiny yellow flower shares its name with all kin in the buttercup family: Ranunculaceae.

There is another myth surrounding Ranunculaceae that tells of a Persian prince who was so beautiful everyone who saw him fell instantly in love. Besides his handsome features, he was said to have had an angelic voice. He sang as he wandered the countryside, delighting the fairies and wood nymphs. Too timid to declare his love for any of the nymphs, he died of shyness. A *Ranunculus* flower appeared where the prince fell dead.

Perhaps his voice was more like a croak, since the scientific name *Ranunculus* comes from the Latin for frog, *rana*.

The name probably refers to the wet places where the amphibians live and many of these plants tend to grow.

In general, plants in this family like moist soil, but not all of them. For example, a sure way to dispatch cousin clematis is to grow it in wet ground. Most genera are herbaceous with soft tissues, but some clematis and yellowroot (*Xanthorhiza simplicissima*) are exceptions.

Like all plant families, the characteristics of the reproductive organs reveal the common connections. Many species have whorls of stigmas with pollen-bearing anthers. Others like columbines (*Aquilegia*) have spurred nectaries that coevolved with pollinators like the butterflies that unwind long proboscises to reach a sweet reward.

According to the Doctrine of Signatures, plants that have medicinal benefits to us humans were once thought to resemble the parts of the body they helped. So *Hepatica*, which has leaves shaped like a liver, has been commonly known as liverwort since the Middle Ages. (*Wort* means plant. *Hep* appears in words relating to the liver, like hepatitis.) But be warned: Plants in the Ranunculaceae family contain the skin irritant pentadienoic lactone, and some may have toxic alkaloids and glycosides. Although poisonous to humans, they do have a benefit to gardeners, since many of the plants in the family are resistant to deer damage.

Members of the family bloom from mid-winter to autumn. Hellebores, winter aconite (*Eranthis* spp.), and pheasant's eye (*Adonis vernalis*) are among the earliest to show. Some of the last to flower are pink or white Japanese anemones with blossoms on tall stems that flutter like butterflies as the tree leaves above them begin to turn.

OPPOSITE Plants in the family Ranunculaceae: white *Helleborus niger*; double red rose-like, and double pink and white *Ranunculus* hybrids; pink and creamy yellow *Aquilegia* (hybrid columbine); green and reddish gray hellebore hybrids; yellow winter aconite *Eranthis hyemalis*. LEFT Rarely grown are the magnificent Japanese wood poppies—*Glaucidium palmatum* and the white form *Glaucidium palmatum* f. *leucanthum*—delicate gems of the forest floor.

Columbines, including the colorful hybrids, are Ranunculaceae family members. *Aquilegia canadensis* (red flowers at right) is a North American species that grows from Texas east to Florida, north through Quebec, and west to Saskatchewan.

LOVEABLE MOP TOPS

When you hear the word *hydrangea*, the big blue, voluptuous mopheads comes to mind. That plant, *Hydrangea macrophylla* (big leaf), blooms beautifully at the seashore, where the ocean moderates temperatures to extend the autumn growing season and protect plants from quick shifts from cool to ice-cold. In my USDA Zone 6 garden, the flower buds are usually destroyed in winter, since the season in the shaded valley is too short for them to ripen or harden. Recent cultivars like 'Endless Summer' flower on old and new wood, blooming twice for many gardeners, once for me. In some years, I also see flowers on the hardier, once-blooming species *H. serrata*, which is similar to *H. macrophylla* but with more slender dark green leaves. It is true that the pH of the soil affects the color of the *H. macrophylla* and *H. serrata* flowers: bluer in acidic soil, pinker in alkaline soil.

Although the name *hydrangea* summons images of varieties with globular flower clusters, species are made up of two kinds of florets—fertile beads surrounded by showy four-petal sterile florets. *H. macrophylla* varieties with fertile *and* sterile flowers are called lacecaps. The mopheads and fluffy varieties have mostly sterile florets.

Prior to the 1860s when the *H. macrophylla* varieties came on the market, the Asian treelike *H. paniculata* was the choice for American gardens, and more specifically, the ubiquitous variety *H. paniculata* 'Grandiflora', nicknamed "Pee-Gee" with its conical flower head or panicle covered with sterile blossoms. My garden's varieties include the early flowering *H. p.* 'Brussels Lace', greenish 'Limelight', large-flowered 'The Swan' (synonym 'Barbara'), dwarf 'Pee Wee', red-tinged 'Pink Diamond', and large and late 'Tardiva'.

I also grow selections of *H. arborescens* (smooth hydrangea), including *H. arborescens* var. *radiata*, which has dark green leaves with platinum undersides. *H. a.* var. *r.* 'Hayes Starburst' has double-sterile florets shooting from the corners of rectangular fertile clusters. The best known is *H. a.* 'Annabelle' with large spherical heads, while *H. a.*

'Grandiflora' has cloud-like sterile panicles. New varieties are always appearing, like *H. a.* 'Invincible Spirit' with slightly fragrant pink blossoms.

H. quercifolia (oakleaf hydrangea) cultivars are also usually white and include the totally sterile 'Snow Queen', large 'Vaughn's Lillie', and remarkable 'Snowflake' with sterile florets that continue to develop new florets in the center of the former ones. There are climbing varieties of *H. anomala* subsp. *petiolaris*. Other climbing family members include plants in the genus *Schizophragma* and the native scrambler *Decomaria*. A thoroughly remarkable, rare cousin, *Deinanthe bifida*, has extraordinary captivating flowers.

OPPOSITE A rare treasure for partial shade is *Deinanthe bifida*, the two-lobed false hydrangea. ABOVE There are scores of family species and varieties (clockwise from top left): *Hydrangea macrophylla* 'Endless Summer'; *Deinanthe bifida*; *H. quercifolia* 'Snowflake'; *H. serrata* cv.; *H. arborescens* var. *radiata* 'Hayes Starburst'; *H. paniculata* 'Brussels Lace'; *H. macrophylla* 'Endless Summer'; *H. serrata* variety; *H. serrata* 'Preziosa'; *Hydrangea anomala* var. *petiolaris* 'Platt Dwarf'.

SWEET AND SHARP

Even Americans who know little about trees can usually recognize a maple by its leaves. Canadians are more familiar with the maple leaf as the symbol on their nation's flag, which most resembles the red maple, a wide-ranging North American species that grows from the Florida Everglades to Southern Newfoundland.

Most people are familiar with the sweet syrup made by boiling the sap of the sugar maple (*A. saccharum*). Actually, all maples can provide sap for syrup, but the sugar maple, which made New England famous for its magnificent autumn color, is considered best.

The sap may be sweet, but the Latin genus name *Acer* means sharp and refers to the points on the leaves. Species in the family Aceraceae live in most parts of the temperate world. But it is arguably the Asian varieties that attract the most gardeners.

Nearly every Japanese garden includes at least one beloved maple, and has for centuries. During the Edo period (1615–1868), some 200 named cultivars were on record. Many of those were lost by the end of World War II. Today, the number of cultivars is up again, to nearly 250.

From a handful of species, *Acer palmatum*, *A. shirasawanum*, and *A. japonicum*, the Japanese selected varieties with an incredible range of leaf size, shape, and color on dwarf trees barely two feet tall to full-sized varieties of more than thirty feet. Tree structures may be slender and upright, mounding, rounded, weeping, spreading, or vase shaped. The dwarfs allow people to collect Japanese maples, even in small gardens, as long as there is sun. Some will tolerate partial shade as long as there are a few hours of sunlight.

The Japanese maples bloom from late winter to spring with small red, pink, or amber flowers that are often overlooked. Leaves in summer may be green, crimson, bronze, or purple, and variegations of white, green, and pink. Leaves turn red or gold in autumn. Winter reveals the graceful branch structure, smooth bark, and colorful twigs of some cultivars.

I tend about a dozen Japanese maples on my property in New Jersey and among them is a huge *A. palmatum* that could be more than 130 years old. That tree leafs out earlier than most there, with brilliant ruby leaves that then turn deep purple. In autumn, the color changes again to bright red and, later than all the other trees, litters the ground with crinkly colorful leaves. Beside the little pond in my Brooklyn, New York, garden, I grow a golden full moon maple, *A. shirasawanum* 'Aureum' with very round, jagged-edged leaves. There is also an *A. japonicum* 'Aconitifolium' with finely lobed leaves resembling the genus *Aconitum* or monkshood. In fall, it looks as if yellow and red dyes are bleeding toward the centers of its green leaves.

OPPOSITE A *Acer palmatum* var. *dissectum* 'Crimson Queen'; B *A. palmatum* 'Nishiki Momiji'; C *A. p.* 'Beni Otake'; D *A. p.* 'Butterflies'; E *A. p.* 'Karasugawa'; F *A. p.* 'Tsukushigata'; G *A. shirasawanum* 'Aureum'; H *A. palmatum* var. *dissectum* 'Red Filigree Lace'; I *A. japonicum* 'Aconitifolium'; J *A. palmatum* 'Nishiki Momiji'; K *A. p.* 'Rugose'; L *A. p.* 'Shishigashira'. LEFT A mature Japanese maple.

AMBER WAVES

The sure sign of germination is a hint of green as a seedling begins to push through the soil. We know most flowering plants have a two-part seedling leaf. Others sprout with a single offering. The symmetrical twin leaves come from plants known as dicots: squash, tomatoes, and walnuts, for example. The single leaf comes from a monocot: plants like palms, orchids, and grasses. Three of our most important food crops—corn, wheat, and rice—are monocots in the grass family Poaceae (formerly Gramineae).

Ornamental grasses became popular, this time around, in the early 1980s. We had discovered that brown is a color too, and leaving grasses standing through the winter with their decorative tassel flowers was a revelation to American gardeners in colder climates that usually had very little to look at through the winter months. An earlier love affair with ornamental grasses was witnessed at the World's Columbian Exposition—the Chicago World's Fair of 1893. Classical architecture, fountains, and artificial lakes were adorned with urns exploding with flowering grasses.

These plants come from the grasslands, where they colonize huge swaths of territory, which should be a warning: Grasses spread and may become invasive. Nearly all of the popular *Miscanthus* varieties, and annual and perennial *Pennisetum* are not recommended for climates where the seeds have time to ripen and self-sow. For that reason, our photographic scan focuses on grass species and varieties that are either native to parts of North America or, for the most part, do not spread aggressively.

The ornamental grasses are annuals or herbaceous perennials with strappy blades and tubular flower stalks. Certain evergreen grass relatives are important timber sources in parts of the world—the bamboos. These plants have hollow stems or culms and segmented nodes. The cold-hardy running types are among the most tenacious invaders and nearly impossible to eradicate. There are non-running, clump-forming tropical bamboos, but in cold climates, only bamboos in the genus *Fargesia* are safe to plant.

Grass-like plants are often included in discussions of true grasses. In wetlands, there are the rushes (Juncaceae) and in moist or shady spots there are sedges (Cyperaceae). To identify which group these plants fall into, native plant lovers have a saying: "Sedges have edges, rushes are round." If you cut the blade of a sedge crosswise, you'll see a triangle. Cut the rush—it is a circle.

OPPOSITE Clockwise from bottom: *Hakonechloa macra* 'All Gold'; *Chasmanthium latifolium*; *Melinis repens*; *Panicum virgatum* 'North Wind'; *P. virgatum* 'Dallas Blues'; slender *Calamagrostis* x *acutiflora* 'Overdam'; feather duster *Chloris virgata**; *Molina caerulea* ssp. *arundinacea* 'Sky Racer'; *Pennisetum massaicum* 'Red Bunny Tails'; *P.* x *advena* 'Fireworks'; *P. vilosum*; *Melinis nerviglumis* 'Savannah'.
ABOVE My grass "fountain" in early summer (left) and winter (right): tall *Miscanthus giganteus* with *M. sinensis* 'Gracillimus'.

*potentially invasive in some climates

TO SLEEP, PERCHANCE TO DREAM

f you had to guess what family the bleeding heart belonged to, poppies would probably not come to mind. Plants in the poppy genus (*Papaver*) are distinctive and easily recognizable, most often with chalice-shaped flowers having four to six petals with species in every color. Annual, biennial, or perennial Papaveraceae genera include *Eschscholzia* (California poppy), *Meconopsis* (Himalayan blue poppy), *Stylophorum* (wood poppy), *Romneya* (tree poppy, Matilija), species of *Papaver* (corn, Icelandic, Oriental poppy, etc.), and *Macleaya*, an odd exception with petal-less flowers.

The bleeding heart was once a member of the main Papaveraceae family, but custody of it and about half of the other species once lumped into the poppy clan has lately been given to the subfamily Fumariaceae. That family name probably derives from the term for smoke or fumes, since some of these plants may have been set alight and inhaled as medicines or hallucinogens.

There is debate as to whether Fumariaceae will one day emerge as a separate family. To add insult to injury, in 2010, an attempt was made to disband the genus *Dicentra*. This group was split into several new genera. The woodland types have been pushed into *Lamprocapnos*, although it is likely the old name will stick around. The climbing types will become either *Ichthyoselmis* or *Dactylicapnos*.

Lamprocapnos flowers are usually distinctive and complex, resulting in descriptive common names such as Dutchman's breeches and squirrel corn. North American bleeding hearts include *L. eximia* and *L. formosa*. There is a climbing bleeding heart vine with dull pink blossoms, formerly *Adluma fungosa*, called Allegheny vine or climbing fumitory. *Lamprocapnos scandens* (which may be moved to *Dactylicapnos*) is a climbing bleeding heart with bright canary yellow flowers. Another genus, *Corydalis*, includes plants that have flowers like small versions of the American bleeding hearts in pink, yellow, cream, purple, or cyan.

Plants in both the Papaveraceae and Fumariaceae family have things in common. They all literally bleed. The poppies often have white latex that drips from the stems when they are cut or broken. Bleeding hearts, named for the shape of their flowers, have translucent amber juice. Another commonality is that most of these plants are poisonous. A familiar example is *Papaver somniferum*, the opium poppy, a hardy annual re-branded as the "breadseed poppy."

OPPOSITE Former poppy family kin: A The old-fashioned bleeding heart (*Lamprocapnos* [formerly *Dicentra*] *spectabilis*); B *Lamprocapnos spectabilis* 'Alba'; C wood poppy (*Stylophorum diphyllum*); D *Corydalis cheilanthifolia**; E *Corydalis ochroleuca*; F *Lamprocapnos* (syn. *Dicentra*) *eximia*. LEFT Typical Papaveracea family members: one Oriental poppy (*Papaver orientalis*, top), two Icelandic poppies (*P. nudicaule*).

*potentially invasive in some climates

THE BIG BREAK-UP

The possible splitting of the poppy family pales in comparison to what has already happened among the lilies. In recent times, Liliaceae was shattered into dozens of families. We used to be able to look at a yucca and say "lily," or a hosta, or even asparagus. Liliaceae united plants with parallel leaf veins and often three-part fragrant flowers. The family was also a convenient place to drop off orphans. Now it is lonelier, a nearly empty nest. *Clintonia* (yellow corn-lily, bead lily), *Erythronium* (trout lily), *Fritillaria*, *Tricyrtis* (toad lily), *Tulipa*, and *Lilium* itself, the garden or true lily, remain in the family.

Common names don't clear up the matter. Many plants with lily in their names never have been in the family, be they water lily, peace lily, or calla lily. Lily-of-the-valley and daylilies once were but are no longer members.

Plants continue to get nudged and prodded by taxonomists, sometimes based on DNA research, to be renamed and divided. Solomon's seal and other *Polygonatum* species are now Ruscaceae. *Disporum* and *Uvularia* are very similar to the Solomon's seals, but have been moved to Colchicaceae. The false Solomon's seal, *Smilacina racemosa*, got its genus changed to *Maianthemum* and became part of Ruscaceae along with the mayflower (*Maianthemum canadense*) and the superficially quite different, old-fashioned cast iron plant (*Aspidistra*).

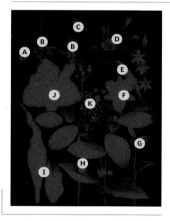

The alliums, which include bulb-forming ornamental and edible plants like onion and garlic, are now Alliaceae. Asparagus is now in Asparagaceae. The botanical jury is still out on the 200 species in the genus *Chlorophytum* (like the spider plant, *Chlorophytum comosum*). Some think Agavaceae should claim it along with *Camassia* (quamash, Indian hyacinth), *Cordyline*, *Furcraea*, *Yucca*, and, believe it or not, *Hosta*.

The flowering bulbs were, perhaps, most agonizingly wrenched away from the lily family. Familiar plants like daffodils, hyacinths, *Leucojum*, *Brodiaea* (*Triteleia*), *Ornithogalum*, and scilla all reside elsewhere now. Other spring-blooming former lilies include three-petal trillium and *Paris*.

If you look at the prominent unbranched veins in the leaves of the lily outcasts, you can see why they were once thought to be closely related. All of this lumping and splitting of plants really doesn't matter to the home gardener. There aren't even that many horticultural generalities to be drawn. For instance, plants in a given family do not always have the same care requirements. On the other hand, genealogy has become a very popular hobby these days.

OPPOSITE Former lily family members: A *Allium sphaerocephalon*; B *Asparagus sprengeri* (ferny stems, flowers, berries); C *Triteleia* (syn. *Brodiaea*) *laxa*; D *Hemerocallis* hybrid; E *Disporum flavens*; F *Hemerocallis* 'Lemon Gem'; G *Polygonatum humile*; H *Uvularia grandiflora*; I *Chlorophytum amaniense*; J *Hemerocallis* 'Spiritual Corridor'; K *Mianthemum* (syn. *Smilacina*) *racemosa*. ABOVE *Endymion hispanicus* (formerly *Scilla campanulata*, *Scilla hispanica*) at the Brooklyn Botanic Garden.

TRUE TO TYPE

Even though the taxonomists have taken many plants out of Liliaceae, there are still exquisite relatives, especially in the genus *Lilium* itself. True or garden lilies may be grown in among other summer perennials. However, the hybrids are prone to fungal diseases and need good air circulation—especially at ground level—and well-drained soil, so how and where they are grown is crucial. I usually plant the bulbs in fall on their sides so that water does not collect in the depression at the top. The stem will come up straight. Dig a hole four to six inches deep. If the soil tends to stay damp all the time in the general area, amend it with a fibrous organic material like coir, and mix in coarse sand or chicken grit.

The lily hybrids need full sun. Some species like *Lilium martagon* are more forgiving, tolerating a bit of shade. *L. formosanum* can reach eight feet and bear large white trumpet flowers followed by candelabra fruits that can be cut and dried for indoor decoration.

There are divisions of garden lilies (*Lilium* spp.). There are the Asiatic hybrids with out-facing flowers; and some martagon hybrids (like 'Mrs. R. O. Backhouse') with small, "Turk's cap" down-facing flowers bearing recurved petals; candidum hybrids resembling parents that include the Madonna lily; American hybrids from North American species; longiflorum hybrids with the Easter lily in the mix; trumpet and aurelian hybrids bred from the Chinese species like *L. regale*, *L. henryi*, and *L. aurelianse* with large, slightly nodding, flaring flowers that are fragrant and more so in the evening; Oriental hybrids based on Japanese native species, including the famous large-flowered 'Stargazer' with white flowers striped and spotted dark pink; Orienpet hybrids, heat-tolerant crosses between the orientals and trumpets or aurelians; and the true, pre-hybridized species.

Lily bulbs in the garden can be dug up and divided when they are dormant, and may even *need* to be split apart if they create many offsets. The plants can also be grown from seeds. They germinate in two different ways: Some, like *L. formosanum* develop a single green leaf soon after fresh

seeds are sown. Others, like *L. martagon,* do not make a leaf, but first develop a tiny underground bulb. After a season of chilling and dormancy (in the refrigerator or outdoors), they produce their first leaf.

OPPOSITE Still the same, lilies stayed in their family: A *Lilium* 'White Henry', a selection of the species; B *L. henryii*; C *L.* 'Leslie Woodruff'; D Orienpet lily hybrid. ABOVE In the garden, hybrid 'African Queen'; *Lilium* 'White Henry'; and *L. henryi.*

Part Three

FORM FOLLOWS FUNCTION

Why do humans have thumbs? Why do cats have long tails? Why do many birds have colorful feathers? These physical features evolved because they serve invaluable purposes for each animal. Our thumbs give us precision grips. Feline tails help cats balance as they leap from one household precipice to the next. Male birds dress up to attract a mate.

Plants evolved helpful characteristics as well. Although they don't have fingers, vines can grab on to surfaces. Some plants need to balance, often sending cantilevered branches in one direction to support growth in another. Showy flowers attract pollinators. We may capitalize on some of these traits—such as shape, form, and stature—for our plantings.

We seek naturally low, spreading plants for ground covers and flowering vines for colorful high points to our compositions. We might want long, dangling trumpet-shaped blossoms in one spot or clusters of glistening stars for another. Some flowers are flat-topped and round; others grow on spikes held above their foliage. Spherical blossoms create masses of color, and floral spires can become energizing exclamation points.

Leaf form is another plant adaptation that we can look to for our designs. Small silvery leaves covered with hairs, powder, or wax evolved to preserve moisture in plants native to windy, dry climates. Broad leaves grew large to gather light in shady, humid habitats.

Once again, we are capitalizing on nature's developments. Intricate, colorful flowers attract us, and they also demonstrate the concept of coevolution, since they developed right along with their pollinators: insects, birds, bats, etc. The blossoms lure their animal partners with the promise of sweet nectar, and in return, genetic material is carried to another member of the plant's species.

One example of coevolution is the relationship between milkweed and monarch butterflies. Milkweed blossoms provide nectar for monarchs, and its leaves feed their larvae. As the caterpillars eat, they ingest a toxin in the plant sap that does not harm them, but makes the larvae unpalatable to predators. Birds learn to recognize the caterpillar's yellow, white, and black bands as an announcement for "do not eat."

OPPOSITE Shapes and sizes vary greatly: (left to right) the long raceme of white flowers on the vine *Wisteria floribunda* 'Longissima Alba'*; ground-hugging sub-shrub *Cotoneaster horizontalis* with tiny leaves and coral red berries; colorful leaves of purple smoke bush, *Cotinus coggygria* 'Velvet Cloak'.

potentially invasive in some climates

DESTINY

Within the complex and nuanced world of botany, there are a few general categories. There are *herbaceous* plants with soft stems, and *woody* plants with hard, permanent growth. Plants we know as annuals live only for one year, while those we call perennials live longer, perhaps for decades—even centuries. In common garden parlance, perennials are cold-hardy, deciduous herbaceous plants—those that have soft tissues, die to the ground for winter, and return in the spring. However, any plant that persists for longer than two years is a perennial, and that includes woody—non-herbaceous—plants.

Botanically, true annuals are *monocarpic*, which means they bear fruit only once. Annuals sprout from a seed, produce flowers and seeds, and then die—all in a single growing season. Marigolds are annuals, as are zinnias. Biennials like foxglove and hollyhocks are monocarpic, but they take two growing seasons to flower, fruit, and die.

Still other plants like bromeliads may live for years before they, too, flower, fruit, and die. *Agave americana* is called the century plant because it lives for decades before it begins its swan song by sending up an impressive ten-foot-tall flower spike and the fruit that follows. Often, by the time plants like these and others—for instance hen-and-chicks (*Sempervivum*)—begin to bloom, they have produced babies, or pups to carry on vegetatively as a backup to sexual reproduction via pollination, fruit, and seeds. (Growing plants from seed is sexual propagation. Growing plants from pieces of plants, like stem cuttings or divisions of roots and plantlets is vegetative, or asexual propagation.)

When we think of the products of flowers—fruits—we picture something edible, fleshy, and sweet, but fruits may either be moist or dry. Anything that contains a seed is a fruit: juicy tomatoes, avocados, pears, and also hazelnuts, vanilla beans, and wheat.

There are many perennials that we use like annuals, because in cold climates they grow for one season and are killed by frost if not dug up and brought into a warmer place for winter. But in their home ranges, plants like geraniums, begonias, and coleus act as true perennials. Rather than calling them annuals, it would be more precise to say "frost-tender," or "tender perennials."

We've all seen flower gardens that seem to be dominated by herbaceous perennials. On close inspection, you may find annuals, as well as tender plants, bulbs, ground covers, and flowering shrubs—woody plants with multiple stems sprouting at or near the ground. These cosmopolitan plantings, often called perennial beds and borders, are better described as "mixed," as in mixed border.

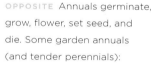

OPPOSITE Annuals germinate, grow, flower, set seed, and die. Some garden annuals (and tender perennials): A *Verbena bonariensis*; B *Thunbergia alata* 'Lemon Star'; C *Emilia coccinea*; D *Nicotiana alata* 'Lime Green'; E *Laurentia axillaris* 'Starshine'; F *Angelonia angustifolia* 'Angelface Blue'; G *Cuphea hyssopifolia*; H *Tagetes tenuifolia* 'Lemon Gem'; I *Exacum affine*; J *Scaevola aemula*; K *Angelonia angustifolia* 'Angelmist Lavender'; L *Angelonia angustifolia* 'Angelina White'; M *Ammi majus*; N *Pentas lanceolata*; O *Lisianthus* hybrid; P marigold *Tagetes* hybrid; Q *Impatiens* 'Seashell Yellow'. ABOVE Top to bottom: orange *Tithonia rotundifolia*, light purple *Centratherum punctatum*, variegated foliage from *Acalypha wilkesiana* 'Hoffmannii', tiny *Alternanthera ficoidea* 'Aurea Nana'.

Annuals in raised beds contained by low-cast concrete walls
are used for color and for cutting in an Austin, Texas, garden
designed by landscape architect James David.

THE FINISHING LINE

Consider the various ways vines climb. Knowing the ways that these plants get where they want to grow can help you choose the right support, and often, the right vine.

Some plants wind their growing shoots around anything—whether a sturdy branch or a length of string. The terminal shoot circles the air, searching for assistance. When it "feels" something, cells on one side of the stem grow at an accelerated pace, which causes the stem to wind. Wisteria vines and beans climb using this seek, discover, and twine method.

Plants like bougainvillea use vigorous new shoots to thread through older stems to hang on to. Roses also grab older canes and on to trellises or fences with their thorns. Other vines, passionflowers for instance, have tendrils. When these modified leaves come in contact with something, they wind around it and then corkscrew to pull the stem in close. The spring tendril also acts as a shock absorber in the wind. Clematis leaf stems behave like tendrils bending around a wire or string to support the vine.

Still other vines have fingertip-like disks that glue themselves onto a surface. Boston ivy attaches with these disks called "holdfasts." True ivy, *Hedera* species, and climbing hydrangea, for example, have small rootlets called adventitious roots that actually grow into the cracks between bricks, onto the surface of stucco, or into tree bark or porous wood shakes to hold on. Vines that grab with holdfasts or rootlets do not make good choices for covering anything besides dry stone walls and will not climb wires or other slender props.

If you are considering a vine to adorn a building, select a safe one that won't pull down the siding. In any event, provide a structure for a vine that will stand several inches in front of the building. Some vines are flexible enough to allow you to lower them when the house needs washing or painting. I've seen some nice trellises that are hinged at the ground, and fold down for maintenance.

With diligent pruning, you can encourage a vine like wisteria to grow as if it were a tree over a sturdy umbrella-shaped form—into a topiary called a standard. But don't be surprised if in response to hard pruning one of the more vigorous varieties of *W. floribunda* or *W. sinensis* sends up a shoot in the lawn—some fifty feet away.

OPPOSITE Summer vines include clockwise from top left: multicolored *Mina lobata*; bitter melon (*Momordica charantia*) with split fruit that has dropped its scarlet seeds; cream and yellow-green *Clematis rehderiana*; snake gourd *Trichosanthes kirilowii*, which also bears frilly white flowers. ABOVE The Art Nouveau-like annual cup-and-saucer vine (*Cobea scandens*).

Magnolia Plantation and Gardens in Charleston, South Carolina, is home to local native *Wisteria frutescens* and the more vigorous *W. sinensis* (shown), which has naturalized through a property that has been in family ownership since 1679.

RACE FOR THE TOP

Vines can be annual or perennial, herbaceous or woody. Regardless of their life span or the strength of their stems, these plants all grow toward the light—usually up, and often quickly. But unlike other skyward plants like trees, vines need something to lean on. Vines can wind around a trellis, drape over a wall, creep along the ground, or weave up through other plants in the garden; think of a small-flowered clematis that threads up through a sturdy climbing rose (page 77). With most of their growth held high, there is plenty of space for complementary plants to grow beneath them.

Annual flowering vines like morning glory, cardinal vine, or moonflower (*Ipomoea* species) could adorn the fence surrounding a vegetable garden, adding some extra color. Creeping ones could fill in between the rows of crops, for instance sweet potato vines (also *Ipomoea*) with black, marbled, or gold foliage. The annual vines may be "taught" to grow up a tower or *tuteur* (French for "tutor") for a vertical accent in the kitchen garden. Of course, some vines bear fruit—annuals like cucumbers, pole beans, or peas or perennials like passion fruit, kiwi, or grapes as long as they are given a sturdy scaffold for support.

Grapevines can become permanent covers for pergolas overhead. There are several ornamental grape selections, for instance silvery *Vitis vinifera* 'Argentea' and red-leafed *V.v.* 'Purpurea' with glowing-embers autumn color. Deciduous climbers like the pipevine (page 122) provide shade in the summer. Flowering vines may decorate a vertical trellis, fence, or wall for a colorful backdrop to a perennial border.

If you must have the infamous wisteria, look for a few of the less thuggish species such as varieties of Asian *Wisteria venusta* (synonym *W. macrobotrya*), or southeastern American *W. frutescens* that won't muscle out your other plants.

Wisteria vines are also notorious for being bloom-shy if there is not enough sunlight, if the soil is too rich, or if roots are absorbing nitrogen fertilizer from the nearby lawn. Abundant foliage and no flowers might indicate high nitrogen. Pruning works for me. I cut my wisterias' new shoots back to four or five leaf nodes from their main stems as often as I can until late summer.

OPPOSITE Perennial vines A *Pathenocissus tricuspidata* 'Lowii'; B *Campsis radicans**; C *C. r.* 'Jersey Peach'*; D *Clematis viorna*; E *Lonicera sempervirens* 'John Clayton'; F *Hedera helix* 'Gold Heart'; G *Glechoma hederacea* 'Dappled Light'; H *Wisteria venusta* (syn. *W. brachybotrys*) 'Alba' (in bud); I *Parthenocissus quinquefolia* 'Variegata'. ABOVE A *Clematis* x *Jackmanii*–type variety spills over a stone wall at North Hill, a private Vermont garden.

*potentially invasive in some climates

THROUGH THICK AND THIN

I n the world of hosta fanciers, the word *substance* is used to describe the thickness or thinness of leaves. Leaves that are sturdy and stiff are said to have "heavy" or "good substance," and are often more resistant to slug and snail damage.

One of the most popular hosta varieties is called 'Sum and Substance.' It has very large yellow-green leaves that form a flattened mound about eighteen inches high. The leaves emerge yellow in spring and then deepen in color, a morphological state termed *viridescence*. (Leaves that lighten through the season are said to be *lutescent*.) In general, golden hostas can tolerate direct sunlight and blue-green darker ones, more shade, but you may have to experiment.

When the leaves of the old standby *H. sieboldiana* 'Elegans' unfurl in the spring, they appear quite blue due to a waxy coating that wears off through the season. The leaves are bumpy and deeply veined. *H. tokudama* and its offspring *H.* 'Love Pat', and *H.* 'Abiqua Drinking Gourd' capture rain and funnel it down to the soil with rough, cup-shaped, and almost corrugated leaves (called *rugose*).

Some plants (including hostas) with beefy leaves, stems, and even flowers may be *tetraploids* having doubled chromosomes. These plants may originate naturally, but more often are made when seeds are exposed to chemicals like colchicum, derived from a fall blooming crocus, or even herbicide residue. The leaves may be twice as thick with flowers larger and more numerous on brawny stalks.

On the other hand, plants with fragile substance may still be appealing. Hollyhocks have nearly filmy petals. And think about the luminous tissue-paper bracts of bougainvillea.

Next time you have a chance to stand in an arbor beneath grape leaves or below a Japanese maple, look up toward the sun and contemplate the layers of transmitted light and shadow.

Light transmission is not something customarily thought about in garden design, but it is another characteristic to explore. I have placed several trees, shrubs, and perennials, not for the light that strikes them and is reflected back to my eyes, but rather for the light that passes through them. In late summer, hardy *Begonia grandis* leaves— green with red veins—planted on the south side of a semi-shaded path look like stained glass. The paperbark maple (*Acer griseum*) has amber, exfoliating bark. I planted this small tree where the long shafts of the autumn and winter afternoon sunlight make the translucent sheets of bark glow.

OPPOSITE Hollyhock flowers have tissue-paper-like translucent petals. Purple sedum has leathery succulent leaves. Opium poppy petals are filmy, but their fruits are hard orbs covered with a powdery, waxy coating. ABOVE Substance is the thickness or thinness of leaves and flowers. Hosta leaves vary, but are generally substantial, for instance in the case of cup-shaped and puckered *Hosta tokudama* below a sliced leaf of *Hosta sieboldii* 'Elegans' showing its substance in cross-section. The atypical leaves of H. 'Red October' has speckled red stems. There are less familiar tiny hostas, as well.

PLUMP AND JUICY

Every cactus is a succulent, but not every succulent is a cactus. A succulent is a plant that stores moisture in its stems and fleshy leaves. Cacti don't even have leaves; they vanished eons ago. Photosynthesis takes place instead through the green skin of modified stems swollen with water. Their leaves are gone but not forgotten; they've turned into the spines that arise from areoles—the physical characteristic that distinguishes cacti from all other plants. The spines are for protection of course, but they also comb moisture from fog and dew.

The drought-loving cacti are indigenous to North American deserts from Mexico north to the Southwest and Colorado, and some species come from the dryland plains of Montana and Alberta, Canada. Good garden practice advocates planting the right plant in the right place. Very fast-draining soil in plenty of sun is a spot for cold-hardy cacti. You can also create the right soil mix in a sunny spot. I grow several cacti in nearly pure three-eighths-inch crushed rock (gravel) to which I've added about a third more garden loam.

Gardeners think of cacti as only coming from hot, dry climates. But there are humidity-loving tropical jungle species like the *Epiphyllum* (page 8). There are also thousands of other frost-tender succulent species from around the world, and many could be additions to frost-free gardens in the South and coastal California, where temperatures do not dip below freezing. *Aeonium, Aloe, Crassula, Delosperma, Dudleya, Euphorbia,* and *Pelargonium* are just a few.

Cold-hardy succulents are either deciduous or evergreen. The evergreen ones, including cacti, expel stored moisture in winter, so that freezing water will not rupture their cells. By winter's end, the shriveled plants are colorless, but in short order, they plump up, grow, and blossom.

Sedum varieties are frequently grown succulents for cold climates. They range from tiny ground covers often called stonecrops, to the eighteen-inch-tall versions of liveforever: *Sedum telephium* and *S. spectabile*. The taller sedum species and hybrids want well-drained soil and good air circulation, similar to companion plants like lavender, Russian sage, coreopsis, and *Rudbeckia* (black-eyed Susan).

Short sedum varieties are traditional rock garden plants, where they may mingle with diminutive "alpines" like rockcress (*Arabis* spp.), sea pink (*Armeria* spp.), basket-of-gold (*Aurinia saxatilis*), pinks (dwarf *Dianthus* spp.), moss pink (*Phlox subulata*), succulent hen-and-chicks (*Sempervivum* varieties), and creeping thyme (*Thymus* spp.). These days, you may find these succulents planted atop buildings as energy-saving "green roofs."

OPPOSITE Hardy succulents: A *Sedum telephium* 'Atropureum'; B *S. telephium*; C *S. spurium* 'Tricolor'; D *S. kamtschaticum*; E *S. spurium*; F *S. makinoi* 'Ogon'; G *Sempervivum* hybrid; H *Opuntia humifusa*; I *O. fragilis*; J *Sedum lineare* 'Variegatum'; K *Euphorbia myrsinites*. LEFT Succulents in Judy Bradley's San Diego water-wise garden with fuzzy *Kalanchoe beharensis*, dark red *Aeonium arboreum* 'Schwarzkopf', and colorful *Echeveria* varieties.

A border of *Aloe vera* plants in an Arizona garden. The tubular blossoms are favorites of many of the hummingbird species that can be seen in the American Southwest.

SHADES OF GRAY

Succulent plants have developed mechanisms to keep moisture in their leaves and stems. Many other plants adapted to retain moisture by developing glaucous or waxy coatings. Some protect their leaves with powder, sometimes called "bloom," like the haze on an Italian prune plum. Another means of protecting leaves in harsh climates is a covering of thousands of white or translucent hairs. All of these forms of surface armor make the leaves reflective.

There are bluish hostas like *H.* 'Halcyon' with a waxy bloom, similar to what makes *Dianthus* varieties appear steely. Fuzzy hairs amplify the platinum appearance of the foliage of *Brunnera* 'Jack Frost' and a few lungwort varieties like *Pulmonaria* 'Spilled Milk' and *P.* 'Majeste'. Softer, furry hairs on lamb's ears (*Stachys bizantina*) and mulleins (*Verbascum* species and varieties) make stroking them irresistible.

Many silver plants come from the arid and windswept Mediterranean (page 175), like the ubiquitous olive tree, or the lesser known cotton lavender (*Santolina chamaecyparissus*). In cold climates where olive trees cannot survive, the weeping silver pear (*Pyrus salicifolia* 'Pendula') is an ingenious alternative, for instance in Andrea Filippone's vegetable garden. The genus *Artemisia* (wormwood) offers many choices with varieties like 'Powis Castle', 'Silver King', 'Silver Queen', 'Silver Brocade', and many others.

Over time, these plants have developed herbal essences as defenses against hillside grazers. The plants did not develop resistance to diseases, probably because the greater air circulation on windswept hillsides kept fungi from getting a foothold. If you have ever grown *Artemisia* 'Silver Mound', you know that the plants are prone to sudden death. The soft foliage is susceptible to fungal diseases. Any impediment to air movement, even from other plants, allows diseases to attack. In dewy gardens, like mine, the hairs of some silvery plants trap water, and if they stay wet too late in the day, they rot.

Perhaps the silver plants should be grown together in a spot with the conditions they crave. Many gardeners create formal all-silver plantings, but they could just as easily be designed as informal amorphous mounded clouds. Of course, silver plants may be integrated into plantings with other annuals, shrubs, trees, and flowering perennials like violet *Geranium* 'Rosanne', *Echinacea purpurea* 'White Swan', and *Achillea* 'Moonshine' with sulfur-yellow flowers and ferny silver foliage.

OPPOSITE Silvery plants include: A *Dianthus plumarius*; B *Phlomis fruticosa*; C *Cynara cardunculus*; D *Phlomis fruticosa*; E *Artemisia arborescens* x *absinthium* 'Powis Castle'; F *Artemisia ludoviciana* 'Silver Queen'; G *Stachys byzantine*; H *Elymus arenarius*; I *Cynara cardunculus*; J *Pycnanthemum muticum*. ABOVE Silvery and gray-green foliage from (bottom to top) *Stachys lanata*, grassy *Festuca glauca*, *Sedum spectabile* (in "broccoli" bud), and flowering lavender Russian sage (*Perovskia atriplicifolia*).

A "silver" planting at Old Westbury Gardens on Long Island features scores of plants with foliage covered in reflective hairs, or a bloom of powder or wax. Many of these plants are herbs that originated in the Mediterranean region of the world.

ON PINES AND NEEDLES

onifers—cone-bearing woody plants like pine, cedar, hemlock, and spruce—adapted to their world by inventing revolutionary ways to do just about everything. These trees bear narrow, thick-skinned needles with waxy coatings to reduce evaporation in windy locations and in cold weather when water may be locked in the frigid soil. The conifers do not rely on insects for pollination; instead, they produce enormous quantities of pollen to be carried far and wide by the wind.

However, these "new" improvements originated about 380 million years ago, between the primitive moisture-loving mosses and ferns and what is arguably the most pleasing of nature's developments: showy flowers. Conifers are called gymnosperms (naked seed) since they do not produce fleshy or dry fruits. Their seeds form on the tips of short stalks or between the scales of their cones.

We think of conifers as having needles; however, ancient cycads have palm-like fronds, and ginkgo trees have broad leaves. Rather than being evergreen, the ginkgo drops its leaves in the autumn, as do some needle-leafed deciduous trees such as swamp cypress (*Taxodium*), larch (*Larix*), and the dawn redwood (*Metasequoia*).

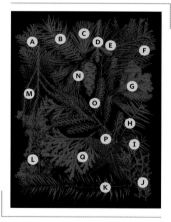

Evergreen trees may be used as singular specimens, or planted in groups for screens and windbreaks. Evergreen shrubs, often pruned trees, serve similar purposes. We are all familiar with hedges of clipped yew (*Taxus* spp. and varieties). These living fences also make excellent backgrounds for flower plantings. Naturally low-growing, spreading *Juniperus horizontalis* and *J. procumbens* may be planted as ground covers.

Some conifers are among the tallest and oldest living things on earth. The same trees may be the sources of diminutive cultivars typified by compact, slow growth—some adding less than an inch per year. These dwarfs may have originated as mutations that appeared on normal tree branches. Particularly prized individuals have to be propagated vegetatively from cuttings to make identical clones. Collectable dwarfs and miniature dwarfs may have innate shapes such as globes, pyramids, or obelisks, and exhibit colored needles with gold or purple casts or white variegations.

OPPOSITE Conifers: A *Chamaecyparis lawsoniana*; B *Cunninghamia lanceolata* 'Glauca'; C *Pinus mugo*; D *Cryptomeria japonica* 'Gyokuryu'; E *Sequoiadendron giganteum* 'Hazel Smith'; F *Chamaecyparis pisifera*; G *Taxodium distichum* 'Peve Minaret'; H *Torreya nucifera* 'Snowcap'; I *Chamaecyparis thyoides* 'Miko'; J *Juniperus communis* 'Gold Cone'; K *Cunninghamia lanceolata*; L *Chamaecyparis obtusa* 'Fernspray Gold'; M *Cryptomeria japonica* 'Ben Franklin'; N *Pinus parviflora* 'Glauca'; O *Abies koreana* 'Horstmann's Silberlocke'; P *Abies pinsapo*; Q *Thujopsis dolbrata* 'Aurea'. ABOVE Not all conifers have needles; *Ginkgo biloba* for example, including cultivars like fishtail 'Saratoga' in front of tubular 'Todd's Broom'.

ONE GOOD FERN DESERVES ANOTHER

We know that foliage is often more important in a garden vista than blooms are. Flowers are fleeting, but foliage lasts all season long or longer, in the case of the needle and broadleaf evergreens. There are evergreen ferns, as well, but most of the choices for our gardens die to the ground in winter and present their coiled, bishop's crook crosiers again in spring.

Most ferns come from the shaded, moist woodland areas of the world, but there are drought-tolerant ferns, desert species, and ones that grow in sunny rock crevices (*Cheilanthes* spp., for example). Hayscented fern (*Dennstaedtia punctilobula*) also likes sun and can often be found growing in open areas like somewhat dry meadows with sweet fern (*Comptonia peregrina*), a creeping subshrub, and little bluestem grass (*Schizachyrium scoparium*).

In shady spots, we're happy to have plants with large solid leaves that evolved to gather as much light as possible.

Ferns, on the other hand, unfold their feathery fronds to absorb light and provide us with unmatched texture in these protected spots.

There are some 12,000 fern species in the world, and these are among the oldest plants on earth. There are ferns with colorful fronds, like the Japanese painted fern (*Athyrium niponicum* 'Pictum' and other varieties). Some of the hardy ferns for gardens are evergreen, for example, the *Polystichum* spp. like Christmas fern. Other useful garden ferns are *Adiantum pedatum* (northern maidenhair fern), *Athyrium filix-femina* (lady fern), *D. erythrosora* (autumn fern), *Onoclea sensibilis* (sensitive fern), *Osmunda cinnamomea* (cinnamon fern), *O. claytoniana* (interrupted fern), *O. regalis* (royal fern), and *Thelypteris noveboracensis* (New York fern).

Some fern allies to grow alongside these old-timers include plants that will provide contrast to their feathery foliage or produce flowers that punctuate the plantings. Worthwhile examples include *Rodgersia* spp., *Trollius* spp., *Brunnera macrophylla* varieties, *Omphalodes cappadocica*, hosta varieties, *Carex* spp., *Milium effusium* 'Aureum', *Primula sieboldii*, *Epimedium* varieties, and shade-tolerant spring-flowering bulbs.

As delicate as some ferns appear, most are fairly sturdy, and a few might even become an aggressive problem. The North American species *Matteuccia struthiopteris* (Ostrich fern) has runners—just below the soil surface—that connect plant to plant. Although slow to establish like many ferns, once it gets going, ostrich fern will colonize as much territory as it can, and even choke out weeds. You may want such a species for a difficult site that is too shady for lawn yet still calls out for a blanketing cover, but be wary (or at least knowledgeable) about what you wish for.

OPPOSITE Ferns have a distinctive leaf or frond, which is usually divided or compound—"pinnate"—like a feather—or when each section is itself divided, bipinnate or tripinnate. The ferns' light and airy appearance lends a specific feel to a planting (and often color) reminiscent of their typical habitat, which is usually cool and shaded. LEFT There are ferns however, that do not grow on the forest floor. Some are rock dwellers and a few live in deserts. Silvery *Cheilanthes lindheimeri* is right at home with succulent *Agave victoria-reginae*.

SIZE MATTERS

The full-page scans in this book are in scale to each other. These photographs show what fits on Ellen's large flatbed scanner. So, the largest leaves in the garden cannot make it onto the glass surface, for instance *Gunnera manicata* (Zones 7–10) with leaves five or more feet across. Small plants could, of course, like the cranberry (*Vaccinium macrocarpon* Zone 2–6), which can be grown as a fruiting ground cover. The cranberry's leaves are the size of your pinky nail. *Macrocarpon* means big fruit, and compared to the leaves, the berry is huge. If hostas had fruits of a similar scale, they would be watermelons. The flowers of the cranberry are small and look like the head of a pink crane, perhaps the source of its common name.

When we think of big leaves in our gardens, hostas come to mind. Of course, there is a range—*H. venusta* leaves could be compared to tablespoons. *H.* 'Sum and Substance' has green-gold leaves about two feet long. Generally, the scale of a landscape is set by surrounding trees, walls, and paving—the permanent elements. But we find ourselves concentrating on the plants at human scale, from our toes to the tops of our heads. The larger foliage establishes the scale of a planting. Distinguish the large leaves with smaller ones and small flowers for lively combinations.

A garden with plants of all the same size might read as an interesting "lake" made of foliage, or as easily, be static and boring. Relieve the monotony with contrasting scale, which creates energy and movement and makes it easy to enjoy as your eyes scan along, delighting in the rhythm of the arrangement.

The idea is to use various sizes of flowers. If you have some giant herbaceous meadow hibiscus with blooms as large as dinner plates, modify their impact with equally large aggregations of blossoms, for example *Hydrangea paniculata* 'Grandiflora'. Massing plants with individual blossoms might also work; perhaps *Hemerocallis* 'Corky' with scores of small fluttering daylily flowers held above the strappy foliage.

It may seem counterintuitive, but a small garden may be more successful if large-leafed plants are used. A small urban garden is the perfect spot for a soothing green oasis. Small, finely detailed plants would only further constrain tight quarters. You don't want a busy composition there, but something smooth and easy to take in.

In narrow quarters, consider grouping the largest leaves closest to the spot where the garden is most often viewed—from the back door of the house. Plants with progressively smaller leaves may be spaced down the path to fool the eye, making the area appear deeper and larger than it really is.

OPPOSITE Diversity in late spring, clockwise from top left: tiny buds and a few flowers line the two-foot flower spike of *Veratrum viridis*; small yellow *Hemerocallis lilioasphodelus*; *Papaver atlanticum*; green primrose *Primula* 'Francesca'; yellow-green leaves of *Caryopteris* x *clandonensis* 'Worcester Gold'; *Hosta* 'Frances Williams' and the ferny leaf of *Sorbaria sorbifolia*. ABOVE Enormous leaves of *Gunnera* sp. for warm-temperate climates that are neither too cold nor too hot.

Contrasts in scale with tiny leaves on plants like boxwood and giant ones from Gunnera, at Geof Beasley's garden, *Bella Madrona*, in Portland, Oregon.

Reproduction is the primary objective of every living thing. Plants do it with seeds. And in order to make seeds, there has to be pollination. There are flowers that are not brightly colored and may not have scents we humans find attractive. Perhaps their pollinators are flies or beetles. A few of these flowers have gone to intricate lengths to make sure pollination happens in just the right way. There are plants that produce intricately shaped blooms so that insects have to enter, move through chambers, and escape having fulfilled the flower's objective—without a reward of nectar.

Aristolochia is a genus of creeping plants and vines, some delicate, some vigorous. There are tropical members of the genus with huge flowers decorated to resemble carrion to attract flies. At the center, there is an opening that appears like a bright light, which leads to a bulbous pocket

lined with hairs angled downward. Flies enter, but they have a hard time exiting. When they finally do escape, they are covered with pollen.

In the Northern Hemisphere, *Aristolochia* species evolved smaller flowers with similar devices like interior hairs or exterior ones like eyelashes. *A. durior* is called Dutchman's pipe for flowers shaped like calabash smoking pipes. (In Victorian times and into the twentieth century, people have grown this deciduous vine on their porches for the shade provided by the large, shingle-like overlapping leaves.)

This plant is the preferred host for the pipevine swallowtail butterfly. One year, the native caterpillars found my plant in New Jersey. I was thrilled to watch some of the heart-shaped leaves devoured by these rare insects. I never did see the butterflies that followed.

There are many other plants with intricately shaped flowers: *Arisaema* species, the Jack-in-the-pulpits, tiny flowers lining the shrouded spadixes. Some of them also have "tails" growing either from the tip of their hoodlike spathes or their floral spadices. These serve as access ramps to help pollinating insects climb directly up and into the inflorescences for pollination.

Don't be certain that the plants have died if nothing sprouts in the spring. I have had a few that seem to have just taken a year off. Like the other plants of the woodland, the *Arisaema* want a humusy soil like the duff of the forest floor ,where they get along famously with more prized plants for woodland gardens in Zones 5–8: bloodroot, wood poppy, mayapple, ferns, and terrestrial orchids.

OPPOSITE Many flowers use craftiness over beauty to get pollinated by inviting flies and beetles to crawl into intricate flowers and wriggle around. (Left to right) Bees might pollinate the subtle green tufts of *Alchemilla mollis*, since they appear in great numbers. Other insects are attracted to the little pipes of *Aristilochia durior*, or the larger hooded spathes of *Arisaema ringens*—with "lips" that are green (rarely), or eggplant-colored. LEFT Precious dark purple *Arisaema sikokianum* and a rare green individual—both with a snow-white spadix.

SPIRES OF INTENTION

Flowers come in many forms, shapes, and sizes. It's up to us to decide how to use them. We may contrast one large flower with many small ones. We may create dynamic rhythm within a planting—using the repetition of elements or waves of undulating forms. We can also announce the high notes and even elevate a scene with the shapes of inflorescences—groupings of multiple flowers on a single stem.

There are herbaceous plants like certain *Veronica* species that produce what appear to be clusters of stalagmites, or inverted icicles. These ascending spires are like exclamation points providing excitement and movement—shifting the viewer's eyes skyward. Delphiniums have a commanding presence with blue or white blossom-laden stems, as does the tender mealycup sage, *Salvia farinacea*, on a much smaller scale. More upstanding perennials include the obedient plant (*Physostegia virginiana*), blazing star (*Liatris* spp.), red hot poker (*Kniphofia* spp.), Culver's root (*Veronicastrum virginicum*), black cohosh (*Actaea* spp., formerly *Cimicifuga*), and *Astilbe* and *Penstemon* species and varieties.

Contrast these vertical flowers with plants that have broad, rounded leaves. A few *Ligularia* species are perfect—providing the textural contrast on their own. Some species (*L. dentata* 'Othello', for instance) have dark water-lily-pad-like leaves and tall stems bearing garish Kodak-yellow daisy flowers. Others species and varieties (*L. stenocephala* 'The Rocket', for example) have toothed triangular leaves with starry lemon yellow flowers covering tall conical spires.

Other vertical herbaceous perennials punctuate a planting with their stature and hold their blossoms at the top rather than have them running up the stems. *Rudbeckia maxima*, for example, sends up towering shafts with yellow coneflowers above silvery blue-green leaves. On the other hand, subtle grace comes from lavender mist meadow rue (*Thalictrum rochebrunianum*), providing a more delicate touch for a bed or border. Here, purple, white, and yellow flowers float on wiry stems some seven to eight feet in the air.

There are shrubs and trees that grow into natural pillars described as columnar. Those that are similar but not quite as narrow are described as fastigiate. These plants grow with parallel, vertical branches. Examples include boxwood (*Buxus*) 'Graham Blandy' and 'Fastigiata', columnar Irish yew (*Taxus baccata* 'Fastigiata'), and a sweetgum tree selection—*Liquidambar styraciflua* 'Slender Silhouette'. This telephone-pole-thin genetic variation was found growing beside a lake in Tennessee by nurseryman Don Shadow. Cuttings were taken and propagated. These sentinels make an unforgettable statement.

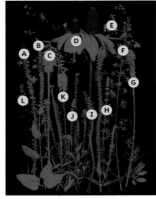

OPPOSITE Short or tall flower spikes in summer: A *Lysimachia atropurpurea*; B *Veronica spicata*; C *Kniphofia* hybrid; D *Rudbeckia maxima*; E *Thalictrum rochebrunianum*; F *Heuchera villosa*; G *Liatris spicata*; H *Salvia superba*; I *Veronicastrum virginicum*; J *Veronica spicata* 'Foxy'; K *Cimicifuga* (syn. *Actea*) *racemosa*; L *Heucherella* hybrid. LEFT A grove of columnar *Liquidambar styraciflua* 'Slender Silhouette'.

asked the fashion designer turned gardening maven and author, Dianne Benson, aka Dianne B., what she's been interested in lately. "My new penchant for circular leaves has led to all sorts of surprise combinations: *Ligularia* 'Othello', and *L.* 'Britt-Marie Crawford' are just right to surround large-leaf trillium," she shared. "The demure flower spike of *Darmera peltata* surprises me in early spring, and then makes way for round crinkle-edged leaves." The ground beneath these plants is covered with shiny round European ginger. The black stems of maidenhair fern (*Adiantum pedatum*) are topped by "circlet upon circlet" of tiny leaflets that give the scene an ethereal quality.

Conventional design advice promotes activity and contrast. For every disk and orb, there should be a spike and spire. But there is soothing effect in Dianne B.'s planting, as the eye flows from one "puddle of floating pads to the next, from plants like *Astilboides tabularis* (like a table) leaves."

Placing rounded forms together may produce a soothing, comforting result. Massing globular flowers adds weight and volume. A mound of flat-flowered chrysanthemum daisies could make a similar anchoring contribution. Numerous pompom blossoms together go a step further: They promote visual harmony.

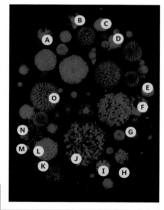

The most symbolically soothing plants might come from the globular seedpods of *Papaver somniferum*, the opium poppy, for obvious reasons. Spherical flowers could also solicit a contrary response. A close inspection of the flower or seed heads of tall *Allium* varieties look like fireworks displays. The effect, if not as raucous as actual pyrotechnics, is certainly energizing.

Rather than moving the planting along or stopping it in its tracks, the allium balls hover and encourage us to linger, as well. More dynamic are the pincushion flowers of the scabiosa varieties, or their tall cousin *Cephalaria gigantea*. There are also the prickly flower heads of globe thistle (*Echinops ritro*), which remain standing after its tiny blossoms have dried and blown away.

An interesting study in contrast might be to create formal square beds edged by dwarf boxwood, and then fill those with floppy, uncontrolled broad round leaves, or lollipop-like spherical flowers. Architectural elements are softened by the amorphous shapes—a nice fusion of class and sex appeal.

OPPOSITE Spheres and circles: A *Cephalnthus occidentalis*; B, D *Hypericum prolificum*; C onion flower head; E *Papaver somniferum* pod; F *Helenium flexuosum* cv.; G *Anethum graveolens*; H *Dalia* 'Stoneleigh Cherry'; I *Helenium autumnale* cv.; J *Allium ampeloprasum*; K *Gomphrena globosa*; L *Tagetes* hybrid; M *Ageratum houstoinianum* 'Album'; N *Allium sphaerocephalon*; O *Echinops ritro*. ABOVE An orange deciduous Knap Hill azalea blooms in front of a fastigiated red beech *Fagus sylvatica* 'Dawyck Purple', and behind the variegated willow *Salix integra* 'Hakuro Nishiki'.

If you go to a public garden or speak to a professional garden designer and ask him or her about color in plantings, you'll probably get an answer like, "I chose what I like," or "I was inspired by a famous garden." Few people will mention color theory. Nevertheless, seeing combinations based on color relationships is another way to discover appealing schemes and guide you to fine-tune color for the effect you're hoping to realize.

For centuries, visual artists have benefited from a reference tool called the color wheel to help them create harmonious compositions of tones and hues. We gardeners can use it too. After all, a well-composed planting is indeed a work of art.

The basic principles of color theory and design are revealed by the hues relative positions and relationships on the wheel. They are there when you need them: Don't feel chained to the wheel. These directives are enlightening, but like many sets of rules, they may be followed or broken.

You may want to choose colors that appeared to you in a dream or remind you of a favorite spot you saw on vacation. Carry a camera or snap a shot with your phone. Inspiration is everywhere: the fabric on a pillow, an Oriental rug. Flip through the pages of fashion magazines. Take a trip to a museum—a painting could inspire a scheme. For a planting at the front of the house, consider your home's exterior and the colors that will look best with that. Look at everything with an eye toward color combinations: the shades, tints, and hues all around us.

Nature is always a good teacher. The woodland has its own palette, as does the sunny meadow. If you feel like putting every color of the rainbow together, do it. And if that Joseph's coat combination doesn't look right, edit. Select some potted species and varieties at the garden center, put them together and move them around. This way, you can arrange color schemes before you buy.

Notions of color have been passed along through the years, but I have to say that some of the nicest combinations in the garden happen by accident, and they always will.

OPPOSITE A favorite subdued combination (counterclockwise from bottom left): *Artemisia ludoviciana* 'Silver King'*, *Ajuga reptans* 'Catlin's Giant', *Athyrium niponicum* 'Pictum', mottled *Geranium phaeum* (leaf)*, *Asarum canadense*, *Cotinus coggygria* 'Velvet Cloak', *Hosta* 'Gold Regal' flowers, feathery leaves of *Cimicifuga* (syn. *Actea*) *simplex* 'Hillside Black Beauty', *Hydrangea serrata* 'Grayswood', tiny *Geranium phaeum* flowers, dark flowers of *Nicotiana* 'Ken's Coffee', *Acanthus hungaricus* flower spike.

CIRCLE OF LIGHT

Although there is some debate as to who initially discovered the visible color spectrum, many believe it was Sir Isaac Newton around 1660 when he split sunlight with a glass prism. What Sir Isaac's prism projected onto the laboratory wall was basically a rainbow—the "ROYGBIV" we learned about in school: red, orange, yellow, green, blue, indigo, and violet. Newton assigned a musical note to each of the colors and, later, connected the beginning and end of the spectral hues to form a circle, the color wheel. (The modern wheel incorporates six major colors.)

Color as we see it is light—the electromagnetic wavelengths reflected by objects back to our eyes and processed by the mechanisms therein. For example, a red rose of Sharon appears red because that is the color of the light bouncing back to us. The small yellow verbascum flowers and steel-blue sea holly reflect those ranges of light. The wheel begins with these three colors spaced evenly in an equilateral triangle.

Red, yellow, and blue (RYB) are reflective hues. Pigments, dyes, and printer's inks are based on cyan, magenta, yellow, and sometimes black (CMYK). Our modern computer screens use additive light-transmitting colors—red, green, and blue (RGB)—for the incredible range displayed.

We take it for granted that red is red, but this a human-centric view. Our retinas have three types of color-sensitive cones that correlate to three primary colors. Our *trichromatic* prejudice might make us feel sorry for color-blind cats and

dogs, but feline supersensitivity allows them to see more in the dark than we can, and dogs "see" with their noses arguably better than we do with our eyes. Insects do not see things as we do, and may even process wavelengths of light we cannot. Bees see so far into the ultraviolet range that some flowers reveal targets and landing lights pointing to their nectaries that are invisible to us.

Between the primary colors are the secondary hues made by blending equal amounts of the first ones: orange between the red and yellow, green between the yellow and blue, and violet between the blue and red. When the primary and secondary colors are mixed, a third set of hues appears. These are the tertiary colors. Equal parts of red and orange make red-orange. The other tertiary colors are yellow-orange; yellow-green, blue-green; blue-violet, red-violet (purple).

OPPOSITE The color wheel breaks wavelengths of light down to its simplest or primary colors; red, yellow, and blue represented here by red *Hybiscus syriacus*, the yellow flowers of a *Verbascum* hybrid and blue *Eryngium planum* 'Blaukappe'. ABOVE Between the primary colors are the secondary and tertiary colors, for example, between red and blue is violet, and between violet and red is red-violet or purple. These secondary and tertiary colors are represented in mid-spring by large blue-violet hybrid clematis blossoms, one violet iris flower, tiny pale red-violet lilacs, and dark purple columbines.

GOING GREEN

ccording to theory, green is a secondary color made from equal parts blue and yellow. An imaginary wheel made just for the garden could view green as a neutral color, since foliage is always present, most often serving as a foil behind or below floral combinations. Green is like the frame for a painting. In a planting scheme based on the three primary hues—red, blue, and yellow—green is there, but doesn't factor into the selection.

In a different situation, green could be essential, for instance if the scheme is an audacious combination of green, orange, and violet. The green in this composition, even if it comes only from boldly striking leaves and not colorful flowers, plays a pivotal role.

There are dark greens that absorb more light and recede into the background. Leaves may also be chartreuse

or yellow-green—the color of emerging foliage in spring—and shine in the foreground. Then there are the variegated leaves—green with white, cream, or yellow, for example.

Of course, not all leaves are green. In the last few decades, plant breeders have introduced even more versions of many plants with colorful leaves. *Weigela* 'Wine and Roses' has maroon leaves, as does the red-leafed peach, several purple beech tree varieties, *Physocarpus opulifolius* 'Diablo', and the hazel variety *Corylus maxima* 'Purpurea'.

In *Shades of Gray* (page 113), we discussed silver and blue-green leaves that have reflective surfaces covered with powder, wax, or thousands of tiny hairs that reflect light. In the scheme based on an Oriental rug, most of the color comes from leaves, and none of them are green. There are khaki leaves splashed claret-red, medium carmine, and unexpected aubergine and purple-taupe.

In addition to the color of leaves, their scale and texture contribute, as we've learned, to the depth and diversity of the garden's infinite variety. The broad leaves may read as a swath of color, while the finer leaves might be seen as pointillist or textural color.

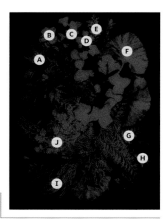

OPPOSITE Green could be the basis of a color scheme with variegation, shades, and tints. A *Adonis amurensis* (leaves); B *Buxus sempervirens* 'Latifolia Maculata'; C *Hedera helix* 'Buttercup'; D Fragaria vesca 'Golden Alexander'; E *Chamaecyparis nootkatensis* 'Variegata'; F *Petasites japonicus* 'Variegatus'; G *Chamaecyparis obtusa* 'Fernspray Gold'; H *Buxus sempervirens* 'Elegantissima'; I *Chamaecyparis pisifera* 'Filifera Aurea'; J *Tanacetum parthenium* 'Aureum'.

LEFT Shades of green in a planting in my New Jersey garden from spring to fall.

Leaves are green, but they may also be silver, gold, yellow, bronze, red, and variegated—all of which make the perennial border planting at the Bellevue Botanical Garden in Bellevue, Washington, striking through the seasons.

ON THE LIGHTER (AND DARKER) SIDE

White and black are missing from the color wheel. Black is theoretically the absence of color—the absorption of all light. White appears when all colors are together, and all light is reflected at once. If you were to spin the color wheel at high speed, white would appear. White is often used as an accent in the garden, either with flowers or more permanent elements like a fence or latticework. Some gardens are made with only white flowers. It is not too hard to arrange when they are all white—from short to tall and relationships of texture and scale.

Whether a hue appears vivid or subdued depends on how saturated the color is. Color value is how light or dark the particular color appears. Maroon is darker in value and pink lighter than their parent hue: red. When mixing paint, adding white to a color pigment creates a tint or pastel. Pale flowers are lighter versions of hues, like ivory from yellow. Likewise, colors might appear as shades—darker versions of colors made when black is added to a hue. Tones are subdued by adding gray, brown, or a color's complement (found directly across from it on the wheel) to the pure, vivid color: army green from green.

What we call black plants are usually ones that are just very dark hues. What appears black in the garden is what we see in contrasting shadows in bright sunlight. There's not much one can do about the high contrast observed on a sunny day. I don't like to photograph a garden in full sun, and frankly, I prefer not to even view one under such conditions. In the subdued light of an overcast day, plants look their best. Colors appear richer, and there is more visible variety. The eye can drift from the front of the planting to the back without being stopped by blinding, washed-out flowers with no apparent detail, or black holes made by shadows.

OPPOSITE "Black" is usually shades of purple and green: (clockwise from top left) *Cotinus coggygria* 'Velvet Cloak', *Cimicifuga simplex* 'Hillside Black Beauty', annual millet *Pennisetum glaucum* 'Purple Majesty', *Acer palmatum* variety, *Hibiscus* x *moscheutos* 'Kopper King', *Ligularia dentata* 'Britt-Marie Crawford', *Ipomoea batatas* 'Blackie' next to heart-shaped *Cercis canadensis* 'Forest Pansy', *Weigela florida* 'Fine Wine' with *Trillium* fruit, daylily flower *Hemerocallis* 'Jungle Beauty', strappy black leaves and pale flowers of *Ophiopogon planiscapus* 'Nigrescens', *Ajuga reptans* 'Catlin's Giant', maroon leaf of beet *Beta vulgaris* 'Bull's Blood', *Begonia* 'Black Fang' to its right and *Geranium maculatum* 'Espresso' above it. ABOVE LEFT When mixing paint colors, adding white creates a pale tint; adding black creates a dark shade. White is represented here by tender, tuberous white dahlias, spidery annual *Cleome* 'Helen Campbell', and feathers of tender perennial *Salvia farinacea* 'Victoria *White*'. ABOVE RIGHT Pale-colored buxom peony blossoms contrast with the little light pink trumpet flowers from old-fashioned beauty bush, *Kolkwitzia amabilis*.

HUE DO YOU LOVE?

A century and a half after Sir Isaac Newton, Johann Wolfgang von Goethe began studying the psychological effects of "perceptive" colors. He noticed that blue gives a feeling of sadness, and yellow, joy. Goethe created his own wheel and divided colors into two groups: the plus side (from yellow-red to red-yellow) and the minus side (from blue-red to red-blue). He claimed colors on the positive side represented excitement and cheerfulness, while those on the negative side were associated with weakness and yearning. Something close to magenta signified dignity and grace. Green was a neutral.

Some designers also divide colors into two families, one being hot, and the other being cold. We think of red as the most vibrant color. Red is emotionally intense. Red makes the heart beat faster. Red is the color of love, perhaps because the heart is red (and so is blood). To create a high-energy planting, red may be partnered with orange and yellow, and quieted with maroon. Blue is the color of the sky and the ocean, those most pacific entities. As Goethe observed, blue is tranquil, peaceful, and unlike red, may cause one's blood pressure to lower.

In tropical regions and in other places with hot climates, vibrant carnival colors can stand out in bright sun. On the other hand, blue, too subtle to hold up to harsh light, could be just the thing to create a cool, relaxing spot for the end of a long day at the office. Blue alone might disappear in evening light, however. You can add light blue and a touch of cool white to brighten a dusky planting.

The most famous "hot" planting in the world is probably the red border at Hidcote Manor in England, designed—beginning in 1907—by its American owner Lawrence Johnston (1871–1958). The red border was known for its sensuous, intense, smoldering colors. The color and art of Johnston's creation owes much of its success to an incredible range of plants that were flooding England at the time. Johnston's art was assembling plants—from bulbs to annuals, perennials, shrubs, vines, trees, and many frost-tender plants with red and smoky maroon foliage that had to be wintered over in greenhouses—with companions that highlighted their best attributes and hid the lesser aspects. It was Johnston who pioneered what we now know as the mixed border.

OPPOSITE Colors on the wheel from red-orange to yellow are said to be warm, those that range from blue to red-violet are considered cool. (Clockwise from top left) Hot *Crocosmia* 'Lucifer'; *Acer palmatum* var. *dissectum* f. *atropurpureum* 'Red Dragon'; yellow Asiatic lily 'Grand Cru'; red Maltese cross (*Lychnis chalcedonia*); *Crocosmia*; red Asiatic lily 'Jazz'; fruit of *Penstemon digitalis* 'Husker's Red'; yellow *Heliopsis* 'Bressingham Doubloon'. ABOVE Cool colors from flowers, left to right: *Amsonia orientalis* (syn. *Rhazya orientalis*); *Amsonia tabernaemontana*; cool pink gas plant (*Dictamus albus*); violet *Iris siberica* 'Caesar's Brother'; white *Dictamus albus* var. 'Albus'.

MONO A MONO

After the writer and renowned gardener Vita Sackville-West created her all-white garden at Sissinghurst Castle in England, a trend began that continues today. A white planting could include snow white and cream to ivory. An all-white arrangement is not hard to create, and even easier to shop for—simply scan catalogs for annuals, perennials, shrubs, and even trees with flowers in that color throughout the seasons and variegated foliage in green and white. But you must deadhead the fading flowers, because brown shows up quickly against the white and detracts from the intended result.

One could choose to stick very carefully to the single-color notion, which would alter as the growing season progressed. An all-pink garden could be achieved with a succession of plants that bloom in that frequently available color. Or, variations on the single color could be allowed so that bright pink might join the arrangement with fuchsia, shocking pink, and rose. A monochromatic color scheme could zero in on one hue and create contrast between pastels and shades, and from flower texture and size, while also taking into account the times that they bloom. Shades, almost like shadow plantings, might bring in rich crimson, burgundy, and subdued maroon.

The focus here is on versions of a single color, and in all cases leaves play their part. For red, white, yellow, and even blue arrangements, berries might be useful. Remember that twigs too have their colors, and for the yellow and white monochromatic arrangements, variation with gold, yellow, or silver and white on green could make an appearance playing the role of dappled light.

OPPOSITE A monochromatic combination from Louise Wrinkle's Alabama garden in winter include (clockwise from top left) witch hazel; yellow spattered leaves of evergreen shrub *Aucuba japonica* 'Variegata'; daffodils; globe clusters of *Edgeworthia chrysantha* 'Winter Gold'; berries of heavenly bamboo *Nandina domestica* 'Leucocarpa'; pansies; yellow-green *Helleborus foetidus* fruits; and *Caltha palustris*. ABOVE (Clockwise from top left) *Deutzia gracillis* 'Variegata'; *D. scabra*; *Lilium martagon* 'Album'; *Hosta* 'Striptease'; *Salix integra* 'Hakuro Nishiki'.

An area with perennial plantings at Frank Cabot's *Les Jardins de Quatre-Vents*, located in La Malbaie in Québec, Canada, features a monochromatic blue border.

CLOSE ENCOUNTERS

olor harmonies are combinations based on hues and their position on the color wheel. The monochromatic scheme incorporated variations of one color. The analogous harmony allows one color to dominate, and brings adjacent colors immediately to the left and right along with light pastels, dark shades, and tones. While the monochromatic planting is calm and soothing, the analogous one is similarly serene, but richer, deeper, and more compelling.

If you were to pick orange, for example, then yellow-orange and red-orange would go into the mix. Pastels and shades of the secondary and tertiary colors elaborate on the theme, so salmon, pumpkin, and rust might be added along with peach, fawn, and amber all the way to sienna and vermillion. This kind of scheme is naturally successful. The colors inevitably go together.

Many daylily varieties come in versions of a cantaloupe color. These plants could simply be massed together with success. But vivid shades could be placed close to the main viewing point, and paler, softer ones drifting into the background—like the hazy tones of distant mountains. The *trompe l'oeil* or "fool-the-eye" effect makes the space seem deeper than it actually is.

Analogous colors are often seen in nature. The various shades of bark are analogous, as are autumn's leaves. Remember, nature is not based on the color wheel; the color wheel is based on nature. Plantings can incorporate the colors of decorative tree bark from amber paperback maple (*Acer griseum*) or river birch (*Betula nigra*). The changing colors of foliage in fall also contribute opportunities with maples, for example, or sweet gum (*Liquidambar* sp.) with yellow, red, and purple leaves at the same time.

OPPOSITE Daylilies often bloom in shades and tints that range from warm pink and pale yellow to orange, melon, and rust.
BELOW LEFT Pink azalea flowers (evergreen *Rhododendron* varieties) swarm around a late star magnolia flower (*Magnolia stellata* variety), and stems with lavender pink, white, and blue Spanish bluebells, *Endymion hispanicus*. BELOW RIGHT Yellow to red late summer annuals including cock's comb *Celosia* 'Chief' (top); and zinnias like large dark orange 'Benary's Giant' series, large yellow-tipped 'Zowie', and small pompom 'Persian Carpet'.

ACCENTUATE THE POSSIBLE

The monochromatic and analogous displays are bound to be successful, but in some cases, they may still seem incomplete. The monochromatic color scheme might appear too homogeneous for some situations. A combo of analogous reds might look too saturated, or overly active and bright. You may need to add an accent.

Part of the success of an accent color is contrast. White can spark just about any planting. Bright white pops in the garden and attracts attention, especially when it is surrounded by primary colors. The color that lies directly across the wheel from the hue—its complement— is known for contrasts, and will supercharge a planting. An arrangement based on blue and blue-violet flowers may seem withdrawn. An accent is called for. White as an accent could steal the show. Orange is blue's complement, but it might look garish and brash compared to the refined blues. For more subtlety, when the complementary accent could be a bit shocking, look to secondary or tertiary colors found nearby. Canary yellow always brings out the best in blues. Yellow might be the intonation to differentiate the blue and blue-violet hues, tints, and shades, and make these analogous colors appear more complex and vivid without overpowering them.

In reverse, to accent an orange scheme, silver, being somewhat white and bluish (based on blue's complement across the wheel), might be just the thing to elevate warm hues in the yellow-orange to red-orange range. Silver provides a sophisticated accent. Metallic foliage goes well with most colors, and looks especially good with vivid, saturated hues and deeper shades.

OPPOSITE An accent color makes a monochromatic scheme pop, or any arrangement for that matter. Cover the yellow daffodils in the image with your hand, then uncover it. The deep blue hyacinths, pale grape hyacinths, near-white striped squill (*Puschkinia scilloides*) and starry blue glory-of-the-snow (*Chinodoxa sardensis*) become more distinguished when yellow is included. ABOVE LEFT White and silver go with everything, the latter tending to be a bit more subtle and perfect for a planting of *Rudbeckia* daisies and their relatives with an orange *Crocosmia* variety (syn. *Monbretia*) with silver dusty miller, *Senecio cineraria* against a background of bronze Japanese maple. ABOVE RIGHT White is always an accommodating accent color. This late summer arrangement of dahlias, zinnias, and holly berries was energized by the addition of white cosmos and one white zinnia that turn hot red to spicy peppermint.

COLORS OF DISTINCTION

The hues directly across from each other on the color wheel are complementary: yellow/violet, blue/orange, red/green and so on. When a complement is used as an accent, expect fireworks. These high-contrast partners are color's more appealing versions of black and white.

You can try a little test to realize how much these colors are truly opposite. Take a piece of construction paper in red and stare at it in bright light. In about a minute, the color-receptive cones in the retina will become weary. Look away, or at a white piece of paper. You will see an afterimage of the color's complement: in this case, green.

When you hope to make one color as strong as it can be, place its complement next to it. Psychedelic and pop artists used the complements, for example a green outline around red lettering, to make the message vibrate.

This high-octane arrangement might be best for a flamboyant planting of tropicals in containers. But the complements can be toned down and used less to incite, and more for balance. In painting, if the complements are mixed together, the result is brown. Fine artists use a translucent wash of a complement over its opposite color to tone it down and diminish reflectivity. The American *plein air* impressionists often used a pale complementary tone in shadow areas.

In plantings, understated shades of complementary colors can provide nuanced contrast: a pairing of dark green and chocolate brown geranium leaves with a purple-brown checkered lily or the guinea hen flower *Fritillaria meleagris* or *Nectaroscordum siculum* ssp. *Bulgaricum*, for example. Burnt orange lilies with indigo monkshood is a complement that could incite compliments.

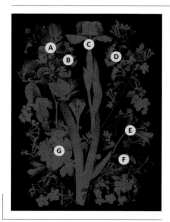

OPPOSITE Colors opposite each other on the color wheel are complementary, they complete a scheme. Across from yellow is violet. A Weeping Camperdown elm tree *Ulmus glabra* 'Camperdownii' (stem scanned upside-down); B small fragrant yellow clove currant flowers, *Ribes odorata*; C an intermediate bearded iris; D *Phlox divaricata*; E fairy bells *Disporum flavens*; F *Corydalis flexuosa*; G Camperdown elm fruits.

ABOVE Shades of mauve and purple-brown with fern green in a subtle complementary arrangement for partial shade, including (clockwise from left) *Euphorbia dulcis* 'Chameleon', *Geranium phaeum** buds, checkered lilies *Fritillaria mileagris*, spotted and blotched leaves from individual *Geranium phaeum* plants.

*potentially invasive in some climates

SPLIT COMPLEMENT/ TRIADIC/TETRADIC

A variation on the complementary scheme calls for adding the adjacent colors to both sides of one of the complement. This arrangement is known as the *split complement*. If you chose yellow and its complement, violet, the variation would be yellow with red-violet, violet, and blue-violet.

Another scheme imagines a triangle laid on top of the color wheel. Basically, this *triadic* scheme uses any three equally spaced colors around the wheel. The attraction of the triadic is that it has an inherent contrast that makes each

of the colors look rich, but unlike the sharp and contrasting differences between colors in the complementary scheme, these remain in balance.

The *double-complementary*, or *tetradic* arrangement, brings together two pairs of color opposites as if an "X" were drawn across the wheel. Imagine a primary and a secondary color are selected, as well as their complements. The points of the "X" would aim toward the four chosen colors. If the first color were yellow, and the second orange, then the third would be violet and the fourth blue.

These esoteric arrangements probably sound like more than you may want to know, but for combinations in planters or window boxes, some of the schemes can be brilliant. It is probably a useful thought to allow one or two colors to dominate, as is the case with some of the other intricate schemes, and consider an accent of white.

OPPOSITE A split-complement color scheme employs three equally spaced colors from the wheel, and in this case (with a little horticultural liberty) rose red *Rosa* 'American Pillar'; the long-blooming lavender-blue *Clematis* 'Betty Corning'; and greens including chartreuse *Cotinus coggygria* 'Golden Spirit'. LEFT A yellow, red-violet to blue-violet tetradic scheme suggested by nurseryman Tony Avent of Plant Delights stars 'Picasso' calla lily and chartreuse-leaved *Buddleia* 'Evil Ways'* introduced by another nurseryman, Sean Hogan of Cistus Nursery. To these, we added (clockwise from left) a hosta stem with blue-violet buds, a plume from the dwarf *Astilbe chinensis* 'Pumila', yellow *Thunbergia alata* 'Sunny Lemon Star', pink *Monarda fistulosa* above *Allium thunbergii* 'Ozawa' and *Lilium* 'Leslie Woodruff' (lower left).

*potentially invasive in some climates

Expert gardener Charles Cresson has a border backed by a white picket fence made of recycled plastic and planted in what could be considered a triadic scheme, with tones of yellow and two colors—blue-violet and red-orange—one third way around the color wheel.

"I hate variegated plants," I used to hear people say. "They look like clowns." I don't hear that anymore. As people put in practice their gardening passion, they discovered that as wonderful as flowers were, they were fleeting. Foliage, on the other hand, could last for months, or even year-round. Gardeners also discovered that shade, far from being a curse, could be a blessing and an opportunity to grow an entirely new group of subtle and fascinating plants. Variegated foliage with stripes, contrasting edges, or splashes and spots of white, yellow, cream, or even silver simulates dappled sunlight and attracts attention in the darker places. Today, people collect these colorful plants (and hosta lovers might even fight over them).

Variegation in a leaf results from a lack of the green pigment chlorophyll. Some plants are variegated due to disease, but this is uncommon. The alteration is usually a cellular mutation that may be propagated through cuttings, or in some cases of genetic variation, even seeds. It might also be chimerical, when a single organism produces two or more genetically different types of meristem tissue—cells at the tip of new growth. In that case, propagation is limited since the ability to produce the variance only occurs at the point of differentiation and therefore cannot be reproduced, for example, from root cuttings.

Variegated leaves are typically white and green, but there are multicolored leaves with red, pink, and yellow over green, like some cannas. There are leaves with zones of color, like the geraniums with dark maroon blotches. Variegation can appear as light color at the edges of the leaves (marginate), or in the center of the leaf (medio variegation). Plants that are striped usually have lines running the length of the leaf, but a few grasses have crosswise dashes.

OPPOSITE A *Canna* 'Pink Sunburst'; B *Kniphofia* hybrids; C *Canna* 'Panache'; D dark red *Cordyline* 'Festival Grass'; E green leaves and flowers of *Yucca filamentosa* 'Color Guard'; F *Aloe* cv.; G *Trachelospermum asiaticum* 'Ogon Nishiki'; H *Coprosma kirkii* 'Variegata'. ABOVE LEFT Chartreuse and variegated cream and green (clockwise): *Quercus robur* 'Concordia'; *Sanguisorba officinalis* 'Lemon Splash'; *Metasequoia glyptostroboides* 'Ogon'; *Filipendula ulmaria* 'Variegata'; *Morus alba* 'Snowflake'; *Hedera helix* 'Buttercup'; *Convallaria majalis* 'Variegata'; *Euonymous japonicus* 'Microphyllus Pulchellus'; *Melissa officinalis* 'Lime'; *Lysimachia punctata* 'Golden Alexander'. ABOVE RIGHT Clockwise in green and white: *Miscanthus sinensis* 'Cosmopolitan'*; *Hydrangea arborescens* var. *radiata*, *Alchemilla alpina* with silver hairs beneath their leaves; *Pachysandra terminalis* 'Variegata'; *Lamium maculatum* 'White Nancy'; *Clethra alnifolia* 'Creel's Calico'; *Disporum sessile* 'Variegata'.

*potentially invasive in some climates

Part Five

SPIRIT OF PLACE

People seem drawn to open pastoral landscapes with gently rolling hills covered by shorn grass. I, too, find that beautiful. I suspect this to be a primordial attraction. In open land, we can see that no predators are hiding behind the scrub to attack and eat us.

However, I like the woods as well. The shadowy forest is a place that fairy tales tell us is filled with hidden dangers and evil spirits—left over from times when there might have been some peril. But we don't have to respond to such inclinations, even if they are in our genes. We can create gardens in any style our climate will allow—be that pasture or forest; Japanese or Italian style; or even floating on water.

There are many ways to bring a sense of a place to the garden. You might create a strictly native planting—a noble pursuit. You could select diverse plants from around the world that fit the conditions offered by your landscape. But you can still build gardens in the style of other regions or countries.

I have to remember that "right plant, right place" is a valuable recommendation. It would be silly to try and grow tropical plants outdoors in Nova Scotia, although they might make a good seasonal container planting, and better, a Panhandle planting. That doesn't mean that a bit of finessing is out of the question: After all, this is horticulture, and like agriculture, making adjustments like amending the soil is acceptable and often necessary.

Most of my property has very sandy soil deposited by the flooding river, but there is clay in one area. The clay stayed moist until rains stopped, and then it got brick-hard. I added compost and three-eighths-inch crushed rock and turned the clay over to a depth of twelve to eighteen inches: That worked. The clay holds moisture, but the gravel improves drainage. A south-facing seventy-foot-long low stone wall around the garden absorbs heat from the sun and radiates it to the plants, which helps me cheat the zone. This place in Zone 6 with forty-five inches of annual precipitation is rather Mediterranean in style with herbs like nepeta, lavender, and thyme.

Meadow species share a mixed border. Florida plants summer in containers, and waterside species grow along the edge of the canal that cuts across my island property.

OPPOSITE Subtle North American plants include yellow daisy *Heliopsis helianthoides* var. *scabra* 'Summer Nights', spiny buttons of *Eryngium yuccafolium* (rattlesnake master), the large blue-violet spire of *Lobelia siphilitica*, smaller *Agastache foeniculum*, and the soft Mexican grass, *Nassella tenuissima**.

*potentially invasive in some climates

INTO THE WOODS

Wherever there is soil and ample rainfall, there are trees. Wherever there are trees, they are in danger. "Any fool can destroy trees," wrote the great naturalist John Muir. "They cannot run away; and if they could, they would still be destroyed—chased and hunted down as long as fun or a dollar could be got out of [them]."

The ancient American forests include the coastal conifer stands of the Northwest, the oak woodlands of California and Texas, the pine woods of the South, and the wooded Appalachian mountain range. My garden lies in the coastal northeastern forests, an area that encompasses the Appalachian Piedmont and coastal plain through seven states from Maryland to southwestern Maine. It is a broadleaf, temperate mixed-hardwood forest characterized by maple, oak, beech, wild cherry, black walnut, hickory, tulip poplar, ash, birch, white pine, and hemlock.

Most of the old-growth woodland has been lost to development. We can replant trees, but cannot bring back the ecosystem they defined. The woods surrounding my property have grown up in the years since this land was last farmed as apple orchards. The understory plants had made a comeback, but have all but disappeared due to browsing deer and, most recently, invasive weeds. Old government surveys of wild areas can often be found at the library, noting genera and species like *Trillium* spp., *Phlox divaricata*, foamflower (*Tiarella* spp.), *Cypripedium* slipper orchids, *Arisaema triphyllum* (Jack-in-the-pulpit), *Carex* spp., columbine (*Aquilegia canadensis*), bloodroot (*Sanguinaria canadensis*), wild ginger (*Asarum* spp.), *Erythronium* spp., mayapple (*Podophyllum peltatum*), *Iris*, Virginia bluebells (*Mertensia virginica*), wood poppy (*Stylophorum diphyllum*), and a dozen fern species.

I've grown many of these plants. None were wild-collected. I grew some from seeds; others were purchased from nearby public wildflower garden fund-raisers and nurseries specializing in propagating local plants. I have a few woodland beds where I tend these plants in the soil beneath a huge white pine to try and preserve their genes while enjoying their remarkable beauty.

The word *soil* as I use it here is not quite accurate; the growing medium is not like garden loam. It's more like the natural "duff" found on the forest floor—humus made of decomposing vegetable matter. Just a few inches deep, the duff becomes quite dry in summer, which is another reason many of these plants, which come up and bloom early in the rainy spring, go semi-dormant or completely disappear by the first days of summer.

OPPOSITE (Clockwise from top left) Woodland ephemerals include white stars on foamflower spikes (*Tiarella cordifolia*) among fern crosiers, hooded green Jack-in-the-pulpits (*Arisaema triphyllum*), yellow trout lilies named for their mottled foliage (*Erythronium americanum*), white European wood anemone (*Anemone nemerosa*), foamflower's maple-shaped leaves. ABOVE My woodland garden with white trillium, Virginia bluebells, yellow wood poppy and Mayapple leaves.

WIDE-OPEN SPACES

Though grasslands can be found in most parts of the world, true prairies are unique to North America. The prairies are often on flat or gently rolling land. There is constant wind and bright sunlight. The amount of annual rainfall is less than for meadows, but more than deserts. The barren short-grass prairies of the Great Plains where the bison once roamed are not places we hope to interpret as gardens. However, the tallgrass prairie, which once covered 250 million Midwest acres, is a design source, even though less than 1 percent of that unique plant community still exists.

The word *prairie* comes from the French for meadow, but this habitat type is not what we find in the eastern meadows. The Midwestern prairie is typified by temperature extremes, low rainfall, and drought. Those influences, along with fire, kept shrubs and trees from getting a foothold. Exceptions can be found in some regions within the prairie, for example northwestern Illinois, that receive a bit more rainfall, allowing trees to dot the landscape. We know these places as savannas.

Fires on the prairies have been common for centuries, either caused by lightning striking the "fuel" of dry, dead grasses and forbs (non-grass flowering plant) killed by autumn frosts, or by Native Americans. These indigenous people often burned sections of the prairie to clear the land for hunting or for security.

You might not care to torch your prairie planting, or hope that lightning strikes, but you have to simulate fire's effects if you want to keep woody plants (and even weeds) from taking over the garden. The native tall grasses and forbs are cool season plants that come up late in the spring. Weeds, mostly European farm pests, sprout earlier. So a mid-spring mowing (or controlled burn) will knock back the weed and tree seedlings.

Plants of the tallgrass prairie include familiar species, many of which have become garden plants, or should be. Take, for example forbs: purple coneflower (*Echinacea purpurea*), Culver's root (*Veronicastrum virginicum*), rattlesnake master (*Eryngium yuccifolium*), cup plant (*Silphium perfoliatum*), black-eyed Susan (*Rudbeckia hirta*), yellow coneflower (*Ratibida pinnata*), *Boltonia asteroides*, sneezeweed (*Helenium autumnale*), *Coreopsis tinctoria*, blazing star (*Liatris* spp.), perennial sunflowers (*Helianthus* spp.), and nodding onion (*Allium cernuum*). Grasses include Indiangrass (*Sorghastrum nutans*), big bluestem (*Andropogon gerardii*), switchgrass (*Panicum virgatum*), little bluestem (*Schizachyrium scoparium*), prairie dropseed (*Sporobolus heterolepis*), sideoats grama (*Bouteloua curtipendula*), prairie brome (*Bromus kalmii*), prairie cordgrass (*Spartina pectinata*), and feather reed grass (*Calamagrostis* spp.).

OPPOSITE The prairie community exists only in North America. Showy plants of the Midwest tallgrass prairie are worthwhile garden plants for much of the country, and may also be assembled for a mid-to-late summer meadow. A *Eupatorium purpureum* subsp. *maculatum*; B *Veronicastrum virginicum*; C *Monarda fistulosa*; D *Eupatorium perfoliatum*; E *Cimicifuga* (syn. *Actea*) *racemosa*; F *Liatris spicata*; G *Panicum virgatum*; H, K *Silphium terebinthinaceum*; I *Asclepias tuberosa*; J *Pycnanthemum muticum*; L *Asclepias incarnata*.

The word "prairie" comes from the French word for meadow, and this form of grassland only exists in North America. The Prairie Garden at the Chicago Botanic Garden has plants like blazing star (*Liatris pycnostachya*) with lilac spires.

THE PEACEFUL PLACE

Several years ago, I traveled to see a meadow preserved by a local conservation group. A wire fence surrounded the area, no-trespassing signs were posted, and water lines had been routed to the place for fire hydrants. But there wasn't any meadow. Instead, a young grove of trees had grown within the fenced area. Nature is not static, and if an area is meant to be preserved, it has to be maintained: conservation with intervention. Meadows are transitional plant communities that grow on cleared land in regions with more rainfall than the Midwestern prairies.

Meadows are but moments in the succession of open land in areas with ample rainfall that will in short order be given over to the "woodies"—shrubs and trees. To remain a meadow, a place has to either be too wet for most trees or maintained by mowing or controlled burns.

A plant community is a natural collection of plants that benefit from the particular characteristics of a site. A community can be as small as a pond and as large as the Amazon rain forest. The prairie and meadows as plant communities both need full sunlight. There are more grasses in the prairie and more forbs (non-grass flowering herbaceous plants) in the meadow. Due to heavier rainfall, the species in meadows do not need to grow deep taproots to reach moisture like those in prairies.

Some of the native meadow plants are familiar to us as species in genera we welcome to our gardens, like monarda, aster, false dragon's teeth or obedience (*Physostegia virginiana*), and rudbeckia. Others are not usually thought of as garden plants, but could be. Some of those plants are goldenrod, sneezeweed (*Helenium autumnale*), New York ironweed (*Vernonia noveboracensis*), butterfly weed (*Asclepias tuberosa*), Joe Pye weed (*Eupatorium maculatum*), wild indigo (*Baptisia australis*), northern sea oats (*Chasmanthium latifolium*), and hayscented fern (*Dennstaedtia punctilobula*).

There are wet meadows (and fens—moist sites in the prairie with alkaline soil) where moisture-loving plants thrive. Few grasses grow there, but grass-like plants do, for instance rushes (*Juncus* spp.), sedges (*Carex* spp., *Scirpus* spp.), and cattails (*Typha latifolia*). The wet meadow is home to giant swamp hibiscus, turtlehead, cardinal flower and great blue lobelia (*Lobelia cardinalis, L. siphilitica*), swamp milkweed (*Asclepias incarnata*), blue flag (*Iris versicolor*), and *I. prismatica*.

Meadows are wildlife bonanzas, providing cover and food. The plants attract butterflies, birds, and other animals.

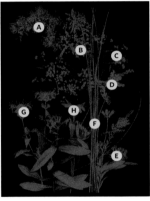

OPPOSITE The Eastern meadows have plants in common with the Midwestern tallgrass prairie community. The difference is moisture. One of the meadow plantings at Willowwood Arboretum (left) in Central New Jersey is home to shorter grasses (little bluestem vs. big bluestem) and colorful flowering plants like A *Eupatorium pupureum* subsp. *maculatum*; B *Scirpus cyperinus*; C *Euthamia graminifolia*; D *Solidago nemoralis*; E *Asclepias tuberosa*; F *Schizachyrium scoparium*; G *Monarda fistilosa*; H *Rudbeckia hirta*.

WET AND WILD

Wetlands are places where moisture is plentiful for most if not all of the year. These places may be seacoasts, ponds, marshes, fens, vernal pools, bogs, swamps, rivers, lakes, and our own backyard water gardens. These moist environs are filled with wonderful plants and often teaming with wildlife of all kinds.

North America has some amazing native shrubs like azaleas and clethra that grow in moist soil at the water's edge. Marginal plants include pickerel rush (*Pontederia cordata*), marsh marigold (*Caltha palustris*), and lizard's tail (*Saururus cernuus*). Floating plants, those with leaves that lie on the surface, include waterlilies (*Nymphaea odorata*), lotus (*Nelumbo lutea*), and spatterdock (*Nuphar lutea*). In the wild, these surface species send roots down into the muck at the shallow bottom.

Some of us lucky gardeners have natural ponds or streams on our properties. The allure of water in the garden inspires more people to bring this element into the landscape. Water in a backyard pond catches a bit of the sky and brings it down to earth. In a shaded urban space, water's ability to reflect light is a real plus. Imagine the sights and sounds of moving water from a fountain or waterfall. The soothing sound is especially welcome where the whoosh of flowing water can take the edge off traffic noise or mask the whir of an air conditioner.

Wetlands are self-sustaining ecosystems. No such luck for a man-made pond. Just to generate moving water, you must defy gravity. But millions have taken up the challenge. Water gardening is an aspect of our outdoor passion that continues to grow in popularity.

If you are planning on putting in a small pond, make it at least three feet deep, as wide and as long as you have room for, and if you hope to grow flowering plants, site it in full sun. The entire excavation will be lined with rubber sheeting.

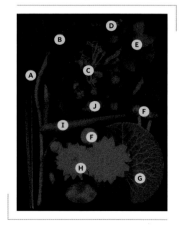

Marginal plants will go into pots that rest on shelves built into the sides of the artificial pond and also covered by the liner. Floating plants go into large, shallow containers filled with dense clay soil (never humus-based potting mix, which floats). Planted pots with moistened soil are lowered onto supports like large inverted clay pots so their rims are about eighteen inches below the water surface for summer. In cold climates, the pot should be further lowered in the fall to about three feet.

OPPOSITE Wetlands range from vernal spring pools to ponds like one in New England where the native plants pictured grew. A *Typha angustifolia**; B *Pontederia cordata*; C *Rhododendron viscosum*; D *Vaccinium corymbosum*; E *Clethra alnifolia*; F *Nuphar lutea*; G,H *Nymphaea odorata*; I *Peltandra virginica*; J *Cephalanthus occidentalis*. ABOVE Native plants in a wood frame and rubber-lined "raised bed" water garden.

*potentially invasive in some climates

Having natural water on the property, like a stream, is wonderful. There's a lot to be said for water—in its right place. Sometimes, I wish I had a little less of it. My property, an island in a river, has been flooded a dozen times over the last fifteen years. I had the "ten-year event," "the hundred-year flood," and once, when the governor called out the National Guard, "the millennial event." I have to wonder, what follows a millennial event?

In between the floods, my property is quite dry. One place that stays wet, however, is the rock-lined canal that cuts across the island and joins the fast and slow branches of the river. This watercourse is basically a stream, and it allows me to grow marginal plants that thrive in shallow water. The plants that live along the edge are "amphibious" like frogs—they live in water and on land depending on the current conditions—high water or low. I grow rodgersia, waterside iris, and primroses (mostly candelabra types, *Primula beesiana*, *P. bulleyana*, and *P. x bulleesiana*). The canal is a garden, not an actual riverbank or shore. I try to be responsible, and not grow exotic plants that might escape.

Ecologists say "the edge is where the action is," and this holds true whether the spot is where the sidewalk meets the lawn, or the dry land meets the stream. An actual shoreline is very important for erosion control, and for the plants and animals that live in this habitat.

Along with native herbaceous plants like watercress (*Nasturtium officinale*), mosses and ferns like New York fern (*Thelypteris noveboracensis*), sedges like *Carex* spp., and rushes like *Juncus* spp., there are native trees and shrubs that hold the bank (and could be choices for a rain garden, page 172). These woody plants have to be very tolerant of flooding and

be able to survive with their roots covered by water for up to 40 percent of the growing season. Tree examples include hazel alder (*Alnus rugosa*), gray birch (*Betula populifolia*), black ash (*Fraxinus nigra*), eastern larch (*Larix laricina*), black spruce (*Picea mariana*), black willow (*Salix nigra*), and common baldcypress (*Taxodium distichum*).

American shrubs that are tolerant of flooding are bog rosemary (*Andromeda polifolia*), chokecherry (*Aronia* spp.), (*Baccharis halimifolia*), buttonbush (*Cephalanthus occidentalis*), summersweet (*Clethra alnifolia*), red osier dogwood (*Cornus stolonifera*), inkberry (*Ilex glabra*), winterberry (*I. verticillata*), Virginia sweetspire (*Itea virginica*), bayberry (*Myrica pensylvanica*), ninebark (*Physocarpus opulifolius*), swamp azalea (*Rhododendron viscosum*), and American elderberry (*Sambucus canadensis*).

OPPOSITE Some ornamental plants for a moist area include:

A *Iris versicolor*; B *Veratrum viridis*; C *Primula x bullessiana*; D *Sambucus canadensis*; E, G *Ligularia japonica* (flower buds and leaf); F *Darmera peltata*.

ABOVE Plants that are a little too glad to reproduce in a moist situation should be kept from areas where seeds might escape into the wild. *Primula japonica** is a garden plant, and not one for wild wetlands away from their homeland.

*potentially invasive in some climates

A shallow pond with moving water at the entrance to Henriette Suhr's garden, Rocky Hills, features waterside plants like iris and primroses with a background of colorful deciduous and evergreen azaleas.

LET IT RAIN

Many gardeners all over the country have realized the importance of water not just for aesthetics or irrigation, but also as a precious resource to be conserved. This awareness has led some people to harvest or capture the rain that falls on their property in cisterns, rain gardens, and bog plantings.

A rain garden is located in the lowest part of the property and designed to collect runoff from roofs, driveways, and the like. Accumulated water is filtered by the soil as it seeps

down to replenish groundwater, is used by plants, or evaporates back to the atmosphere.

If the landscape soil is heavily compacted, then a rain garden medium has to be brought in. Excavate a depression in the soil. The hole can be just about any size and depth, and should be filled with a moisture-retentive but well-drained medium consisting roughly of 25 percent compost, 50 percent coarse sand, and 25 percent excavated garden loam. Conventional gutters and downspouts can be channeled into underground French drains from which some of the water will seep into the earth as it travels to the site and more will drain toward the rain garden.

Plants selected for this area must be able to tolerate periods of wet and dry: native meadow wildflowers, ferns, sedges, rushes, and moisture-tolerant shrubs and trees (page 166).

Another type of retention planting is a bog garden, which must be sited in full sun in a spot that does not flood, and will not be subject to chemical run-off from the lawn. Dig a bowl-shaped hole one to two feet deep and at least five feet in diameter. The hollow may be lined with special pond clay—packed and pounded inside of the bowl. A rubber garden pond liner or even plastic sheeting can be used instead of clay. In those cases, line the soil bowl with a layer of sand, lay down the liner, and punch drainage holes all over—bottom and sides. To allow rainwater to flow into the bowl, the liner should not extend above the level of the surrounding ground.

To mimic the bog's decomposing humus, the medium should be highly acidic. Peat moss (while an inferior, acidic, and quick-to-degrade soil amendment) could be useful here mixed three to one with coarse sand. Plants for the bog garden want a high-acid, low oxygen, and nutrient-deficient environment (like the wiry cranberry, carnivorous pitcher plants, and sundews).

The countries bordering the Mediterranean Sea have a special climate, but one that is not unique to that part of the globe. Specific weather patterns and temperature conditions are shared by a few places within latitude 40 degrees north and 40 degrees south. These areas include the southwestern tip of Africa, a dot at the center of New Zealand, parts of Chile and China, Western Australia, and the coast of California.

In the countries touching the sea itself—Spain, Italy, Israel, Turkey, Algeria, Morocco, and others—the Moorish or Islamic style continues to bear a powerful influence. Cloistered gardens surrounded by walls, or in courtyards, with a central water runnel and fountain, evolved in part as responses to social and environmental factors: a need for privacy and security, weather and water.

With sufficient irrigation, the Mediterranean area is ideal for growing a wide range of food crops from spring through summer. No wonder agricultural crops have been cultivated there for thousands of years, helping civilizations develop and flourish. When plants put down roots, so do people.

Sea travel encouraged trade.

Many foods associated with one country originated elsewhere, like Ireland's potato. Eggplant is popular in the Middle East and probably made it to Italy from there. Italy is associated with New World fruits like tomatoes, peppers, and zucchini from Central America. In a French fairy tale, Cinderella stepped out of a coach transformed from a pumpkin. Spain and Florida are famed for citrus, which came from Asia.

Although the Mediterranean is a subtropical region, many of its plants can tolerate colder climates, and cultivars have been selected that are bone-hardy: herbs

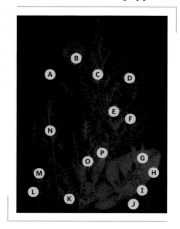

like lavender (*Lavandula angustifolia*), a host of *Artemisia* varieties, lamb's ears (*Stachys bizantina*), and many silver-leafed plants (page 113). The key is to provide excellent drainage year-round. When I think of Italy's gardens, I picture Italian cypress (*Cupressus sempervirens*), those tall, slender evergreens that shoot up in the semiformal villa landscapes. Other people might think of red ripe tomatoes, or fragrant herbs. Many herbs familiar in Italy can also be grown in North America, like sage, oregano, marjoram, thyme, fennel, parsley, and mint.

OPPOSITE Mediterranean and similar plants A edible fig; B *Achillea* species (from the Greek hero Achilles); C *Artemisia ludoviciana* 'Silver King'*; D *Lychnis coronaria*; E *Tanacetum partheneum* 'Aureum'; F *Gypsophila repens*; G *Olea europaea*; H *Stachys byzantina* 'Helene von Stein'; I *Santolina chamaecyparissus*; J *S. virens*; K *Tanacetum vulgare*; M *Salvia officinalis* 'Icterina'; N *Achillea* 'Schwellenberg'; O *Lavandula angustifolia*; P *Origanum vulgare* 'Aureum'. ABOVE Members of the Solanaceae family: tomatoes 'Japanese Black Trifele', 'Yellow Pear', purple 'Black Cherry', and plum 'Juliette'; eggplants 'Italian Long', pale round 'Rosa Bianca', small Asian 'Ping Tung'.

*potentially invasive in some climates

Chanticleer, the magnificent public garden in Wayne, Pennsylvania, has many newly designed plantings around a former estate, including this Moorish-style fountain and runnel beside the main house.

PARADISE FOUND

Gardeners in Coastal California think that their climate is so special, so unlike the rest of the country that they have little in common with people who tend the soil elsewhere: And they are right. Gardeners west of the Rocky Mountains even have their own growing zone map based not on the climate zones determined by the United States Department of Agriculture, but on twenty-four divisions established by *Sunset Magazine*.

These gardeners face significant challenges: mudslides in winter, low rainfall in summer, earthquakes, and wildfires.

Despite those impediments, California is a gardener's paradise. With warm, sunny hillsides, Californians can grow a host of plants from Australia, South Africa, and the Mediterranean: figs, olives, citrus, walnuts, and of course, wine grapes. The climate is also ideal for invasive exotic plants, which have overrun many of the state's some 5,000 native trees, shrubs, grasses, annuals and perennials, bulbs, and herbs. The situation is not quite as dire as it is in Hawaii, which could stand as a warning.

The best gardens to house the myriad exotic, noninvasive plants might be urban plantings. These mini-botanical gardens could be thought of as zoos. Imagine a place like Berkeley in the East Bay across from San Francisco where it is warm enough to grow some citrus and bananas, but cool enough to have a few lilac varieties and apples. There are succulents: agave, aloe, tropical aeonium, and echeveria. You can see palms there and clumping bamboo. There are the immensely popular strap-leafed New Zealand flax (*Phormium* varieties related to lilies), the horsetail-like "restios," and the more familiar fuchsia, jasmine, confederate jasmine (*Trachelospermum jasminoides*), tree ferns, and flowering maples (*Abutilon* varieties). Abutilons, related to hibiscus, have nodding flowers and species coming from Central and South America, China, India, California, and even Hawaii.

If I had land in California, I might try to grow native plants like the late-winter-blooming *Garrya* spp. with flower tassels that look almost like icicles, coastal redwoods, Douglas iris, flannel bush, and others in the outer areas of the property, while keeping more tender exotics closer to the house. California native plants may be recognized for specific epithets like *californica, occidentalis, douglasii,* or *fremontii*.

For those who garden up the coast in Oregon and Washington State, the climate resembles Great Britain's. I have to admit a bit of environmental jealousy toward folks who can grow the plants we see in English books and magazines.

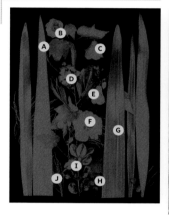

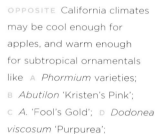

OPPOSITE California climates may be cool enough for apples, and warm enough for subtropical ornamentals like A *Phormium* varieties; B *Abutilon* 'Kristen's Pink'; C *A.* 'Fool's Gold'; D *Dodonea viscosum* 'Purpurea'; E *Abutilon* 'Seashell'; F *A.* 'Kristin's Pink'; G *Phormium* varieties; H *Coprosma* 'Roy's Red'; I *C.* 'Pink Surprise'; J giant redwood *Sequoiadendron giganteum* 'Hazel Smith'. ABOVE In a Berkeley garden by Brandon Tyson: *Brahea armata* (Mexican blue palm), coral flowers of *Aloe distans*, and rosettes of *Echeveria imbricata*.

Bob Clark's Oakland, California, garden combines art with horticulture. The climate—neither too cold nor too warm—allows for plants that are cold hardy like pink flowering cherries, and ones that are frost tender like yellow angel's trumpet (*Brugmansia sp.*) with huge, flaring flowers.

NATURE REFINED

The Japanese Tea Garden in San Francisco's Golden Gate Park, designed in 1894 by Makoto Hagiwara, is the oldest such garden in the United States. Hagiwara imported one thousand flowering cherry trees along with other native plants from his East-Asian homeland. He lived in and cared for the gardens until 1942, when he and his family were forced into an internment camp.

The best known U.S. planting of Japanese trees is around the Tidal Basin in Washington, D.C., a man-made inlet created in the late nineteenth century. The view is dominated by the Jefferson Memorial to the south, and in early April by flowering cherries around the banks. In 1912, the people of Japan gave 3,020 trees to the people of the United States. The original gift included nearly a dozen varieties, but is dominated, today, by pinkish white Yoshino (*Somei-yoshino*). The cherry tree, or "sakura," is a symbol of the fleeting nature of life. In Japan, the celebration of the trees peaks not when they bloom, but when the blossoms shatter and litter the ground with pink and white petals.

When we think of Japanese gardens, we picture the elements of the style: cloud-pruned shrubs, moon bridges, statues of Buddha, stone lanterns, bamboo fences, koi ponds, and waterfalls. Alternately, the quiet, contemplative Zen gardens with floors of carefully raked gravel come to mind.

As for Japanese plants, North America and Europe must have been connected to those islands long ago, for many Western species have counterparts there. The overwhelming number of analogous species occur in the eastern United States in genera such as *Jeffersonia*, *Podophyllum* (mayapple), *Arisaema* (Jack-in-the-pulpit), *Pachysandra*, *Viburnum*, *Asarum* (wild ginger), and even the cherry trees (*Prunus* spp.).

You cannot establish a true Japanese garden outside of Japan, but like many of the places that inspire us, we can adapt special features in the Japanese style to our home landscapes. Consider certain concepts: enclosure, reduced scale, controlled angles of view, and symbolism. Nature is revered, distilled, and presented in miniature. Another feature is "borrowed scenery." You may not have a snow-capped mountain in the background of your garden, but neighboring trees can be "brought" into the landscape with thoughtful framing.

Western notions like symmetry are eschewed—mirroring in a natural landscape only exists in reflections in water. We may not be able to decipher all aspects of the subtle symbolism, but the overriding ethic is clear—produce an entire "world" in a garden.

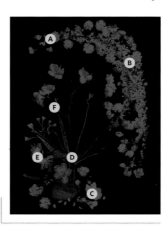

OPPOSITE Notable cold-hardy Asian plants: A double pink weeping Higon cherry (*Prunus subhirtella* 'Pendula Plena Rosea'); B *Spiraea thunbergii*; C *Prunus* 'Shirotae'; D non-running hardy bamboo *Fargesia nitida*; E *Rhododendron mucronulatum*; F *R. m.* cv. LEFT The cherry blossom holiday celebrates petal fall.

NATURE REVERED

Traditional Chinese gardens are built, rather than planted, and based on nature. Instead of yielding to the happenstance of the wild, nature as a ruling force is formally dictated. The architecture of the garden usually includes a mound, a pond, and a pavilion. Plants are brought in as the secondary layer. The senses are addressed by framing views from the dwelling windows, aromas from fragrant flowers, and even the pebble paving is arranged for its feel beneath the feet. Finally, a single *taihu* rock is carefully placed in the space. Mountains and rocks play a special role in art, design, myth, poetry, and Chinese scholarship.

"China is, indeed, *The Mother of Gardens*," wrote Ernest Henry Wilson in a book bearing that title. On his expeditions to find plants in China, Wilson collected 65,000 specimens, introducing to westerners 1,500 plants, including dogwoods, rhododendron, forsythia, primroses, clematis, lilies, and peonies. Most of the peonies we grow in our gardens have been bred from Japanese cultivars, which themselves were developed from Chinese varieties. The Japanese borrowed from the Chinese for art, gardens, and plants—refining what they found to make it theirs.

Peonies were grown in Chinese gardens as far back as 1000 BCE as medicinal plants, and as ornamentals during the Sui Dynasty (605–617). The peony could be considered the unofficial national floral emblem of China, where it is revered in literature, poetry, and art—as a primary decorative element in porcelains, screen paintings, clothing, and tapestries.

Chinese Classical gardens were built by and for the scholar class—bureaucrats, officials, and civil servants—and first appeared during the Eastern Han Dynasty (25–220 CE), around the same time as the adoption of Confucianism. After the fall of this dynasty, the scholar class retreated to their gardens, which became private places for contemplation.

It was during the long period between the Eastern Han Dynasty and the Tang Dynasty (618–907) that the classical Chinese garden style matured and expanded. The Song Dynasties (960–1279) were considered the "golden age" of garden design as high art flourished across the country.

During this time, the central idea was to create a sense of distance, of the infinite. The Japanese adopted a quintessential principle of incorporating a framed vista, the Chinese phrase for which is *jie jing*. Another term that expresses the rules for asymmetrical arrangement is feng shui—balancing patterns of yin and yang, and the flow of chi (the life force).

OPPOSITE Peonies, and especially woody tree peonies are revered in Chinese Scholar gardens (clockwise from bottom right) 'Coral Terrace', 'Multi-colored Butterfly' and 'Guardian of the Monastery' with an English variety of an Asian: *Dicentra* (syn. *Lamprocapnos*) *spectabilis*—'Gold Heart'. ABOVE A detail of an example of the Chinese miniature rock art of *Penjing*.

ON THE ROCKS

Japanese rock gardens are dry landscapes, what we call Zen gardens. The Chinese practice a similar form called *Penjing*—related to bonsai—in which a large stone is "planted" on a tray or in a garden, to stand in for a jagged mountain, and artfully decorated with plants. Americans may have a fuzzier notion of what constitutes a rock garden as being any garden with rocks strewn around, what the British call a rockery. (To make rocks look natural, I sometimes bury two-thirds or more underground.) A true rock or alpine garden requires considerable thought and attention.

The plants selected from nature are those that grow in tight spaces, at high elevations, next to and among rocks. These species are usually dwarfed by evolution to help them survive in poor soil, high wind, and drastic temperature extremes. They are protected in winter by insulating snow cover. They include some of the herbaceous plants and scruffy subshrubs that grow above the tree line—hence "alpines."

Consider the conditions these plants are exposed to in the thin air above the timberline. Summer temperatures are low, but in the dry air above the clouds and pollution, the sun is barely filtered. Leaves are tiny to conserve moisture; plants grow very close to the ground. Water is often tied up in snow or frozen earth. More of the plants are below ground than above, with taproots plunging deep into the earth in search of available moisture and food. In this arid climate, it can take years for fallen leaves and dead plants to decompose, leaving the soil without nutrients or layers of humus.

Summers are short and winters long. Most flowering occurs in the late spring, and all at once so the alpine "meadows" are ablaze in color. "Spring," however, might occur in August.

All of that hard work results in jewellike plants and spectacular flowers to attract pollinators while they can. Some alpine plants and those from similar if less extreme environments may be encouraged to survive in milder climates. Heat is the enemy. The essential requirement is superior drainage—50 percent soil, 50 percent coarse sand or grit. A guaranteed snow cover in winter can't hurt.

More genera with dwarf species include *Androsace, Antennaria, Aquilegia, Arabis, Arenaria, Campanula, Delosperma, Draba, Gentiana, Geranium, Hebe, Helianthemum, Lewisia, Penstemon, Phlox, Potentilla, Sempervivum, Thymus, Veronica,* and *Viola.*

OPPOSITE A *Anthyllis montana* 'Rubra'; B *Leontopodium alpinum* (Edelweiss); C *Salvia* 'Sensation Rose'; D, E *Saxifraga crustata*; F *Eriogonum ovalifolium* (syn. *Paronychia ovalifolium, Amaracea supalifolium*); G *Opuntia fragilis*; H *Thalictrum kiusianum*; I *Scutellaria prostrata*; J *Edraianthus serpyllifolia*; K *Dianthus* x 'Brigadier'. ABOVE Dark pink *Armeria maratima* and tiny sedums on a stone wall.

As gardeners, we look to the larger world around us for inspiration, to history, literature, art, loved ones, and nature itself. Our ornamental gardens combine plants for color or environmental conditions, collections of weird and lovable species, or just about anything that turns us on. Perhaps, you might be moved to grow the flowers named in the works of William Shakespeare, the cottage gardens he knew, or the formal gardens of his queen. In Victorian times, a style emerged using the new plants from Britain's colonies. Later, the Arts & Crafts movement promoted naturalistic plantings countering the former fashion.

A sensual garden might concentrate on plants for fragrance, flowers with perfume, and leaves that impart their own special scents. An evening garden might be made as a place to relax after work with flowers that bloom at night, filling the darkness with fragrance. Many of the evening scented flowers are also white in order to attract their moth pollinators.

During the day, a butterfly planting would attract those colorful pollinators and also feed their larvae—caterpillars. And a hummingbird garden could provide nectar-rich plants with the hues and shapes that attract these beautiful birds. What about some of the other creatures that may play in the garden—children? We talk about plants for kids: ones that grow really fast and big, and others that look like they have smiling faces. A pizza garden might be just the thing with tomatoes, basil, and garlic.

There might be very personal creations, for instance, plantings inspired by people, reminders of your grandmother's garden. Perhaps the memories are of tasty vegetables or maybe of candied violets and rose petals.

Got shade? You might want to make a secret garden as a place to escape from the heat of summer or the commotion of your busy day. Too subtle for you? How about a sunny cutting garden filled with flowers you'll grow to gather for arrangements indoors?

These are some of the themes that we can bring to our landscapes. You may think of others. The scans and the accompanying garden photos are filled with ideas for combinations that will help you create new visions for your own little universe.

OPPOSITE Irritating or even potentially poisonous plants may also have medicinal uses. (Clockwise from top left) *Lonicera periclymenum* 'Serotina Florida'; *Allium* 'Hair'; *Digitalis lutea*; *D. parviflora*; *D. lanata*; *Cotinus coggygria* (threadlike flowers); *Hedera helix* 'Blue Moon'; *H. h.* 'Gold Heart'; *Achillea millefolium* 'Apricot Delight'.

THE SWEET SMELL
OF SUCCESS

Many flowers are fragrant, and evolved to smell in a way we (and their pollinators) find irresistible. You might plant a sensory garden with fuzzy-leafed herbs that must be handled in order to release their smells, like scented geraniums (*Pelargonium* varieties). There could be a spice garden with cultivars of dianthus—pinks—that contain eugenol, a chemical compound with a clove-like aroma.

A planting could be based on night-fragrant exemplars for the patio. Look for white flowers like nicotiana, datura, and white petunias that attract moths and other creatures of the night. Some flowers do not even open until their insect associates are active. Moonflower (*Ipomoea alba*), for example, and four-o'clocks (*Mirabilis jalapa*), which got their common name from the time the buds unfurl.

Many tender perennials have perfumed flowers. These plants spend their summers outdoors in northern gardens, where they are planted in large containers or in flower beds. Others, like the bulbs of tuberose, will be stored dormant in cool basements for winter. Some potted plants, like citrus trees that blossom with the lengthening daylight hours in winter and heliotrope with perfume that could be described as cherry, vanilla, and baby powder, go to a sunny window indoors or to a greenhouse. Many of these plants can live year-round in subtropical gardens around the Gulf of Mexico. A favorite of mine is *Hoja santa* (*Piper auritum*), a large shrubby relative of the source of black pepper, with large heart-shaped leaves that, when crushed, summon another common name: root beer bush.

A host of annuals smell too, including stock, mignonette (*Reseda odorata*), and sweet alyssum (*Lobularia maritima*), whose honey-like fragrance fills my sister's neighborhood in Northern California.

Cold-hardy perennials for fragrance include snakeroot (*Actea*, syn. *Cimicifuga* spp.), bouncing bet (*Saponaria officinalis*), fragrant Solomon's seal (*Polygonatum odoratum*), phlox (species and varieties), daylilies, some hostas (i.e. *H. plantaginea*), lavender, garden lilies, lily-of-the-valley, daffodils (especially cultivars of *Narcissus jonquilla*), hyacinths, and many tulip varieties.

Trees and shrubs also have fragrant flowers, of course. Examples are flowering almond and apricot, black locust, magnolias, and linden trees. Shrubs include paper bush (*Edgeworthia spp.*), winter viburnum species, winterhazel (*Corylopsis glabrescens*), witch hazel (*Hamamelis* varieties), tea olive (*Osmanthus fragrans*), daphne species, buffalo or clove currant (*Ribes odoratum* with the same odiferous chemical that's in the dianthus), mock orange (*Philadelphus* varieties), Carolina sweetshrub (*Calycanthus floridus*), Mexican orange (*Choisya ternata*), sweet pepperbush (*Clethra* spp.), and of course, the celebrated lilacs and roses.

OPPOSITE Fragrance is in the nose of the beholder, and behold the variety: A *Phlox paniculata* 'David'; B *Passiflora alatocaerulea*; C *Hosta plantaginea*; D *Clethra alnifolia* 'Rosea'; E *Dianthus plumaris* hybrids; F *Pelargonium citrosum* 'Mint Rose'; G *Geranium macrorrhizum*; H *Hydrangea arborescens* 'Invincibelle Spirit'; I *Heliotropium arborescens* cv.; J *Clethra alnifolia* 'Creel's Calico'; K *Piper auritum*; L *Vitex negundo* 'Heterophylla' (rub the stems to release the scent); M *Abelia mosanensis*; N *Daphne burkwoodii* 'Briggs Moonlight'; O *Rosa* 'Pink Knockout'.

THE NOSE KNOWS
THE ROSE

When we meet a rose in a garden, today, if it has any scent at all, it smells mostly of fruit and tea. That's a sketchy description of the scent of a hybrid tea rose. These roses were a sensation from the start when they were introduced in the 1800s. Unlike the once-blooming, old shrub roses that European and American gardeners knew, these roses rebloomed throughout the season. Prior to 1867, when the first hybrid tea rose, 'La France', was introduced, fruit and tea were not what people knew as the scent of a rose. If you have ever smelled rose water, you may have a better idea of what the old roses were like: It has a dusty, flowery, perfume smell that seems dry and sweet, intense and delicate at the same time. You can almost feel it in your nose. I grow an old rose in my garden. It is a little centifolia called 'Petite de Hollande'. Centifolia roses contribute essential oils used in perfume.

There is a downside to having a notable fragrance. Flowers that fill the air with scent are actually decomposing, evaporating and allowing their molecules to drift off into the air for us to sample. But sniff a dozen cut long-stemmed roses, today, which have been bred to last nearly two weeks, and you won't smell anything.

As plant hybridizers worked to develop longer-lasting cut roses, the recessive gene for fragrance was lost. Breeding for long stems also compromised scent. In the garden, too, scent is drifting away. Most recent attempts to produce disease-resistant, long-blooming bushes also sacrificed the recessive gene for fragrance. Humans undid in a century the perfume it took roses thousands of years to develop.

Maybe people today do not know what they are missing. American gardeners want healthy, low-maintenance, and long-flowering bushes. As long as they do, plants like the original *Rosa* 'Knock-Out' will dominate the market, even though it has no scent.

There are a few rose growers who are trying to get fragrance back while keeping some of the positive, recent developments. David Austin in England has produced dozens of fragrant shrub roses he considers the best of old and new. Tom Carruth in Los Angeles has bred some sweet-smelling varieties like peppermint striped 'Scentimental' for Weeks Roses, the grower that also recently introduced a rose called 'Night Owl' with red-violet flowers and a kind of pineapple and spice fragrance.

OPPOSITE Modern roses all too often do not have a fragrance. For an antique fragrance, much like rose water, small double 'Petite de Hollande' is a favorite in my garden. A new one is dark purplish-red 'Night Owl' with a hybrid tea fragrance— tea touched by pineapple and spice. When these roses are blooming, companions like white mock-orange varieties (*Philadelphus* 'Belle Etoile', for example) blossom as do clove-scented *Dianthus*. Then, the flowers on wands of lavender begin to open (left to right: *Lavandula angustifolia, L. a.* 'Munstead', *L.* 'Hidcote Pink'). ABOVE Fragrant cut roses with daphne, mountain mint, and butterfly bush.

DAZZLING ENTICEMENTS

Although the fragrant flowers of the butterfly bush (*Buddleia* varieties) produce nectar for adults, their leaves offer nothing to caterpillars, unlike the native butterfly weed (*Asclepias tuberosa*), which feeds both the larvae and adults. Unfortunately, some of the the *Buddleia* species also pose a problem as a potentially invasive exotics in climates where their seeds have a long enough season to ripen and self-sow. All in all, it's best to look for native, regional and local plant species if you're in the market for orange, yellow, lavender, or lilac-colored fragrant flowers.

A true butterfly garden should have flowers with nectar, and also leaves to feed caterpillars. You can't have butterflies without their larvae, and in a way, you can't have birds without caterpillars. Birds need protein, especially when they are babies, and that means they need to find insects to eat.

As mentioned earlier, there are caterpillars that birds do not eat, however. These are species like the monarch that have evolved over the years to exclusively feed on plants in the genus *Asclepias*. The leaves contain toxins to which the caterpillars have become immune. Birds have learned that certain markings on colorful caterpillars indicate that they are unpalatable. The monarchs' dependence on a specific food points out another reason to seek the host plant species that coevolved along with the insects.

Other relationships abound. Spicebush swallowtail caterpillars feed on *Lindera benzoin* (spicebush) and sassafras. The pipevine swallowtail is attracted to *Aristolochia durior*—the pipevine. Tiger swallowtails favor the waterside buttonbush, *Cephalanthus occidentalis*. Many butterfly larvae and adults like the black swallowtail are attracted to members of the Umbelliferae—the carrot and parsley family—typified by umbrella-shaped inflorescences and ferny leaves.

Some butterflies do not care for pretty plants or nectar. They prefer to sip tree sap. Others feed on dung or carrion. There are fungus eaters, and ones that lick aphid honeydew—the secretions of these and other plant lice. There are even butterflies that do not eat at all. Those species may live only for a day or two and survive on nutrient reserves from their larval stage.

Besides planting butterfly attractors, you can place pieces of overripe banana outdoors in a dish to gather them when they are in the neighborhood. Very often, the insects will be just as happy to find a spot of moist ground to "mud-puddle" in, and in the morning they also like to bask on a sun-struck rock.

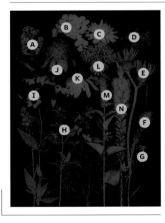

OPPOSITE The best plants for butterflies not only entice them with flowers and nectar, but may offer leaves for larva to eat. Some colorful butterfly-attracting plants include: A *Eupatorium purpureum*; B *Phlox paniculata* 'Nora Leigh'; C *Rudbeckia laciniata* var. 'Hortensia Golden Glow'; D *Monarda* 'Berry Red'; E *Inula magnifica*; F *Liatris spicata*; G *Coreopsis lanceolata* 'Moonbeam'; H *Monarda didyma* 'Raspberry Wine'; I *Rudbeckia triloba*; J *Echinacea purpurea* 'Razzmatazz'; K *Echinacea purpurea* 'The Swan'; L *Asclepias incarnata*; M *Agastache foeniculum* x *rugosa* 'Blue Fortune'; N *Liatris spicata* 'Alba'. **LEFT** Two-tailed swallowtail butterfly (*Papilio multicaudata*) on purple coneflower (*Echinacea purpurea*).

GOOD VIBRATIONS

f you live in the American Southwest, you may see dozens of migrating hummingbird species. Gardeners east of the Mississippi and north may recognize only a few. The wonderful ruby-throated hummingbird (*Archilochus colubris*), named for the male's shimmering iridescent crimson neckband, is the species most often seen.

Hummingbirds are the garden's smallest avian visitors. The average weight of a ruby-throat is three to four grams, less than a nickel. The "hum" for which they are named is the sound of their wings, which depending on the size of the species, beat up to 100 times per second. The unique movement of the wings allows the birds to zoom through the garden and to hover as they feed. It takes a lot of fuel to support this effort, which is why the birds seek their own weight in high-energy sugar water and nectar every day. The birds also eat insects for protein.

The birds sip nectar with their long, darting tongues from flowers like those of the trumpet vine (*Campsis radicans* and varieties), and pollinate the flowers in return. About 8,000 North and South American plant species depend exclusively on hummingbirds for pollination. Hummers will visit tubular and flaring blossoms that offer a rich reward. So you may find them feeding at the dark blue *Salvia guaranitica,* or on honeysuckle vines like *Lonicera periclymenum* var. *serotina* 'Florida' and the local scarlet native *L. sempervirens,* along with its ever-blooming yellow variety 'John Clayton'.

You can plant a few fragrant deciduous azaleas for your hummingbird garden: sweet azalea (*Rhododendron arborescens*) and the swamp azalea (*R. viscosum*). The birds will zoom to the small tubular flowers of red hot poker (*Kniphofia* spp.), even if the variety has cream or yellow blossoms.

Birds see colors pretty much as we do, and the longer wavelengths of red light allow that color to be perceived from a great distance. Commercial hummingbird feeders are usually red for this reason. (Skip the red dyed sugar water, and make your own solution: one part sugar to three parts water to attract them in spring, one to four to keep them healthy—no color needed). You'll notice that the birds do not feed exclusively on red flowers. The quantity of nectar and the shape of the flower trump hue.

I always get excited when hummingbirds return in spring. Banding experiments identifying individual birds have shown that they return to their place of birth.

OPPOSITE Plants that attract hummingbirds A *Lonicera sempervirens;* B *Ipomoea multifida;* C *Nicotiana alata;* D *Impatiens pallida;* E *Kniphofia galpinii* hybrid; F *Monarda didyma* 'Raspberry Wine'; G *Cuphea ignea;* H *Pentas lanceolata* 'Red'; I *Salvia farinacea;* J *Perovskia atriplicifolia;* K *Fuchsia* hybrid; L *Hybiscus syriacus* 'Red Heart'. RIGHT A male ruby-throated hummingbird stands guard atop *Cornus kousa* 'Wolf Eyes'.

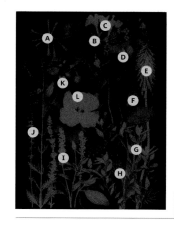

DON'T EAT THE DAISIES—
TRY THE DAYLILIES

Eating flowers sounds like a somewhat new idea, but humankind has been doing it for centuries. The artichoke is a flower bud, and broccoli is covered with buds. Eating less conventional edible flowers, colorful ones often as garnishes for salads and other dishes, is in fact a more recent mode. Once you've tasted a peppery nasturtium, for instance, you'll find that many flowers may offer more than just their pretty faces. Flowers may be used in drinks, soups, jellies, syrups, flavored oils, vinegars, or fritters.

Not every flower is edible, though. As we've learned, many plants are poisonous to humans. Also, don't eat anything that may have been sprayed with pesticides or herbicides. So, nothing from the florist or picked from the side of the road. And, I am sorry to say, you cannot eat flowers just because they are served in a restaurant. I have witnessed ivy used as a garnish, and worse, oleander—both toxic plants. As a general rule: if in doubt, leave it out.

How about establishing a corner of the garden dedicated to edible flowers? On page 239, you'll find a list of edible flowers describing their flavors or contributions to the table.

When summer's zucchini plants begin to produce in earnest, you may end up with more fruits than your family can handle, but not if you harvest flowers to eat. Squash blossoms are wonderful filled with flavored ricotta cheese, dipped in batter, and deep fried.

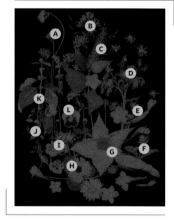

For garnishes, pick flowers in the morning when they are filled with moisture. If you plan to use them soon, float the flowers, cut with a little bit of stem intact, in a bowl of water. To store flowers longer, place them face up on a moistened paper towel set in a covered plastic or glass storage container in the refrigerator.

In most cases, you will be using small flowers whole or pulling petals off of larger ones. Remove fibrous bracts on blossoms like roses, and use the petals. To candy lilacs, rose petals, and violets, dip them in beaten egg white, cover them completely with white sugar, and place them on a rack to dry.

You may want to pluck out the slimy stamens and pistils of larger flowers like daylilies. In one case, however, the part one might think to remove is desirable: The stigma of *Crocus sativus* is the source of the valuable spice saffron.

OPPOSITE The theme of a garden design could be one devoted to edible flowers: A *Allium schoenoprasum* (chives); B *Origanum vulgare* (oregano); C *Agastache foeniculum* (anise hyssop); D *Borago officinalis* (borage); E *Cucumis sativis* 'Diva' (cucumber); F *Ocimum basilicum* (basil); G *Curcubita pepo* cv. (summer squash); H *Calendula officinalis*; I *Tropaeolum majus* 'Peach Melba' (nasturtium); J *Mentha piperita* 'Variegata' (peppermint); K *Ocimum basilicum* 'Lemon'; L *Viola* cv. (pansy). ABOVE Daylilies, and especially yellow ones, are tasty in salads. Flower buds are used in stir-fry.

SECRET GARDENS

cannot deny the healing power of gardens. In Frances Hodgson Burnett's 1911 novel *The Secret Garden*, a sickly orphaned girl discovers a walled garden on the grounds of her uncle's estate. The garden had been tended by her late aunt, and anyone who comes in contact with it, including the girl, her uncle, and her cousin (both of whom are also suffering from various ailments), is cured of any emotional or physical maladies. Everyone lives happily ever after, naturally.

A secret garden can be any secluded place hidden away from the gaze of regular garden visitors where the person who tends the plants can find a few moments of solace and a respite from the tasks and heat of summer.

To me, that means a shady spot where it is often ten to fifteen degrees cooler than in the sunny open spaces. In the protected garden, ferns of all sorts can be planted along with Solomon's seal (*Polygonatum* spp.), false Solomon's seal (*Maianthemum racemosa* syn. *Smilacina racemosa*), and a host of ferns. If you want to include nonnative shade-tolerant plants, then hostas of all types can be cultivated along with their companions like *Pulmonaria* spp.,

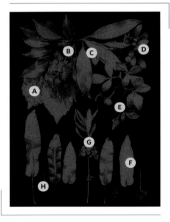

Epimedium spp., astilbe, heuchera, geranium, Asian bleeding heart (*Dicentra spectabilis*, syn. *Lamprocapnos spectabilis*), and the delightful martagon lilies.

The secret or private area doesn't have to be surrounded by a wall, although who wouldn't want a walled garden or perhaps an old stone barn foundation?

You can plant modern screens of shrubs like *Trochodendron*, and *Aucuba* or native *Illicium* in Zone 7; *Kalmia* and *Poncirus* in Zone 6 and warmer. I recommend a "bio-hedge," a planting of mostly deciduous local shrubs that serve as wildlife hiding places, living spaces, and often bird buffets with berried plants. In my area, shrubs include: dogwood, witch

hazel, spicebush, blueberry, bayberry, winterberry holly, serviceberry, chokecherry, elderberry, viburnum, and wild roses.

OPPOSITE A handful of mostly green plants recommended for Zone 7 have been prodded by Nick Nickou to thrive in his Zone 6 garden. A *Aucuba japonica* 'Variegata'; B *Trochodendron araliodes*; C *Illicium floridanum* 'Album'; D *Skimmia japonica*; E *Poncirus trifoliate* 'Flying Dragon'; F Hart's tongue fern fronds (*Asplenium scolopendrium*); G *Kalmia angustifolia*; H dried *Illicium* fruits. ABOVE For the shaded Secret Garden. Clockwise from top left: *Ploygonatum odoratum* 'Variegatum'; silvery Japanese painted fern, *Athyrium japonicum-pictum*; crested male fern, *Dryopteris affinis* 'Cristata'; bronze autumn fern, *Dryopteris erythrosora*; false solomon's seal with berries, *Mianthemum* (syn. *Smilacena*) *racemosa*.

LITERALLY LITERARY

William Shakespeare mentioned more than 200 plants in his works. There is speculation as to whether he was an avid gardener, and some say that this apparent knowledge of plants proves that he was. But these folks might be overlooking the fact that most Elizabethans had a familiarity of plants that would put us to shame. In Shakespeare's time, plants were more than pretty: They were food sources and important medicinals. There are many herbs mentioned in the plays and sonnets, such as mint, marjoram, savory, and lavender. Shakespeare also uses plants and flowers in similes to describe a character's mood, or in metaphors for situations. As Juliet says,

> *"What's in a name?*
> *that which we call a rose*
> *By any other name would smell as sweet."*

Among the best known flowery lines are those that appear in *A Midsummer Night's Dream*:

> *"I know a bank where the wild thyme blows,*
> *Where oxlips and the nodding violet grows,*
> *Quite over-canopied with luscious woodbine,*
> *With sweet musk-roses and with eglantine:*
> *There sleeps Titania sometime of the night,*
> *Lull'd in these flowers with dances and delight."*

The wild thyme is most likely *Thymus vulgaris*; the pale yellow oxlip is *Primula elatior*; woodbine could have been the morning glory–like bindweed or honeysuckle; the eglantine is probably *Rosa eglanteria*.

A "Shakespeare Garden" is simply a planting in which the flowers selected to grow are among those mentioned by the Bard. For instance, he refers to the ubiquitous European cowslip (*Primula veris*) seven times, and this comely fragrant flower of spring would be an important resident of any arrangement inspired by his works. Late daffodils, tulips, violets, columbine, and pulmonaria (lungwort), would be good companions for the oxlip and cowslip primroses.

The design can be just about anything you like. In keeping with Shakespeare's time, one plan could be based on the model of an Elizabethan knot garden, where low hedges made of clipped woody herbs are encouraged to grow in ways that make them appear as if they go up, over, and under each other in a pattern resembling a Celtic knot. The ground within the borders of low hedges may be planted with some of the shorter flowering plants Shakespeare wrote about, or even cabbages and lettuce.

A nonliving element might be brought in to become the central feature of the planting. The ornament might be a sundial, fountain or, perhaps, a bust of the man himself.

OPPOSITE Literary themes for gardens include plantings that bring together varieties mentioned in the works of Shakespeare. Clockwise from top left: columbines, tulip, blue-violet and white lungwort varieties, small and large violets, and at the center, the famous yellow cowslip. ABOVE Poisonous *Aconitum napellus* with antique names like monkshood, wolf's bane, or "aconite" as in *Henry IV.*

The descendant of the French patterned parterre and English knot gardens is found in formal plantings like those of Colonial America. The name boxwood comes from the density of the wood, which has been used to make chess pieces, long-lasting tools, and small containers. The plants will slowly grow large in time. The most popular ones have been the so-called American boxwood (*Buxus sempervirens*) and the English variety (*Buxus sempervirens* 'Suffruticosa'). Neither of these plants originated in the countries noted in their common names, but in Eurasia. The English one has been popular for centuries, for its small leaves and shrub size, growing into balls that can be lined up and clipped for a low hedge. (Boxwoods have an endless reserve of dormant buds that sprout when plants are pruned into nearly any configuration.) But in recent times, English boxwood has developed increased susceptibility to pests and decline from environmental stresses.

There are many others that are more rugged but still dwarf in size. Some have tiny leaves and grow to about one foot tall and two feet wide in fifteen years, such as 'Grace Hendrick Phillips', 'Morris Dwarf', 'Morris Midget', 'Kingsville Dwarf', and 'Tide Hill'. "Spreading" varieties include *B. microphylla* 'Jim Stauffer' and *B. sempervirens* 'Vardar Valley'.

A bit taller are medium varieties like *B. sinica* var. *insularis* 'Nana' and blue-green *B. s.* var. *i.* 'Justin Brouwers' growing to two feet. 'Wanford Page' is gold in spring, 'Golden Dream' is variegated yellow and green, and *B. sempervirens* 'Elegantissima' is cream and gray-green and grows to around three feet. There are selections of yet another species, for example, *Buxus macrophylla* var. *japonica* 'Green Beauty'. Cold hardy hybrids growing taller than two feet include 'Green Mountain', 'Green Velvet', and 'Glencoe'. Upright types include the species *Buxus sempervirens*, conical 'Dee Runk', super-hardy columnar 'Graham Blandy' (with fragrant flowers), and the narrow 'Fastigiata', a superior seletion. 'Rotundifolia' is a large-leafed variety that looks like dense privet.

Once established, boxwoods are drought tolerant. The shrubs like a somewhat alkaline soil—similar to lawn grass. A good tip is to never plant them too deep—if anything, higher than they grew in the nursery—a very unusual recommendation. Boxwoods can take a bit of shade, and are nearly deer-proof, which has increased their popularity to the point that they can now be found at the big box stores.

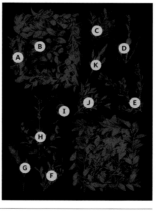

OPPOSITE Boxwood is making a comeback. A *Buxus sempervirens* 'Elegantissima'; B *B. sempervirens*; C *B. s.* var. *suffruticosa* (so-called English boxwood); D *B. microphylla* var. *koreana* x *B. s.* 'Green Mountain'; E *B. m.* 'Peergold' (syn. 'Golden Dream'); F *B. sinca* var. *insularis* 'Tide Hill'; G *B. sempervirens* 'Graham Blandy'; H *B. s.* 'Latifolia Maculatum'; I *B. s.* 'Rotundifolia'; J *B. microphylla* 'Kingsville Dawrf'; K *B. sinca* var. *insularis* 'Justin Brouwers'. LEFT Pruned 'Green Gem'.

HEALTH AND BEAUTY

Plants have always played an essential role in our lives—providing food and often shelter, not to mention the fact that they produce the very air we breathe. Among the important plants to humans, herbs and spices have always been held in high regard. Until the nineteenth century, spices were used to preserve food, and herbs were our primary sources of medicines. So, the herb garden was considered as essential as the food garden.

When a country sent out ships to find and colonize "new" lands, one of the first tasks upon arrival was to set up a test garden. Botanical gardens were originally organized plots for growing collected plants. These herb and food gardens were set up for research and development with formal rows and beds. The formality of a botanical garden, or a "physic"—referring to the science of healing—can be seen today at the Chelsea Physic Garden, which was founded in London in 1673 as the Apothecaries' Garden. The purpose was to train apprentices in identifying and disseminating plants. By the 1700s the garden had initiated an international seed exchange, which continues to this day.

The convention of the formal layout for an herb garden endures in public and private plantings. Herb gardens are most often made up of geometric beds enclosed by low hedges of clipped woody fragrant shrubs and subshrubs like lavender, germander (*Teucrium*), or boxwood. This plan is very much like the early monastery gardens, which often had four or more square beds—usually made around a central water source like a well—and cruciform paths.

I do not have a formal herb garden. I grow herbs as if they were simply ornamental plants, especially in my gravel garden. There, I can find culinary, medici-

nal, and fragrant herbs like lavender, several thyme varieties, sage, foxglove, anise hyssop (*Agastache foeniculum*), bee balm (*Monarda* varieties), oregano, marjoram, and dianthus (pinks). Woody plants include willow, ginkgo, cut-leaf chaste tree (*Vitex negundo* 'Laciniata'), Chinese quince (*Pseudocydonia sinensis*), grapes, elderberry, and roses. Annuals include basil and cilantro.

I grow mints in containers, because they are aggressive runners. I have peppermint, spearmint ('Kentucky Colonel'), and a few glaucous blue-green mountain mints (*Pycnanthemum* ssp.) with a strong menthol fragrance—released when the leaves are crushed. Mint relatives like lemon balm (*Melissa officinalis*) are also best kept in check, and grown in pots.

OPPOSITE Ornamental and useful plants: A *Origanum marjoram* (marjoram); B *Anethum graveolens* (dill); C *Ocimum basilicum* (basil); D *Satureja montana* (winter savory); E *Artemisia dracunculus* (tarragon); F, G, H *Thymus* varieties (thyme); I *Petroselinum crispum* var. *neapolitanum* (Italian parsley); J *Nepeta cataria* (catnip); K *Origanum vulgare* (oregano). ABOVE Rampant mint should be planted in a restricted area.

WHAT DOESN'T KILL YOU MAKES YOU . . .

One critter's treasure is another's toxin. Like fragrance, color, and other aspects of plants we find attractive, the essential oils that make many plants appealing to us for imparting fragrance to soap or perfume did not evolve for our benefit. These properties may be natural insect deterrents. Many of the most fragrant plants are from the Mediterranean region, where browsing animals scamper up the hot, dry hillsides sampling anything they come across. Pungent-tasting and strong-smelling plants like rosemary, thyme, and lavender have the best chance of being passed over. Aromatic or bitter qualities might also be more than unappetizing; they might be warnings of danger.

Whenever anyone writes about medicinal plants, there has to be a cautionary caveat. Do not eat anything you are not familiar with. Many of our best-loved garden plants can be harmful if ingested. Some members of the Fabaceae family are favorite edibles, like garden peas. Others, wisteria for instance, should not be consumed. Some plants may have harmful parts. Rhubarb is a good example: The stems are edible; the leaves are not.

Narcissus and hyacinths are poisonous, which is why deer rarely eat them (they love tulips, however). Oleander is toxic. Larkspur and monkshood can be sickening. Lily-of-the-valley is poisonous, as well. Some plants pose other problems. The herb rue (*Ruta graveolens*) tastes bitter, but it also may cause a skin rash. Rue is phototoxic and may produce blistering if touched in sunlight.

Eating too much of one plant could be lethal, while eating a little could be healthful. Some plants that are poisonous are also life-giving sources of medicines. It has been estimated that as many as one out of every six pharmaceuticals were originally derived from plants. A great example is foxglove (*Digitalis parviflora*): Too much of this plant will stop a person's heart if eaten, but a little bit properly administered is an important cardiac drug.

Hippocrates (460–377 BCE), the father of medicine, left records of a powder made from the bark and leaves of the willow tree (*Salix alba*) to relieve headaches, pains, and fevers. In 1828, Johann Buchner, isolated a tiny amount of needle-like crystals, which he called salicin. A buffered version of the miracle drug, acetylsalicylic acid, was patented as Asprin in 1900 by the Bayer company.

OPPOSITE Among the risky or beneficial plants are: A *Lilium martagon*; B *Artemisia ludoviciana* 'Silver King'*; C *Lonicera periclymenum* 'Serotina Florida'; D *Zantedeschia* 'Crystal Blush'; E *Euphorbia dulcis* 'Chamaeleon'; F *Corydalis lutea*; G *Solenostemon* (syn. *Coleus*) *scutellarioides*; H *Tanecetum parthenium*; I *Lilium* 'Mrs. R. O. Backhouse'. LEFT Flowering nasturtium blossoms are edible; those of tall green euphorbia are *not*!

*potentially invasive in some climates

DEDICATED FOLLOWERS OF FASHION

The Victorian style of planting resulted from several concurrent developments and influences. The British built their empire with colonies around the globe, many of them in tropical climates, which resulted in access to new, frost-tender plants to add to English collections. To keep the plants alive over winter, or to start new ones from seeds and cuttings, the gardeners needed greenhouses. The Industrial Revolution brought affordable glass and extruded iron for these structures. It took quite a bit of energy for manufacturing and to heat the greenhouses, contributing to already polluted air in cities like London.

The English were also influenced by the French parterre style, from the same word as parquet used in flooring designs. The popular style that developed was the carpet-bedding scheme, in which hundreds of plants of the same variety were laid out in paisley patterns and geometric shapes.

Bedding schemes flourished among the new middle class, and neighbors challenged each other, daring to be outdone. Today, bedding only seems popular in institutional plantings, historical re-creations, and theme parks. But if you live in an old house, a version might be fun to develop.

For the most part, these plantings rely on short annuals, like red hothouse geraniums (*Pelargonium*) from South Africa, marigolds, wax begonias, lantana, caladium, and petunias from South America; coleus from southeast Asia; and other exotics, as well as tall tender perennials used as central focal points: big plants like canna, banana, *Brugmansia*, or agave.

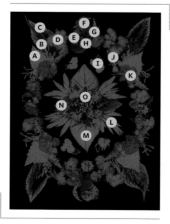

However popular it may have been, there were some contemporary gardeners who complained about the contrived Victorian style. William Robinson was moved to write books railing against mass production and the unnatural carpet bedding, championing instead a more naturalistic style. He started a magazine, *The Garden*, and published a popular book called *The Wild Garden*, which was followed with even greater success by the *English Flower Garden*. His disciple Gertrude Jekyll, a proponent of what has come to be called the Arts & Crafts style, continued his work both at his magazine and in the designs she made with her protégé, the architect Sir Edwin Lutyens.

OPPOSITE Displays of "carpet bedding" could have varieties of: A coleus; B lavender cotton (*Santolina chamaecyparissus*); C, F wheatstraw celosia; D ageratum; E red wax begonias; G lantana; H chenille plant (*Acalypha*); H lantana; I white wax begonia; J *Salvia farinacea*; K hothouse geranium—"pellies"; L canna flower buds; M, N *Caladium*; O coleus. ABOVE A planted Victorian urn with geraniums, spiky dracaena, and trailing variegated *Vinca major*.

Victorian bedding is rarely seen, today, but is still found at the historical Mohonk Mountain House in New Paltz, New York—a family-operated resort founded in 1869. Thousands of annuals are planted in designs that change every year, like this one with *Agave americana* 'Variegata' as the central feature.

FOLK ART

The original cottage garden style emerged in England prior to the Elizabethan era. Unlike the informal style of the Arts & Crafts garden, with which it has much in common, the structure was not an intentional backlash movement countering the contemporary formal knot gardens. Neither were these gardens composed for beauty and pleasure. There was no desire to create a formal design or to develop a grand estate—the idea was to supplement whatever foodstuffs the family could obtain. These plantings were functional gardens with plots for herbs and food close to the house—likely a thatch-roofed cottage.

The early cottage gardens combined vegetable plants, fruit trees, perhaps a beehive. There might have been a well for water and even space for some livestock, possibly a pig-sty. Plants included traditional herbs grown for medicine, flavoring, pest control, fragrance, and even as sources for dye.

Some of the common herbs were feverfew, lungwort, angelica, sweet woodruff, lavender, thyme, wormwood, catmint, lovage, hyssop, and soapwort.

These simple barnyard gardens became more uniform in structure and appearance with the growing national prosperity during Elizabeth I's reign. The utilitarian gardens took on a romantic look that is today the essential element of the English-cottage form.

As the style evolved, less attention was paid to practical considerations. For example, a rose-covered arbor might decorate the entry gate. Simple dirt paths became paved with discarded brick or pieces of stone in random patterns. There might be a central feature—instead of the watering well—possibly a sundial.

Flowers appeared not only on the useful plants, but some grown purely for decoration were shoehorned into the mix. Ornamental plants to consider might be the familiar delphinium, crocus, carnations, sweet William, marguerite, lily, peony, campanula, monkshood, primrose, veronica, lily-of-the-valley, and daisies.

In time, even the grand estates adopted a bit of the cottage garden aesthetic for their landscapes and created small plantings in the style. Some of these estates were actually entire villages with shops and artisans supporting the manor, and cottage plantings enhanced the local charm.

OPPOSITE Old-time cottage gardens offer a style we think of as an English Garden. Plants that would be useful in early summer include: A *Spiraea x bumalda*; B *Campanula punctata*; C *Penstemon digitalis*; D *Geranium* 'Johnson's Blue'; E *Cerastium tomentosum*; F *Geranium sanguineum* var. *striatum*; G *Lupinus polyphyllus*; H *Oenothera speciosus*; I *Veronica spicata*; J *Asclepias incarnata*. LEFT Sandi Blaze's "English" garden in Connecticut.

BACK TO THE FUTURE

The "modern" cottage garden could refer to the style's revival in the 1870s as another counteraction not only in response to Victorian bedding, but also to the Industrial Revolution itself. Some people felt called to return to the land, back to the pre-industrialization days for health, handiwork, and design inspiration. "Hand-made" was the byword of the day. The leaders of the Aesthetic Movement and its descendant, the Arts & Crafts movement, believed that nothing should be mass-produced, and encouraged the reemergence of the home artisan. Naturally, that meant home gardens, as well.

One principal director of both movements in art and design was William Morris, who created fabric and wallpaper based on the flowers he knew from his own garden and those that surrounded the humble cottages of Southeast England. Like William Robinson, Morris was a critic of Victorian schemes, describing them as ". . . an aberration of the human mind which otherwise I should have been ashamed to warn you of. It is technically called carpet-bedding. Need I explain further? I had rather not, for when I think of it even, when I am quite alone, I blush with shame at the thought."

Those flowers making their way into the fabric and wallpapers by Morris were the favored of the time: sunflowers, hollyhock, iris, pansies, geranium, Solomon's seal, evening primrose, marigold, tulips, lupine, and of course, roses.

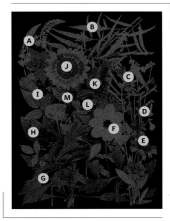

Today's cottage garden style does not focus on food production, but retains the idea of mingling as many disparate varieties as possible in close quarters. Tender perennials and oversize annuals have found their way into these maximalist plantings. You might see tall cannas and blood bananas, and strange red-leafed hibiscus and its cousins: giant red okra and red-leafed cotton.

The relaxed cottage garden look is still with us. The hominess can be enhanced with a casual abandon of encouraging many plants to self-sow—to drop their seeds to the ground in hope that they will sprout and emerge to bloom in the following years. This is an egalitarian scheme in which any plant is accepted as long as it can duke it out with its neighbors for a space to grow.

OPPOSITE The modern take on the cottage garden mixes unusual edibles, perennials, vivid annuals and shrubs. A *Bulbine frutescens* 'Yellow'; B *Rhus typhina* 'Tiger Eyes'; C *Nicotiana* x *sanderae* 'Baby Bella'; D *N. langsdorfii*; E *Gaillardia* 'Burgundy'; F *Dahlia* 'Mystic Illusion'; G *Solenostemon* (syn. *Coleus*) *scutellarioides* 'Lancelot Velvet Mocha'; H *Capsicum annuum* 'Black Pearl'; I *Rosa* 'Pink Knockout'; J *Helianthus* 'Ring of Fire'; K *Hibiscus acetosella* 'Red Shield'; L *Brassica oleracea* 'Scarlet'; M purple basil. ABOVE The source of these plants was New Jersey's Frelinghuysen Arboretum.

SAY IT WITH FLOWERS

There was a time when people communicated their feelings with a twig, a leaf, or some cut flowers. The notion of representing a thought with flowers is as old as antiquity. For this reason, flowers were often depicted as symbols in paintings. For example, lilies represented the vessel or the Virgin Mary in Christian images. And Shakespeare's *Hamlet* reveals the symbolism surrounding some plants:

> *"There's rosemary, that's for remembrance;*
> *pray, love, remember: and there is pansies,*
> *that's for thoughts."*

Ellen Hoverkamp created a memorial image for a friend's late mother based on the viola, known in England by the name "heartsease." An area of the garden could be dedicated to a loved one who has passed, with the commemorative flowers and plants to interpret loss or the qualities of the person who has died.

One of the earliest publications on what was sometimes called "floriography," was written by Madame Charlotte de la Tour in France in 1819. In *Le Language Des Fleur* she gave advice on sending coded messages to lovers well before the days of FTD. The messages weren't always positive: "Love in vain" was represented by the marigold—rejection by a yellow carnation.

Of the hundreds of books published on the subject, 1884's *The Language of Flowers* illustrated by Kate Greenaway was probably the most popular and the source that remains best known today.

Unfortunately, there is no official Oxford Dictionary of plant meanings. You have to find a reference that seems appealing, or gather a few from the library and establish some consistency. If a yellow rose means the same thing in several books, then choose that most common interpretation.

You can create a planting based on an idea and expressed through the symbolic meanings of plants. Perhaps a planting that interprets "peace" might be desired—starring the olive branch. Fortunately, many plants represent aspects of fondness. There could be plants that denote familial affection. A friendship garden could be selected around signifiers of fondness, caring, loyalty, fidelity, and camaraderie. I think a garden dedicated to love could be quite evocative, as so many plants stand for amorous affection.

OPPOSITE A "Heartsease" (another name for pansy) bouquet was made with flowers gathered from a memorial planting to soothe a saddened soul. ABOVE Plants were used in courtship: Purple lilac denotes "stirrings of love." White lilac symbolizes "modest and pure emotions." See page 243 for more translations.

THE NAKED GARDENER

A garden planted for cut flowers can be set up like a vegetable patch with rows of blossoms grown for harvest. Or, the garden may look more, well, like a flower garden. Just bear in mind that this place may not be one of your showiest plantings. As soon as the flowers look good, it's time to cut them. Perhaps we should call this naked gardening.

Most cutting gardens rely on annuals, bulbs, and perennials. Flowers should have long stems and last well after cutting. Just as for a vegetable garden, plant the varieties that you really like and not just things that sound appealing in the catalog. If you don't want red salvia in every room of your house, don't plant them. If the scent of marigolds bothers you, leave that out. (I like their aroma.) Include plants with attractive foliage, like hostas, dusty miller, and even feathery asparagus and bold kale.

I contend that an arrangement of cut flowers can be made from just about every garden on just about every day of the year. Just think of holly, ivy, and other berried or evergreen plants; those that dry well such as grasses; and plants with attractive seed heads. Throughout the rest of the year, you can always cut enough stems for a bouquet or two, if not enough to fill the entire house with vases. If you have the space, include a few extras of your favorites. These plants can be in their own special small bed or right in among their cousins in the mixed border.

Not all plants are what might be called "cut and come again" flowers, but many are. If it bothers you to cut them, just think of it as regenerative pruning.

Annuals and tender perennials for cutting include love-lies-bleeding, *Ammi majus*, bells of Ireland, calendula, feather celosia, Bachelor's buttons or cornflower, cleome, cosmos, lisianthus (*Eustoma* hybrids), globe amaranth, annual baby's breath, marigold, stock, salpiglossis, *Salvia farinacea*, scabiosa, snapdragon, statice, sunflower, sweet pea, and zinnia.

Hardy perennial flowers for cutting could be achillea, aster, carnation, chrysanthemum, foxglove, purple coneflower, echinops, eryngium, goldenrod, baby's breath, lavender, lupine, phlox, and rudbeckia.

OPPOSITE Plants for a cutting garden: A *Celosia* 'Bombay Pink'; B *Antirrhinum* 'Rocket Mix'; C *Helichrysum bracteatum*; D *Echinops ritro*; E *Limonium sinuatum* 'Forever Happy'; F *Gerbera* 'California Mixed Colors'; G *Zinnia* hybrids; H *Ageratum* hybrid; I *Antirrhinum* 'Madame Butterfly'; J *Gomphrena globosa* 'Las Vegas'; K *Phlox paniculata* 'David'; L *Helianthus* 'Valentine' and bud; M *Centaurea cyanus*; N *Platycodon grandiflorus*; O *Tanacetum vulgare*.
RIGHT Flowers for cutting include pink and red dahlias and white hydrangeas.

INSPIRATION FROM THE MASTERS

There was one part of the late English designer Rosemary Verey's garden that was well known and reproduced around the world. An allee, a double row of laburnum trees (golden chain) at Barnsley House arched at the top to connect into a leafy roof above a walkway. When the trees flowered, their chains of bright yellow blossoms dripped from the tunnel's ceiling. Verey planted tall alliums with flowers like dusty purple popcorn balls to bloom on either side of the path beneath the yellow pea flowers.

Bright yellow and mauve are a combination that is criticized from time to time as being too much of a contrast—kind of vulgar. I can't agree. And frankly, all of that is a matter of personal taste.

You may not have a place for a tunnel of laburnum, but one laburnum tree with allium planted beneath it will tell the story. I don't think of this as stealing; it is taking inspiration from the masters, and Mrs. Verey borrowed the idea, herself, from Bodnant Garden in Wales.

Look to the work of an artists like the Belgian landscape architect Jacques Wirtz for a totally different experience. His carved serpentine hedges of boxwood or beech make strong sculptural statements in the landscape. If both of these conventions seem like they would take a long time to create—get started.

That bit of wisdom came to me from another gardener, Helen Stoddard. She lived in a fantasy designed by the Boston landscape architect Fletcher Steele in 1948. Like many gardeners, Stoddard was frugal. I remember visiting her when she was well into her seventies. She was planting magnolia whips, small trees, on a hillside where she planned to place a bench. Her friends suggested she plant larger trees, implying that she might not be around to enjoy them, but she ignored their advice.

The lesson for me was to not wonder whether I should plant something that will take years to mature, or if I should be planting trees at all. Instead, I plant them for me, and for upcoming generations to enjoy and use the fresh air they produce. If we don't plant trees, there will be no giants to admire one hundred or more years in the future. But when I wonder about such things, I think of Helen Stoddard.

I visited her garden again shortly before she died. She was sitting on that bench in the shade from those trees she'd planted years before.

OPPOSITE A combination of plants inspired by Rosemary Verey's Laburnum Walk at Barnsely House in Gloucestershire, England, includes, top to bottom: yellow *Laburnum* x *watereri*; *Allium aflatunense*; *A. schoenoprasum*; variegated ground cover *Ajuga reptans* 'Toffee Chip'; leafy bracts follow the double white flowers of *Anemone nemerosa* 'Bracteata Pleniflora'. LEFT Rosemary Verey's famed Laburnum Walk.

ZONE DENIAL

I n the early 1930s, the Women's Auxiliary of the New York Botanical Garden engaged the landscape architect Ellen Biddle Shipman to design a long, mixed border of trees, shrubs, and perennials running the 260-foot length of the southeast side of the garden's conservatory. Known as The Ladies' Border, the plantings were redesigned in 2002 by Lynden B. Miller, the city's leading designer of public installations who has created works for Bryant and Battery parks among others. Today, this border functions as an experimental hardiness test garden featuring species and varieties that are questionably suitable for winter in the Bronx, New York.

Protected by the conservatory to the north and in full sun for most of the day, a surprising number of heat-loving plants thrive in this area where they have not been expected to survive. Camellias bloom in winter. Rosemary plants flourish and are nearly always evergreen. *Eucomis* varieties, called pineapple lilies, are bulbs that winter over and bloom every year, and the crape myrtles familiar to southern gardens bloom in amazing variety.

This area could be considered a microclimate, and you may have a few places in your garden where you too could try and cheat the USDA hardiness zone recommendations. A south-facing spot (ideally up against the foundation of the house) might be a place to plant half-hardy bulbs. Even planting next to a large boulder might add half a zone. A corner with a windbreak of shrubs could be a spot for a broadleaf evergreen *Mahonia* with leaves and flower buds that are often wind-burned in winter. A useful niche might be on high ground where cold air drains away.

Bodies of water, even as small as a pond, can alter the air temperature. Lakes and oceans have their own mitigating influences. A lake helps mitigate rapid changes in air temperature. The oceans take much longer to cool down in winter and to warm up in spring. The ocean provides more viewing time in fall before a frost puts an end to that season and, later, protects precocious bloomers by keeping the air cool so their buds do not emerge too early and get damaged by frost.

We gardeners often dare to grow things that conventional wisdom warns us not to. Tony Avent, the co-owner of Plant Delights Nursery in North Carolina, often challenges both wisdom and climates. His motto: "I consider every plant hardy until I have killed it myself . . . at least three times."

OPPOSITE Push the limits of your garden's USDA zone by finding a microclimate where plants that like it a bit warmer may flourish. A, C *Stachyuris* 'Magpie' fruit and variegated leaves; B the color-changing flowers of *Nicotiana mutabilis*; D *Lagerstroemia* 'Cherry Dazzle'; E *Geranium* 'Jolly Bee'; F *Hesperola parviflora*. ABOVE The Ladies' Border at the New York Botanical Garden challenges the climate zones.

TENDER IS THE NIGHT-BLOOMING JASMINE

The Victorians loved their equatorial, non-hardy perennials (page 211), but the era of bedding schemes and giant tropical plants passed. Later, in the first half of the twentieth-century, American gardeners customarily planted summer-flowering corms, tubers, and rhizomes like gladiola, dahlia, and canna. But the idea of digging up and cold-storing the underground parts of the plants seemed too hard and too old-fashioned for postwar suburbanites. By 1960, you were more likely to know someone with a bomb shelter than a root cellar.

Tropical plants for summer gardens became a sensation in the 1990s thanks to nursery owners like Tony Avent, Dan Hinkley, Dennis Schrader, and Kathy Pufahl; garden directors like Marco Stufano, Chris Woods, Robert Wong, and Doug Rurhen; and garden writers like Steve Silk, Rob Proctor, and others. *Global warming* came to North American gardens before most of us had heard the term.

Canna/banana gardens sprouted up everywhere, with plants some people called "temperennials," or as we now refer to them, tender perennials. New varieties appeared, for example cannas with striped or stippled foliage, fancy-leafed begonias, *Acalypha* (chenille plant), tropical euphorbia, flowering maple, gold-leafed jasmine, passion flowers, angel's trumpets (*Brugmansia* varieties), night-blooming jasmine, firecracker plants (*Cuphea* spp.), black sweet potato vines, strange pepper relatives (*Solanum* spp.), and one hundred varieties of coleus (*Solenostemon*).

It was a revolution, and the fad became a trend that led to a conventional part of gardening. Late summer and early fall used to be quiet times in the garden with nothing showy until the muffins of fall chrysanthemums turned up in gas station plantings. Now, pretty much everyone includes tropical plants for late-season displays in their garden schemes.

Some of us let the tender plants die—killed by the cold after their long season. Others take cuttings to carry through the winter, and certainly dig up rhizomes to store in a cool corner of the basement, or even in the vegetable crisper of the refrigerator (in a bag marked "do not eat").

OPPOSITE Steve Silk's tropicals include: A *Jasminum officinalis* 'Fiona Sunrise'; B *Colocasia esculenta* 'Illustris'; C *Musa acuminate* var. *sumatrana* (syn. M. *zebrina*); D *Cestrum* 'Orange Peel'; E *Hibiscus acetosella*; F *Hedychium* 'Tara'; G *Tibouchina urvilleana*; H *Acalphyla wilkesiana* 'Kona Coast'; I *Begonia* 'Fireworks'; J *Euphorbia* x *martinii* 'Ascot Rainbow'; K *Impatiens* 'Applause Orange Blaze'; L *Alternanthera ficoidea* 'Yellow Fine Leaf'; M *Begonia* 'Little Brother Montgomery'; N *Passiflora* 'Lady Margaret'; O *Anisodontea* cv.; P *Canna* 'Tropicana'; Q *Bulbine frutescens*; R *Abutilon* 'Voodoo'; S *Mandevilla* 'Sun Parasol Crimson'; T *Solenostemon scutellarioides* 'Electric Lime'; U *Plumbago auriculata*.

ABOVE A big banana and bromeliads at Chanticleer in Wayne, Pennsylvania.

PARADISE CONTAINED

Planting in pots isn't new. The ancient Egyptians and Romans grew plants in containers, and Louis XIV had an orangerie built at Versailles to winter-over 1,700 citrus trees and date palms in tubs. Contained plantings as decorative elements came into vogue in the Victorian era. The gigantic terracotta pots at Biltmore House in Asheville, North Carolina, are a tour de force. The latest trend for pots of plants blasted onto the scene early in this century.

One plant in one pot may be used as a formal accent, for instance potted orange trees could go at the four corners of a rectangular swimming pool. Clustering and staging summering houseplants is a way to create a decorative seasonal display. The current convention, however, is to have each container overflowing with an abundant mix of disparate plants.

The design principle is similar to creating a garden's island bed. Tall plants go in the center, or the back for arrangements to be viewed from one side, shorter plants around those, and standing in for a ground cover, a low-growing specimen that trails over the planter's edge and down to the ground. These plants might include a palm or banana for the middle, colorful annuals and tender perennials such as variegated copper *Acalypha* (chenille plant) and vivid coleus (*Solenostemon*) with *Vinca major* spilling over the rim.

Color can be the guide. Select favorite plants in color schemes like the ones in the garden bed. Consider the starry pink flowers of pentas with taxicab-yellow lantana and silver *Dichondra argentea* cascading like a waterfall to the ground.

This is a case when more will ultimately be best, but resist the urge to overplant from the beginning. If you have a pot that looks great in spring, don't expect a good show through the summer. It might be best to make seasonal planters. Use forced bulbs and pansies during the cool beginning of the growing season. Plan to have tender perennials like black sugar cane and pom-pom dahlias at the ready for potting in early summer.

You'll need a planting "soil" that holds moisture and nutrition, provides air to roots, and is not too heavy (unlike garden soil, which would squeeze out the oxygen and make the container difficult to move). I recommend a soil-less medium based on humus and a drainage material, such as compost or coir and coarse sand or perlite. Container plantings can be gluttons, so use fertilizer through the growing season.

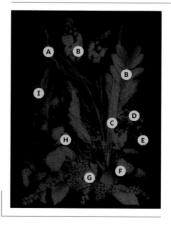

OPPOSITE Plants for containers could include: A *Eupatorium capillifolium*; B *Senna didymobotrya* (flower and leaf); C *Phormium* cv.; D *Galphimia gracillis*; E *Euphorbia* 'Flame'; F *Lantana camara* 'Samantha'; G *Lonicera nitida* 'Baggesen's Gold'; H *Alamanda cathartica*; I *Globba winitii*.

LEFT Planted pots by Louis Bauer at Wave Hill, the public garden in the Bronx, New York.

MAGNIFICENT OBSESSION

There may be no more satisfying thing than to pluck a fruit or vegetable from your own garden and sample it fresh off the vine. Talk about devotion. Vegetable gardening might just be the most challenging outdoor version of our pastime, and that goes double if you hope to do it organically and sustainably, as we all do.

It starts with soil. You can dig or double dig, turning over the soil in two layers and adding organic matter. Or you can make raised beds in which you bring in your enriched soil and fill bottomless wooden boxes set on the ground with sides that are from ten to thirty inches high. But the most modern approach, no-till, preserves the inherent structure of the soil by not disturbing it. Each season, compost is added to

the surface as plants are plugged into the earth, then the bed is mulched. In time, the compost incorporates through the same processes that built the soil through the years.

My garden is shady. I have few places where there is enough sunlight to grow tomatoes, which I allow to sprawl over makeshift supports up on the driveway. I grow winter squash on the southern edge of large plastic, faux terracotta pots, or a half whiskey barrel, and not alone. I plant upright ornamentals like *Colocasia* (elephant ears), and let the squash vines sprawl down over the container's edge. My growing medium is soil-less: two parts coir, one part compost, and one part perlite. Vegetable plants, and especially those in containers, are "gross-feeders," so they get frequent doses of a balanced, organic liquid fertilizer like a kelp and fish emulsion.

Some of the challenges of growing food are avoided by using containers. I can move them if need be for more sunlight. I can pick off bugs if they appear (without bending). Having edibles in several places helps keep the critters at bay.

A conventional vegetable garden will need a fence to keep out bunnies—buried about one foot underground, and coming up about two feet above it. (For groundhogs, also called woodchucks, add a Jack Russell terrier.) Then there are the things you cannot control, like the weather. One year, rain ruins your crops. The next, drought takes its toll,. When the weather forecaster says "another beautiful day without a cloud in the sky," I want to scream.

OPPOSITE Vegetable gardening is having a Renaissance in the United States, and this time around, there is an emphasis on ornamental and edible qualities of unusual and beautiful fruits and edible leaves along with flowering plants. Quirky peppers might find roses between their rows. All sorts of squashes and gourds like 'Goblin Eggs' and colorful 'Carnival' add much to a garden where cabbage and kale deliver edible foliage.
LEFT Colorful greens: parsley, red leaf lettuce, beets, and kale.

A vegetable garden by Long Island designer Lisa Stamm included edible and ornamental plants for harvest and was contained by a Belgian fence—cordoned apple tree espalier in a woven pattern.

SMILING FACES

The first way to engage children in gardening is to show them some quirky flowers. Point out the faces one can see in pansies—once called little brothers. Make the snapdragon flowers talk by squeezing the sides of the blossoms. Show how the inflorescence of the obedient plant (*Physostegia virginiana*) may be bent in one direction or another and hold that shape. Pick some herbs and share the fragrance when the leaves are crushed.

Kids can be a bit impatient, so select some fast-sprouting seeds to sow indoors in late winter like beans or sunflowers. In cool weather outdoors, plant radishes, and when the weather warms, marigolds.

Children are fascinated by exaggerations of scale—enlarged versions of familiar things or shrunken ones. Grow some giant plants and some tiny ones: huge sunflowers for example, or little grape tomatoes. Be sure to grow a few things that children will be able to harvest, cook, and eat. Grow strange fruits and vegetables like gourds, rainbow Swiss chard, or purple carrots. Make a bamboo-tepee as a fort and cover it with scarlet-runner beans with flowers that last for months followed by fruit.

Plant a tree with an older child that will be his or her very own. The tree won't instantly grow to maturity, but there will be occasions to visit the plant as it gets taller and perhaps blossoms. Planting trees with children can help them realize that these are living things worthy of respect.

Visit some giant trees in your area. Encourage kids to learn their names. In the fall, make a scrapbook of pressed fallen leaves in their autumn glory. Collecting leaves is a great activity. Compare different leaf shapes and sizes and learn to identify trees

The most important thing is to get kids outdoors. It seems to me that we are now into the second generation of people who have little connection with nature, and worse, fear it. Some children seem to have been taught that nature is dangerous; that germs are out to get them and predators hide behind every bush. Take a young child outdoors before he or she is three years old. Turn over a rock in search of an interesting insect or a wriggly worm. You may help capture the imagination of a young person and arouse a curiosity and fascination with the natural world that will last a lifetime.

OPPOSITE Children find funny-looking vegetables alluring. Grow purple broccoli with kids and they might even eat it. Try purple pole beans, and some of these quirky edibles (from left) *Beta vulgaris* 'Golden' beet; sliced yellow *Daucus carota* subsp. *sativus* 'Rainbow Mix' carrot; orange *D. c.* subsp. *s.* 'Rainbow Mix' carrot; white *Pastinaca sativa* 'Hollow Crown' parsnip; bull's eye slices of beet *Beta vulgaris* 'Chioggia'. LEFT Sunflowers sprout quickly from sown seed, in a matter of days, and easily grow large to the delight of kids.

Afterword

With years of experience, seasoned gardeners may be able to conceptualize combinations for planting designs before they ever put spade to earth. Rather than wondering what steps there might be to take, we've brought suggestions with the hope that you can skip ahead on the path to success.

This book is not a standard "how-to" manual, but rather an aesthetic "what-to" reference. *Natural Companions* is like a travel guide suggesting possible itineraries, directing you to fascinating places and things to see on your journey. Our goal is to illustrate some artistic points of interest along the way, relationships for plantings and design.

I recommend starting from the ground up—with the soil. Plants, and especially the ornamental perennials we rely upon for excitement throughout the growing season, want a well-drained, moisture-retentive medium with a lot of organic matter. Compost from leaves and perhaps some well-rotted cow manure will be enormously valuable. If the soil is sandy, or there is too much clay, incorporate compost and well-rotted cow manure.

I also suggest bringing in as much of any one variety of annual, herbaceous perennial and groundcover that you can for the middle layer and the front of the planting that draws the most attention. We hope to have them grow in colonies, as they would in nature.

It is likely that in time, you will discover the stalwart, reliable plants for your garden that you can arrange with other species and varieties for the most triumphant combinations. Within these pages, we hope you find information, stories, and most of all, inspiring ways to help each plant boost its neighbors, look its best, and enhance your natural refuge. Combining plants is definitely an art, and like all art forms, it takes practice to master. Good art also requires taking some risks, so don't be afraid to dive in and experiment.

Even professionals tinker with outdoor arrangements. After all, we don't necessarily want our gardens to ever really be finished; this is a passion we hope to practice for a lifetime.

The images in this book present flowers and foliage that will look good growing together. As you wander through the book, make lists of combinations that appeal to you, and jot down names of plants in the photographs that you hope to replicate.

Whether it's color associations, ideas for themes, or collections of fantastic plants that drive your arrangements, you'll revisit *Natural Companions* time and again. I know that returning to the images in this book will be a perennial delight for years to come.

OPPOSITE A tetradic color scheme with yellow-green and magenta to blue-violet: A *Lamium maculatum* 'Anne Greenaway'; B *Thalictrum flavum* subsp. *glaucum*; c *Ranunculus acris**; D *Thermopsis caroliniana*; E *Hypericum* sp.; F *Petasites japonicus* 'Variegatus'*; G *Geranium* x *cantabrigiense* 'Karmina'; H *Chamaecyparis pisifera* 'Filifera Aurea Nana'; I *Polemonium reptans* 'Stairway to Heaven'; J *Campanula glomerata* 'Joan Elliot'; K *Baptisia* 'Purple Smoke'.

*potentially invasive in some climates

Appendix
EDIBLE FLOWERS

ANGELICA (*Angelica archangelica*) is grown for its stems, which can be candied, but the flowers are used in Chinese dishes and as a salad garnish for their licorice/celery flavor

BASIL (*Ocimum basilicum*) flowers taste like mild versions of the leaves.

BEE BALM (*Monarda* spp.) flower tastes vary depending on color and species, from oregano crossed with mint to lemon and orange. Use as an oregano substitute.

BORAGE (*Borago officinalis*) blue star-shaped flowers have a cucumber flavor. Try in chilled soups, or punch, and gin and tonic.

BURNET (*Sanguisorba minor*) petals also taste like cucumbers.

CALENDULA is the pot marigold. Add petals to soups.

CHERVIL (*Anthriscus cerefolium*) flowers are best eaten fresh for their delicate anise flavor on salads.

CHINESE HIBISCUS (*Hibiscus rosa-sinensis*) tastes a bit like cranberries, rose hips, or lemon and is an ingredient in many herbal teas.

CHIVE BLOSSOMS (*Allium schoenoprasum*) and other allium flowers can be used as mild onion substitutes in salads or to flavor vinegars.

CHRYSANTHEMUMS petals are a tad bitter, tangy, and peppery, a bit like cauliflower. Blanch before using.

CITRUS BLOSSOMS are very fragrant and can be overpowering. The petals may be distilled for flower water to be used in Middle Eastern confections.

CORNFLOWERS, also called bachelor's buttons (*Centaurea cyanus*), have a mild clove flavor. Use as a garnish.

DANDELIONS (*Taraxacum officinale*) should be picked when young or just opening for their honey-like flavor.

DAYLILIES (*Hemerocallis* species and varieties) can be picked as buds and stir-fried, or tear petals for a garnish that tastes like sweet lettuce. I find yellow flowers taste best.

DILL (*Anethum graveolens*) flowers have a strong flavor good for adding to dips, cold soups, and fish.

FENNEL (*Foeniculum vulgare*) umbels have an anise flavor that can be used with desserts.

GARDEN SORREL (*Rumex acetosa*) flowers taste lemony, like the leaves, and are great for garnishing cream soups.

IMPATIENS (*Impatiens walleriana*) blossoms are a bit sweet and may be used mostly as a garnish.

JOHNNY JUMP-UPS (*Viola tricolor*) have pretty, tiny pansy-like flowers that are very often used for garnishing soft cheeses and have a slight wintergreen flavor.

OPPOSITE Peppery nasturtium flowers are great tossed in salads and for garnishing cold soups. **ABOVE** The flowers of most culinary herbs (see page 206) are also edible and often offer lighter versions of the flavors of the leaves.

LAVENDER (*Lavandula angustifolia*) flowers are more floral and less medicinal than their leafy counterparts and can be used to flavor ice cream.

LILAC (*Syringa vulgaris*) blossoms may have a lemony flavor, but they vary greatly. Most often the tiny flowers are candied.

MARIGOLD (*Tagetes tenuifolia*) petals are used as a substitute for saffron with a mild citrus flavor.

MARJORAM (*Origanum majorana*) flowers are used like the leaves.

MINT (*Mentha* spp.) blossoms vary according to the variety, like the leaves. The flavor is a bit milder.

NASTURTIUMS (*Tropaeolum majus*) flowers have a terrific peppery, watercress-like taste that varies by color and variety. They can be stuffed with soft cheeses.

OREGANO (*Origanum vulgare*) flowers are milder than the leaves, but may be used in the same way.

PANSY (*Viola* x *wittrockiana*) blossoms have a mild taste, like Johnny jump-ups diluted, somewhat wintergreen or perhaps just "green."

PINKS (*Dianthus* varieties) taste a bit like clove—candy or steep in wine.

ROSEMARY (*Rosmarinus officinalis*), like oregano and marjoram, has flowers that provide a similar taste in a milder form.

ROSES (*Rosa* species and varieties) vary from species to species. All are edible (but watch out for pesticide residue). Use petals as garnish, freeze them in ice cubes for drinks, and mix colored parts of petals with butter for a scented spread. Rose water is used in Middle Eastern candies and cakes.

SAFFLOWER (*Carthamus tinctorius*) flowers are dried for a saffron substitute that will add color to dishes.

SAGE (*Salvia officinalis*) blossoms have a milder taste than the leaves.

SAVORY (*Satureja hortensis*) flowers are hot and peppery.

SUNFLOWER (*Helianthus annuus*) flower buds can be picked and steamed like little artichokes.

THYME (*Thymus* spp.) flowers, like sage, are a gentler version of the plant's leaves and stems.

VIOLET (*Viola* spp.) flowers have a perfume flavor, and may be candied to garnish desserts.

YUCCA (*Yucca* spp.) petals are mild with a hint of sweetness like an artichoke.

LANGUAGE OF FLOWERS

Picture a planting that expresses ideas or tells stories. The inspiration for the meanings may have been folklore or mythology, literature, religion, or the morphology of the plant—its physical characteristics. Imagine what a constricting vine might communicate. The nicest arrangement of plants and flowers probably would express romance and love. Here are some of the plants to tell that story.

Language of flowers for a romantic garden:

ACACIA (YELLOW) secret love

ANGELICA you are my inspiration

APPLE BLOSSOM I prefer you

BABY'S BREATH our everlasting love

BACHELOR'S BUTTONS hope in love

CARNATION (PINK) I will remember you

CATMINT intoxication with love

COREOPSIS always cheerful

DAFFODIL I send my regards

DOGWOOD our love will endure adversity

FERN sincerity

HELIOTROPE I am devoted to you only

HONEYSUCKLE my affection for you is boundless

IRIS (YELLOW) my love is passionate

IVY wedded love, fidelity

JONQUIL desire

LILAC (PURPLE) I feel the first stirrings of love

LILAC (WHITE) modest and pure emotions

PEACH BLOSSOM I am yours

ROSE (RED) I love you; passionate love

TULIP love

TULIP (RED) declaration of love

TULIP (YELLOW) I am hopelessly in love

VERONICA I shall remain true

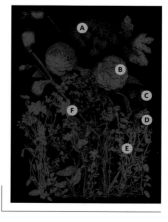

OPPOSITE To pledge one's love with flowers, plants included could be: A angelica; B red rose; C heliotrope; D bachelor's button or cornflower; E catmint; F coreopsis. **ABOVE** Yellow tulips, ferns, and violets all have sentimental meanings according to lore.

Acknowledgments

We want to thank all of the gardeners, designers, authors, nurserymen, and dear friends who have shared ideas, encouragement, and plants:

Tony Avent
Parker Andes
Ann Armstrong
Suzy Bales
Marilyn Barlow
Bartlett Arboretum
Louis Bauer
John Beirne
Tony Bielaczyc
David Blatty
Sandi Blaze
Barbra Blossom
Kevin Bost
Ed Bowen
Martha Bradshaw
Broken Arrow Nursery
Inez Burne
Anna Christian
Susan Cohan
Stephanie Cohen
Sean Conway
Regina D'Amico and
    George Bussman
Nancy D'Oench
Carole Dubiell
Nancy DuBrule-Clemente
Janet Dudley
Dudley Farm Market
Lynn Fiorentino

Juana Flagg
T. Fleisher
John Franke
Frelinghuysen Arboretum
Friends of Elizabeth Park
Gay Gasser
Carrie Gilbertie
Gilbertie's Herb Gardens
Judy Glattstien
Greenwood Gardens
Cheryl Grady
Thomas Graywasz
John Gwynne
Gaby Hall
Carol Hanby and
    Dr. Nickolas Nickou
Ric Ide and Matt Mirisola
Kate Jamison
Richard and Sally Jaynes
Dervla Kelly
Patricia and Timothy King
Timothy King Jr.
Susan Lee
Joan Hepburn Levy
Allison Maltese
Steven McGuire
Theodore Mankovich
Florence Marrone
Marci Martin

Carmelo and Joan Mazzotta
Grant Meyer
Mary Meyer
Eric Morgan
Morris County Park
    Commission
Phyllis Naples
The New York Botanical
    Garden
Joy Newton
Pearl Paperno
Lesley Parness
Virginia Pepper Purviance
Dennis Reilly
Rosemarie Reilly
Donna and David Reis
Judy Richardson
Pat Rolston
Barbara Rossi
Michael Russo and
    Raymond Lenox
Gelene Scarborough
Kristin Schleiter
Jane Seeley
Select Seeds
John Shalvoy
Steve Silk
Chris Simonsen
Leslie Stoker

Stonington Farmer's
    Market
Henriette Suhr
Timothy Tilghman
Trout Lily Farm
Mary Treat
Treat's Market
Wave Hill
George Waffle
Pamela Weil
Jeanne Will
Willowwood Arboretum
Louise Wrinkle
Elisabeth Zander
John Zeigler

Agent, Kris Dahl, ICM

OPPOSITE Clockwise from top left: *Epimedium* hybrids—flowers and leaves; *Euphorbia dulcis* 'Chameleon'; *E. polychroma*; various *Heuchera* leaves and *Trillium luteum*; *Aquilegia canadensis*.

Index

A

Abelia mosanensis, 190
Abies koreana 'Horstmann's Silberlocke', 114
Abies pinsapo, 114
Abutilon 'Kristen's Pink', 178
Abutilon 'Seashell', 178
Abutilon 'Voodoo', 226
Acacia species, 71
Acalphyla wilkesiana 'Kona Coast', 226
Acalypha (chenille plant), 210
Acalypha wilkesiana 'Hoffmannii', 95
Acanthus hungaricus, 128
accent colors, 146, 147
Aceraceae family, 82
Acer (genus), 82
Acer griseum (paperbark maple), 105
Acer japonicum 'Aconitifolium', 9, 46, 82, 83
Acer palmatum, 82, 83, 136
  'Beni Otake', 83
  'Butterflies', 83
  'Karasugawa', 83
  'Nishiki Momiji', 83
  'Rugose', 83
  'Sango Kaku' (coral-bark, maple), 52
  'Shishigashira' (lion's head maple), 47, 83
  'Tsukushigata', 83
Acer palmatum var. *dissectum*
  'Crimson Queen', 83
  'Red Filigree Lace', 83
Acer palmatum var. *dissectum* f. *atropurpureum* 'Red Dragon', 138

Acer rubrum (red maple), 27
Acer saccharum (sugar maple), 82
Acer sawanum, 82
Acer shirasawanum 'Aureum', 82, 83
Achillea millefolium
  'Apricot Delight', 188
  'Terra Cotta', 68
Achillea 'Schwellenberg', 174
Achillea sibirica var. *kamtschatica*, 68
Achillea species, 174
A Clematis x *Jackmanii*, 103
Aconitum napellus, 203
Adiantum pedatum (maidenhair fern), 127
Adonis amurensis, 133
Adonis vernalis (pheasant's eye), 76
Aeonium arboreum 'Schwarzkopf', 106
Agastache foeniculum (anise hyssop), 156, 198
Agastache foeniculum x *rugosa* 'Blue Fortune', 195
Agave americana 'Variegata', 12, 95, 212–13
Ageratum genus, 210
Ageratum houstoinianum 'Album', 126
Ageratum hybrid, 220
Ajuga reptans
  'Bronze Beauty', 54
  'Catlin's Giant', 128, 136
  'Toffee Chip', 223
Alabama, 22, 24, 140
Alamanda cathartica, 228
Albizia julibrissin (mimosa), 71

Alchemilla alpina, 155
Alchemilla mollis, 18, 72, 122
Alliaceae family, 89
Allium aflatunense, 30–31, 223
Allium ampeloprasum, 126
Allium genus, 89, 127, 222
Allium 'Hair', 188
Allium schoenoprasum (chives), 198, 223
Allium sphaerocephalon, 88, 126
Allium thunbergii 'Ozawa', 150
Alocasia amazonica 'Polly', 67
Aloe 'Blue Elf', 12
Aloe cv, 154
Aloe distans, 179
Aloe vera, 108–09
Alternanthera ficoidea
  'Aurea Nana', 95
  'Yellow Fine Leaf', 226
Amelanchier tree (shadblow), 72
American boxwood (*Buxus sempervirens*), 205
'American Pillar', 75
Ammi majus (Queen Anne's lace–like), 40, 94
amphibia, 169
Amsonia hubrichtii (yellow fruit of Chinese quince), 50, 51
Amsonia orientalis (syn. *Rhazya orientalis*), 139
Amsonia tabernaemontana, 139
analogous colors, 144, 145, 147
Andromeda (genera), 59
Anemone japonica, 46

Anemone nemerosa, 158, 223
Anethum graveolens (dill), 126, 206
Angelonia angustifolia
  'Angelface Blue', 94
  'Angelina White', 94
  'Angelmist Lavender', 94
anise hyssop (*Agastache foeniculum*), 156, 198
Anisodontea cv, 226
annuals, 16, 96–97, 191, 212–13
  defined, 95
  F1 hybrids, 65
  fragrant, 191
  for naked gardening, 221
  ornamental grasses as, 85
  from seed, 40
  to sow in spring, 33
  vines, 103
Antarctica, 69
Antennaria neglecta, 32
Anthemis tinctoria 'Sauce Hollandaise', 68
Anthurium spp., *Aglaonema* (Chinese evergreen), 66
Anthyllis montana 'Rubra', 186
Antirrhinum 'Madame Butterfly', 220
Antirrhinum 'Rocket Mix', 220
Apothecaries' Garden, 207
apricot tree (*Prunus mume*), 72
Aquilegia canadensis (columbines), 76, 78–79, 78–79, 245

Araceae family, 66, *67*
Aralia elata
    'Aureovariegata', *18*
Archilochus colubris
    (ruby-throated
    hummingbird), *197*
Arisaema dracontium, 66
Arisaema fargesii
    inflorescence, *67*
Arisaema genus, 66, *123*
Arisaema (Jack-in-the-
    pulpits), 66, *123*, *158*,
    159, *182*
Arisaema ringens, *122*
Arisaema sikokianum, *123*
Aristilochia durior, *122*, 123
Aristolochia genus, 123
Armeria maratima, *187*
arrowhead vines
    (*Syngonium podophyllum*
    varieties), 66
Artemisia arborescens x
    absinthium 'Powis
    Castle', *110*
Artemisia dracunculus
    (tarragon), *206*
Artemisia genus
    (wormwood), III
Artemisia ludoviciana 'Silver
    King', *128*, *174*, *209*
Artemisia ludoviciana 'Silver
    Queen', *110*
Arum italicum, *52*
Asarum canadense, *128*
Asclepias (genus), *194*
Asclepias incarnata, *160*,
    195, *215*
Asclepias tuberosa, *160*, *165*,
    194
Asheville, NC, *229*
Asparagaceae family, 89
Asparagus sprenge, *88*
aspirin, 208
Asplenium scolopendrium
    (Hart's tongue fern
    fronds), *201*
Asteraceae family, 69
Aster genus, 69
asters, *47*, 47
Astilbe chinensis 'Pumila',
    150
Athyrium japonicum-pictum
    (Japanese painted fern),
    200

Athyrium niponicum
    'Pictum', *128*
A. triphyllum, 66
Aucuba japonica 'Variegata',
    140, *201*
Austin, David, 34, 75, *75*,
    193
Austin, TX, *96–97*
autumn, 42, 43, 44, 45, 46,
    47, *48–49*, 50, 51, 144
autumn crocus or meadow
    saffron (*Colchicum*
    'Water Lily'), 44
Avent, Tony, 150, 225, 227
azaleas, 27, *56*, 59, *127*, *145*,
    170–71, 197

B ————————————

bachelor's button or
    cornflower, 242
bamboo plants, 85, *140*, 183
banana plant, 227
Baptisia
    'Carolina Moonlight', 71
    'Chocolate Chip', 70
    'Purple Smoke', *236*
barberry (*Berberis*), 65
Barnsley house, 222, *223*
basil (*Ocimum basilicum*),
    21, *198*, 206, *216*
Bauer, Louis, *229*
beans, *51*, 71
Beasley, Geof, *120–21*
beauty and health plants,
    206, *207*
bees, 17, 123, 131
beets, 230, 234
Begonia, 210
    'Black Fang', *136*
    'Fireworks', *226*
    grandis, 45, *105*
    'Little Brother
        Montgomery', *226*
Bellevue Botanical Garden,
    WA, *134–35*
Benson, Dianne, 127
Berberidaceae family, 65
Berberis (barberry), 65
Berkeley, CA, 179, *179*
berries, *47*, *51*, 59, *140*, *147*
Beta vulgaris, *136*, 234
Biltmore House, NC, *229*
bipinnate leaves, 71
Birmingham, AL, 22

bitter melon (*Momordica
    charantia*), 99
black (color), *51*, *136*, *137*
Blaze, Sandi, 12, *25*, 214
blazing star (*Liatris
    pycnostachya*), *162–63*
bleeding heart (*Dicentra
    [syn. Lamprocapnos]
    spectabilis* 'Alba'), 28
bleeding heart (*Dicentra
    eximia*), 20, *86*, *87*
bluebeard shrub
    (*Caryopteris* x
    clandonensis 'Worcester
    Gold'), 10, *11*, 34, *37*, *118*
Boehmeria nipononivea
    'Kogane Mushi'
    (variegated nettle), *42*, 43
Boltonia asteroides
    'Nally's Lime Dots',
        42, 43
    'Pink', *69*
    'Snowbank', *69*
borage (*Borago officinalis*),
    198
Bowles, E.A. (gardener), 55
boxwood (*Buxus
    sempervirens*), *120–21*,
    205
Bradley, Judy, *106*
Brahea armata (Mexican
    blue palm), *179*
Brassica oleracea 'Scarlet',
    216
breadseed poppy (opium
    poppy), *86*, *104*
bromeliads, 227
Brooklyn Botanic Garden,
    NY, 89
Brugmansia sp. (yellow
    angel's trumpet), *180–81*
Brunnera macrophylla
    'Hadspen Cream', *32*
*Bryophyllum
    daigremontianum*, 12
Buchner, Johann, 208
Buddleia (butterfly bush),
    150, 194
Bulbine frutescens, *216*, *226*
bulbs, 14, 27, 28, 44, 55,
    89, 91, 225
Burnett, Frances Hodgson,
    200
Burpee, Mr., 65

buttercup cousins, *54*, 55, *76*
butterfly bush (*Buddleia*
    varieties), 194
butterfly gardens, 189, 194,
    195
butterfly weed (*Asclepias
    tuberosa*), 194
Buxus microphylla
    'Kingsville Dawrf', *204*
Buxus sempervirens
    (boxwood), 133, 204, *205*
    'Graham Blandy', *204*
    'Green Gem', *205*
    'Latifolia Maculatum',
        133, 204
    'Peergold' (syn. 'Golden
        Dream'), *204*
    'Rotundifolia', *204*
    'Suffruticosa', *204*
Buxus sempervirens var.
    insularis 'Tide Hill', *204*
Buxus sinca var. *insularis*
    'Justin Brouwers', *204*

C ————————————

Cabot, Frank, *142–43*
cacti, *106*, *107*
Caladium, 67, 210
Calamagrostis x *acutiflora*
    'Overdam', *84*
C. alba 'Argenteo-
    marginata' or
    'Elegantissima', 53
Calendula officinalis, *198*
California, 25, 106, 178, 179,
    180–81, 182
calla lilies, 67, 150, 209
Caltha palustris, *140*
Calycalycanthus x *raulstonii*
    (*Sinocalycanthus*
    'Venus'), 64, *65*
Calycanthus floridus
    (Carolina sweetshrub),
    64, *65*
Camellia japonica, 22, 24, *52*
camellias, 52, *53*
Campanula garganica
    'Dickson's Gold', *18*, *36*
Campanula glomerata 'Joan
    Elliot', *236*
Campanula punctata, *215*
Camperdown elm
    tree (*Ulmus glabra*
    'Camperdownii'), *148*

Campis radicans, 102
'Candidum' leaf *Caladium* x *hortulanum,* 67
Canna, 210, 227
   'Panache', 154
   'Pink Sunburst', 154
   'Tropicana', 226
Canning, Scott, 43
Capsicum annuum 'Black Pearl, 216
carnivorous plants, 173
Carolina rose (*Rosa carolina*), 75
Carolina sweetshrub (*Calycanthus floridus*), 64, 65
carrot (*Daucus carota* subsp. *sativus* 'Rainbow Mix'), 234
Carruth, Tom, 193
Caryopteris x *clandonensis* 'Worcester Gold' (bluebeard shrub), 10, 11, 34, 37, 118
Cassia didymabotrya, 12
caterpillars, 194
catmint (*Nepeta* 'Walker's Low') otherwise known as *catnip* (*Nepeta cataria*), 13, 34, 37, 37, 72, 206, 242
Celosia 'Bombay Pink', 220
Celosia 'Chief' (cock's comb), 144
Centaurea cyanus, 68, 220
Centratherum punctatum, 95
Cephalanthus occidentalis, 166
Cephalaria gigantea, 127
Cephalnthus occidentalis, 126
Cerastium tomentosum, 215
Cercidiphyllum japonicum 'Pendula', 23
Cercis canadensis, 14
   'Alba' (redbud), 20
   'Forest Pansy', 136
   'Silver Cloud', 62, 63
Cestrum 'Orange Peel', 226
C. florida 'Athens', 65
Chaenomeles speciosa varieties (quince), 22, 26, 27
Chaenomeles x *superba,* 55, 73

Chamaecyparis lawsoniana, 114
Chamaecyparis nootkatensis 'Variegata', 133
Chamaecyparis obtusa 'Fernspray Gold', 114, 133
Chamaecyparis pisifera, 114, 133, 236
Chamaecypari thyoides 'Miko', 114
Chanticleer, Wayne PA, 176–77, 227
Charleston, SC, 60–61, 100–101
Charlesworth, Geoffrey, 27
Chasmanthium latifolium, 84
Chelsea Physic Garden, London, 207
chenille plant (*Acalypha*), 210
cherry trees, 182, 182, 183
Chicago Botanic Garden, IL 162–63
Chicago World's Fair of 1893, 85
children, 234, 235
Chimonanthus praecox (wintersweet) (evergreen), 53
Chinese dogwood (*Cornus kousa*), 34
Chinese evergreen (*Anthurium* spp., *Aglaonema*), 66
Chinese gardens, 185, 187
Chinese lily species, 91
Chinese quince (*Pseudocydonia sinensis*), 47, 47, 51
Chinese quince yellow fruit (*Amsonia hubrichtii*), 50, 51
Chinese sweetshrub (*Sinocalycanthus chinensis*), 65
Chinodoxa sardensis (glory-of-the-snow), 146
Chionodoxa forbesii 'Pink Giant', 27, 27
chives (*Allium schoenoprasum*), 198
Chloris virgata, 84

chlorophyll, plants without, 59, 59
Chlorophytum amaniense, 88
Chlorophytum genus, 89
Chrysanthemums, 47
Chrysanthemum x *koreana* 'Single Apricot', 46
Cimicifuga simplex 'Hillside Black Beauty', 136
Cimicifuga (syn. *Actea*) *racemosa,* 125, 160
Cimicifuga (syn. *Actea*) *simplex* 'Hillside Black Beauty', 128
circular plants, 126, 127
Cistus Nursery, 150
Citrofortunella mitis 'Variegata', 12
Clark, Bob, 180–81
clematis, 76, 131
Clematis 'Betty Corning', 151
Clematis rehderiana, 99
Clematis terniflora, 42
Clematis viorna, 102
Clematis x *triternata* 'Rubromarginata', 65
Cleome 'Helen Campbell', 137
Clethra alnifolia, 155, 166, 190
Cobea scandens (vine), 98
C. occidentalis (California sweetshrub), 65
cock's comb (*Celosia* 'Chief'), 145
Colchicaceae family, 89
Colchicum autumnale, 45
Colchicum speciosum 'Album', 45
Colchicum 'Water Lily' (autumn crocus or meadow saffron), 44
Colocascia esculenta, 66, 67, 226
color theory and design, 132, 133, 152–53
   analogous color and, 144, 145, 147
   black and white colors, 136, 137
   color as guide, 229
   color blind animals and, 131

   complementary colors and, 148, 149
   discovered by, 131
   monochromatic color, 140, 141, 142–43, 144
   overview, 17, 18, 19–21, 129
   psychological effects of colors and, 138, 139
   split complementary colors, 150, 151
columbines (*Aquilegia*), 76, 77, 78–79, 131, 202, 202
combining plants, 11–14, 237
comfrey (*Symphytum x uplandicum* 'Axminster Gold'), 11
complementary colors, 148, 149, 150
Compositae family, 69
compositions, designing, 11–14
conifers, 114, 115
Connecticut, 12, 25, 43, 214
'Constance Spry', 75
containers for plants, 229
Convallaria majalis 'Variegata', 155
Coprosma kirkii 'Variegata', 154
Coprosma 'Pink Surprise', 178
Coprosma 'Roy's Red', 178
coral-bark maple (*Acer palmatum* 'Sango Kaku'), 52
Cordyline 'Festival Grass', 154
Coreopsis, 242
   'Red Shift', 68
   'Sienna Sunset', 68
Coreopsis grandiflora 'Sunray', 68
Coreopsis lanceolata 'Moonbeam', 195
Cornelian cherry (*Cornus mas*) (evergreen), 53
Cornus (dogwood), 19
Cornus florida 'Cherokee Sunset', 18, 19
Cornus kousa (Chinese dogwood), 34, 197
Cornus mas (Cornelian cherry) (evergreen), 53

Cornus sericea 'Silver and Gold' (yellow twig dogwood), 52
Cornus stolonifera 'Flavarima', 53
Cornus x rutgersensis 'Stellar Pink', 29
Corydalis cheilanthifolia, 87
Corydalis flexuosa, 148
Corydalis genus, 86
Corydalis lutea, 209
Corydalis ochroleuca, 87
Corylus maxima 'Purpurea', 28, 132
Cotinus coggygria, 92, 128, 136, 151, 188
Cotoneaster horizontalis, 92
cottage gardens, 214, 215, 216, 217
cowslip, 202, 202
crab apple (probably Malus 'Prairie Fire'), 9
cranberry (Vaccinium macrocarpon), 119, 173
Cresson, Charles, 152–53
Crocosmia, 42, 43, 138, 147
Cryptomeria japonica 'Ben Franklin', 114
'Gyokuryu', 114
C. sanguinea 'Midwinter Fire', 53
cucumber (Cucumis sativis 'Diva'), 198
Cucumis sativis 'Diva' (cucumber), 198
culinary herbs, 7, 207, 239
Cullina, Bill, 39
cultivars, 57, 62, 81, 115
See also specific cultivars by name
Cunninghamia lanceolata, 114
Cuphea hyssopifolia, 94
Cuphea ignea, 196
Cupressus sempervirens (Italian cypress), 175
Curcubita pepo cv. (summer squash), 198
Cyclamen hederifolium, 45
Cynara cardunculus, 110
Cyperaceae (sedges), 85
Cypripedium reginae (orchid), 36

Cypripedium species (lady slipper orchids), 37

D ———————————————

daffodils, 24, 25, 25, 140, 146
Dahlia 'Mystic Illusion', 216
dahlias, 40, 137, 147, 221
daisies, 147, 156
daisy-like flowers, 69
Dalia 'Stoneleigh Cherry', 126
Daphne burkwoodii 'Briggs Moonlight', 190
Daphne odorata 'Variegata', 22, 24
Darmera peltata, 127, 168
Daucus carota subsp sativus 'Rainbow Mix' (carrot), 234
David, James, 96–97
daylilies, 145, 199, 199
Decomaria (hydrangea scrambler), 81
Deinanthe bifida (hydrangea), 80, 81, 81
Delphiniums, 125
Deutzia gracillis 'Variegata', 141
Deutzia 'Magicien', 9
Deutzia scabra, 141
Dianthus plumarius, 110, 190
Dianthus x 'Brigadier', 186
Dicentra [syn. Lamprocapnos] spectabilis 'Alba' (bleeding heart), 28
Dicentra eximia (bleeding heart), 20, 86, 87
dicot plants, 85
dicotyledons, 66
Dictamus albus, 139
Dieffenbachia (dumb cane), 66
Digitalis grandiflora (foxglove), 38, 39
Digitalis lanata, 188
Digitalis lutea, 188
Digitalis parviflora (foxglove), 188, 208
dill (Anethum graveolens), 126, 206
Disporum flavens, 88, 148
Disporum sessile 'Variegata', 155

'Distant Drums' (rose), 74
DNA research, 16, 59, 89
Dodonea viscosum 'Purpurea', 178
dogwood (Cornus), 19, 52, 53
Dolichos lablab (syn. Lablab purpureus) (hyacinth bean), 51
double-complementary colors, 150
Druse, Ken, 9, 11–13, 14, 17, 19–21
canal garden of, 172
floods on property of, 169
gardens of, 132, 157, 159, 159, 169
grass 'fountain' of, 85
inspired by masters, 222
roses and, 75
sister of, 191
vegetable gardens and, 230
Dryopteris affinis 'Cristata', 200
Dryopteris erythrosora, 200
dumb cane (Dieffenbachia), 66
Dutch iris (I. x hollandica 'Oriental Beauty'), 30–31
dwarf boxwood, dwarf trees, 115, 127

E ———————————————

Echeveria, 106, 179
Echinacea purpurea 'Green Envy', 62, 63
'Razzmatazz', 195
'The Swan', 195
Echinops ritro (globe thistle), 126, 127, 220
Edgeworthia chrysantha, 24, 140
edible flowers, 198, 199, 208, 238, 239–40, 241
Edraianthus serpyllifolia, 186
eggplants, 175, 175
Elizabethan gardens, 202, 203
Elymus arenarius, 110
Emilia coccinea, 94
emotions, 139
Endymion hispanicus

(formerly Scilla campanulata, Scilla hispanica), 89, 145
England, 139, 141, 207, 211, 222, 222, 223
English boxwood (Buxus sempervirens 'Suffruticosa'), 205
English rose 'Royal Wedding' and 'English Garden', 74
Enkianthus campanulatus var. sikkokianus, 56
Epimedium hybrids, 245
Epiphyllum (cacti), 8, 106
Eranthis hyemalis, 54, 55
Eranthis spp. (winter aconite), 76
Erica carnea (spring heath) (evergreen), 53
Ericaceae family, 56, 59
Eriogonum ovalifolium (syn. Paronychia ovalifolium, Amaracea supalifolium), 186
E. russeliana, 20
Eryngium planum 'Blaukappe', 17, 68, 130
Eryngium yuccafolium, 68, 156
Erythronium americanum, 158
Eubotrys racemosa, 56
Euonymous japonicus 'Microphyllus Pulchellus', 155
Eupatorium capillifolium, 228
Eupatorium perfoliatum, 160
Eupatorium pupureum subsp. maculatum, 165
Eupatorium purpureum, 160, 195
Euphorbia dulcis 'Chameleon', 149, 209, 245
Euphorbia 'Flame', 228
Euphorbia marginata, 42
Euphorbia myrsinties, 107
Euphorbia polychroma, 245
Euphorbia rigida, 12
Euphorbia x martinii 'Ascot Rainbow', 226
Eustoma often called Lisianthus, 20

Euthamia graminifolia, 165
evergreens, 52, 53, 59, 115
Exacum affine, 94
Exochorda racemosa 'The
    Pearl', 73
extreme weather, 179, 187

F

F1 hybrids, 65
Fabaceae family, 70, 71, 208
Fagus sylvatica 'Dawyck
    Purple' (red beech), 127
false indigo, 71
false solomon's seal, 88, 200
families
    largest of all, 69
    overview, 14, 16, 57
    spelling and
        pronunciation of, 59
    of trees, 82, 83
    *See also specific families
        by name*
Fargesia nitida, 183
fashion style gardens, 211
feathery pinnate leaves, 71
female/male plants, 66
feng shui, 185
ferns, 34, 46, 116, 116, 117,
    118, 127, 200, 200, 201,
    243
fertilization, 65, 66, 115, 123
Festuca glauca, 111
figs, 174
Filipendula rubra (queen of
    the prairie), 72
Filipendula ulmaria, 36, 37,
    155
Filippone, Andrea, 111
fishtail willow (*Salix
    sachalinensis* 'Sekka'), 52
floating water plants, 167
flooding, 169
floribunda roses, 75
floriography, 219, 243
"flower" arrangements, 51
flowers, 124, 125
    black and white colors
        and, 136, 137
    for butterfly gardens,
        194
    children and, 235
    for cutting, 221
    daisy-like, 69
    development of, 115

edible, 198, 199, 208,
    238, 239–40, 241
expressing meaning
    with, 219, 243
language of, 243
rayless, 69
of roses, 72
round or prickly, 126, 127
summer, 40, 41
winter, 55
foliage. *See* leaves
folk art gardens, 214, 215
'Fool's Gold', 178
form follows function,
    overview, 16–17, 93
foxglove, 38, 39, 208
Fragaria vesca 'Golden
    Alexander', 133
fragrant gardens, 190, 191,
    192
Frelinghuysen Arboretum,
    NJ, 217
Fritillaria mileagris, 149
frogs, 76, 169
frost, 14, 20, 43, 47, 51, 95,
    106, 113, 180–81, 211, 225
fruit, 72, 95
Fuchsia hybrid, 196
Fumariaceae family, 86
functionality, 93, 98, 103
fungal diseases, 91, 111
fungicides, 34
futuristic gardens, 216, 217

G

Gaillardia 'Burgundy', 216
Galanthus nivalis
    (snowdrop), 54, 55
Galanthus plicatus 'E.A.
    Bowles', 55
Galphimia gracillis, 228
Gardener's Eye, The (Lacy),
    23
genera, 57, 59, 65
*See also specific genera by
    name*
Geranium 'Johnson's Blue',
    215
Geranium 'Jolly Bee', 224
Geranium macrorrhizum, 190
Geranium maculatum
    'Espresso', 136
Geranium phaeum, 128, 149
geraniums, hothouse, 210, 211

Geranium sanguineum var.
    striatum, 215
Geranium x *cantabrigiense*
    'Karmina', 236
Gerbera 'California Mixed
    Colors', 220
germination, 85
Geum, 26, 72
ghost bramble (*Rubus
    thibetanus*), 52
Ginkgo biloba, 115
Glaucidium palmatum and
    *Glaucidium palmatum
    f. leucanthum* (Japanese
    wood poppies), 76
Glechoma hederacea
    'Dappled Light', 102
Globba winitii, 228
globe amaranth
    (*Gomphrena*
    'Strawberry Fields'), 40
globe thistle (*Echinops
    ritro*), 126, 127
glory-of-the-snow, 27, 146
Golden Gate Park, CA, 182
gold-leafed bluebeard
    shrub (*Caryopteris* x
    clandonensis 'Worcester
    Gold'), 10, 11, 34, 37, 118
Gomphrena globosa, 126, 220
Gomphrena 'Strawberry
    Fields' (globe
    amaranth), 40
gourds, 99, 231
Gramineae (now Poaceae)
    (grass family), 84, 85, 85
Grape holly (*Mahonia*), 65
grapevine (*Vitis vinifera*),
    37, 103
grass family (Poaceae), 84,
    85, 85, 156
Greenaway, Kate, 219
green (color), 132, 133
"green roofs", 106
greens, 32, 33, 230
Greenwood Gardens,
    New Jersey, 55
Gunnera sp., 119, 120–21
gymnosperms (naked
    seed), 115
Gypsophila repens, 174

H

Hagiwara, Makoto, 182

Hakone, or Japanese forest
    grass (*Hakonechloa
    macra* 'All Gold'), 38,
    39, 84
Hamamelis vernalis (witch
    hazel), 53
Hamamelis x *intermedia*
    (witch hazel), 53, 53
Hart's tongue fern
    fronds (*Asplenium
    scolopendrium*), 201
Haskell, Allen, 27
healing gardens, 189, 200,
    201
health and beauty plants,
    206, 207
"Heartsease" (pansy), 218
Hedera helix 'Blue Moon',
    54, 188
Hedera helix 'Buttercup',
    133, 155
Hedera helix 'Gold Heart',
    102, 188
Hedychium 'Tara', 226
Heims, Dan, 62
heirloom tulips, 28
Helenium autumnale cv, 126
Helenium flexuosum cv, 126
Helianthus 'Lemon Queen'
    (sunflower), 10, 11
Helianthus 'Ring of Fire', 216
Helianthus 'Valentine', 220
Helichrysum bracteatum, 220
Heliopsis 'Bressingham
    Doubloon', 138
Heliopsis helianthoides var.
    scabra 'Summer Nights'
    (daisy), 156
heliotrope, 242
Heliotropium arborescens
    cv, 190
hellebores, 76, 77
Helleborus foetidus, 55
Helleborus foetidus fruits, 140
Helleborus niger, 55, 77
Helleborus orientalis, 55
Helleborus x *hybridus*, 55
Hemerocallis
    hybrid, 88
    'Jungle Beauty', 136
    'Lemon Gem', 88
    'Spiritual Corridor', 88
Hemerocallis lilioasphodelus,
    118

Hepatica (liverwort), *76*
herbaceous perennials, 11, 13, 27, *48–49*, 50, 72, 73, 95, 124, 237
herbs, *112–13*, 175, 206, 207, 214, *239*
Hesperola parviflora, 224
Heuchera villosa, 125
Heucherella hybrid, 125
Heuchera leaves, 245
Hibiscus acetosella, 216, 226
Hibiscus syriacus, 17
Hibiscus x *moscheutos* 'Kopper King', *136*
Hidcote Manor, England, 139
Hinkley, Dan, 13
Hippocrates, 208
Hogan, Sean, 150
holly berries, 147
Hollyhock flowers, *104, 105*
Hosta 'Gold Regal' flowers, *128*
hosta leaves, *105, 105*
Hosta plantaginea, 190
hostas, 111, *118, 119*, 150, 200
Hosta 'Striptease', *141*
Houstonia caerulea, 32
Hoverkamp, Ellen, 9, 11–12, 19, 21, 23, 119, 219
hummingbird gardens, 189, *196, 197*
hyacinth bean (*Dolichos lablab*) (syn. *Lablab purpureus*), 51
hyacinths, 27, *27, 146*, 208
Hybiscus syriacus, *130, 196*
hybrid musk 'Sally Homes' (rose), *74*
hybrids, 77
    defined, 65
    fertilization of, 65
    lilies, 91
    roses, 75
    See also specific hybrids by name
hybrid tea 'Sunset Celebration' (rose), *74*
Hydrangea anomala var. *petiolaris* 'Platt Dwarf', *81*
Hydrangea arborescens 'Invincible Spirit', *81*, 190
Hydrangea arborescens var. *radiata* 'Hayes Starburst', *81, 81*, 155

Hydrangea macrophylla, *39*, *81, 81*
Hydrangea paniculata 'Brussels Lace', *81, 81*
Hydrangea paniculata 'Grandiflora', *81, 81*, 119
Hydrangea paniculata 'Limelight', *10, 11, 14*, *81, 81*
Hydrangea quercifolia (oakleaf hydrangea) 'Snowflake', 'Snow Queen' and 'Vaughn's Lillie', *63, 81, 81*
hydrangeas, 14, *39*, 46, *80, 81, 81*, 221
Hydrangea serrata, *81, 81, 81*, 128
Hypericum prolificum, *126, 236*

Icelandic poppies (*Papaver nudicaule*), 86
Ilex verticilata 'Aurantiaca', *47*
Ilex vomitoria (yaupon holly), 24
Illicium floridanum 'Album', *201*
Illicium fruits, *201*
Impatiens 'Applause Orange Blaze', *226*
Impatiens pallida, *196*
Impatiens 'Seashell Yellow', *94*
Indian pipe (*Monotropa uniflora*), *59, 59*
Indigofera psuedotinctoria 'Rose Carpet', *70*
inflorescence, *66, 67*
insect deterrents, 208
insects/insecticides, 34, 123, *173*
inspiration, color and, 129
inter/intraspecific, 65
Inula magnifica, *195*
invasive plants, 19, *20–21*, 51, 75, 85, 86, 93, 103, 149, 150, 155, 157, 167, *169*, 175, 179, 194, 208, 237
Ipomoea batatas 'Blackie', *136*

Ipomoea multifida, *196*
irises, *30–31, 131, 139*, 148, 168, *170–71*
Italian cypress (*Cupressus sempervirens*), 175
Italian parsley (*Petroselinum crispum* var. *neapolitanum*), 206
Italy, 174, 175
I. x *hollandica* 'Oriental Beauty' (Dutch iris), *30–31*

Jack-in-the-pulpits (*Arisaema*), *66*, 158
Jacob's ladder (*Polemonium reptans* 'Stairway to Heaven'), *38, 39*
Japanese Andromeda (*Pieris japonica*), *55*, 59
Japanese aster (*Kalimeris yomena* 'Fuji Snow'), *47*
Japanese forest grass (*Hakonechloa macra* 'All Gold'), *38, 39*
Japanese gardens, 182, 187
Japanese lily species, 91
Japanese maple, 26, *82, 82, 83*, 105, 147
Japanese painted fern (*Athyrium japonicum-pictum*), *200*
Japanese skunk cabbage (*Lysichiton americanum, L. camtschatcensis*), *66, 66*
Japanese Tea Garden, Golden Gate Park, CA, 182
Japanese wood poppies (*Glaucidium palmatum* and *Glaucidium palmatum f. leucanthum*), *76*
jasmine, blooming, 227
jasmine, winter (*Jasminum nudiflorum*) (evergreen), 53
Jasminum nudiflorum (winter jasmine) (evergreen), 53
Jasminum officinalis 'Fiona Sunrise', *226*
Jekyll, Gertrude, 11, 19, 211

Jerusalem sage (*Phlomis russeliana*), *38, 39*
Johnston, Lawrence, 139
Jones, Robert, 13
Juncaceae (rushes), 85
jungle cacti, 106
Juniperus communis 'Gold Cone', *114*

K

Kalanchoe beharensis, 106
Kalimeris yomena 'Fuji Snow' (Japanese aster), *47*
Kalmia angustifolia, 201
Kalmia latifolia (Nurseryman Dick Jayne's mountain laurel), *59*
Keringoshima koreana, *45*
Kerria japonica, *73*
Knap Hill azalea, *127*
Kniphofia galpinii hybrid, *196*
Kniphofia hybrid, *125, 154*
Kolkwitzia amabilis, *137*
Koster, Tom, 25

L

laburnum trees (golden chain), 222, *223*
Laburnum Walk, England, *222, 222, 223*
Laburnum x *watereri*, *223*
Lachenalia aloides, *12*
Lacy, Allen, 23
Ladies' Border, New York Botanical Garden, *225*
lady's slipper orchid (*Cypripedium reginae* var. *albolabium*), *37, 62*
Lagerstroemia 'Cherry Dazzle', *224*
Lamium maculatum 'Anne Greenaway', *236*
Lamium maculatum 'White Nancy', *155*
Lamprocapnos genus, 86
Lamprocapnos spectabilis 'Alba', *87*
Lamprocapnos (syn. *Dicentra*) *eximia*, *87*
Language of Flowers, The (Greenaway, Kate), *219*

lantana, 210

Lantana camara
  'Samantha', 228

lateriflorus 'Lady in Black',
  69

Latin names, 39, 57, 59, 62,
  65, 69, 89, 91

Laurentia axillaris
  'Starshine', 94

Lavandula angustifolia, 174,
  192

Lavandula 'Hidcote Pink',
  240

lavender cotton (*Santolina
  chamaecyparissus*), 210

lavender flowered catmint,
  Nepeta spp., 72

lavender Russian sage
  (*Perovskia atriplicifolia*),
  111

leaves, 117, 118, 119, *119*
  circular, 126, *127*
  colors of, 132, *134–35*
  compound, 71
  contrasted with vertical
    plants, 124
  hosta, 105
  variegated, 155

legumes, 71

Le Language Des Fleur (de la
  Tour), 219

Leontopodium alpinum
  (Edelweiss), 186

Les Jardins de Quatre-Vents,
  Québec, *142–43*

lettuces, *32, 33*, 230
  See also greens

Leucojum vernum, 24, 55

Liatris pycnostachya (blazing
  star), *162–63*

Liatris spicata, 125, 160, 195

light transmission, 105
  black and white colors
    and, 136, *137*
  color as, 131
  hummingbirds and, 197

Ligularia 'Britt Marie
  Crawford', *34*

Ligularia dentata 'Britt-
  Marie Crawford', *136*

Ligularia genus, 124, 127

Ligularia japonica, 68, 168

Ligularia species, 17

lilacs, 28, 131, 219

Liliaceae family (lilies), 59,
  89, 90, 91, 138, 141, 150,
  158, 209

Lilium 'African Queen', 91

Lilium genus, 91

Lilium henryi, 91

Lilium henryii, 90

Lilium 'Leslie Woodruff',
  90, 150

Lilium martagon, 141, 209

Lilium 'Mrs. R. O.
  Backhouse', 209

Lilium 'White Henry', 90,
  91

Limonium sinuatum
  'Forever Happy', 220

Lindera glauca, 46

lion's head maple
  (*Acer palmatum*
  'Shishiagashira'), 47

Liquidambar styraciflua
  'Slender Silhouette', 124

Lisianthus hybrid, 94

Lisianthus often called
  Eustoma, 20

literary gardens, 202, 203

liverwort (*Hepatica*), 76

Lobelia siphilitica, 156

Lobularia maritima (sweet
  alyssum), 191

London, 207, 211

Long Island, NY, *112–13*

Lonicera fragrantissima
  (winter honeysuckle)
  (evergreen), 53

Lonicera nitida 'Baggesen's
  Gold', 228

Lonicera periclymenum
  'Serotina Florida', *188*,
  209

Lonicera sempervirens, 102,
  196

Loropetalum chinensis var.
  rubrum, 42, 43

Louis XIV, 229

lungwort, 202, *202*

Lupinus hybrids, 70

Lupinus polyphyllus, 215

Lutyens, Sir Edwin, 211

Lychnis chalcedonia (Maltese
  cross), 138

Lychnis coronaria, 174

Lysichiton americanum,
  L. camtschatcensis

(Japanese skunk
  cabbage), 66

Lysichiton americanus
  (skunk cabbage,
  Western U.S.), 66

Lysimachia atropurpurea, 125

Lysimachia punctata
  'Alexander', *38*, 155

M

Magnolia grandiflora 'Edith
  Bogue' (Southern
  magnolia), *50*, 51

Magnolia Plantation and
  Gardens, SC, *100–101*

Magnolia stellata (star
  magnolia flower), 27, 145

Mahonia, 46, 54, 65

maidenhair fern (*Adiantum
  pedatum*), 127

male/female plants, 66

Maltese cross (*Lychnis
  chalcedonia*), 138

Malus 'Prairie Fire' (crab
  apple), *9*

Mandevilla 'Sun Parasol
  Crimson', 226

maple, coral-bark (*Acer
  palmatum* 'Sango
  Kaku'), 52

maple trees, 82, *82, 83*, 105

marigold *Tagetes* hybrid, 94

marjoram (*Origanum
  marjoram*), 206

McCormac, Jim, 25

meadow saffron or autumn
  crocus (*Colchicum*
  'Water Lily'), 44

mealycup sage (*Salvia
  farinacea*), 125

medicinal plants, 76, 206,
  207, 208

Mediterranean, 111, *112–13*,
  174, 175, *176–77*

Melinis nerviglumis
  'Savannah', 84

Melinis repens, 84

Melissa officinalis 'Lime', 155

Mentha piperita 'Variegata'
  (peppermint), *198*

Mertensia virginica 'Alba',
  19, 20

Mesembryanthemum spp.,
  69

Metasequoia glyptostroboides
  'Ogon', 155

Mexican blue palm (*Brahea
  armata*), 179

Meyer, Grant, 12, *12*

Mianthemum (syn.
  Smilacina) *racemosa*,
  88, 200

microclimates, 225

Middleton Place, SC, *60–61*

milkweed, 93

Miller, Lynden B., 225

mimosa (*Albizia julibrissin*),
  71

Mimosa pudica, 71

Mina lobata (vine), 99

miniature 'Constellation'
  (rose), 74

mini-flora (patio) roses, 75

mints, 198, 206, 207
  See also catmint (*Nepeta*
    'Walker's Low')

Miscanthus sinensis
  'Cosmopolitan', 155

mixed beds and borders, 95

modern cottage gardens,
  216, 217

Mohonk Mountain House,
  NY, 12, *212–13*

Molina caerulea ssp.
  arundinacea 'Sky
  Racer', 84

Momordica charantia (bitter
  melon), 99

Monarda 'Berry Red', 195

Monarda didyma 'Raspberry
  Wine', 195, *196*

Monarda fistulosa, 150, 160,
  165

monastery gardens, 207

monocarpic annuals, 95

monochromatic color, 140,
  141, *142–43*, 144, 147

monocotyledons, 66, 85

Monotropa uniflora (Indian
  pipe), 59, *59*

morphology, 16–17

Morris, William, 217

Morus alba 'Snowflake', 155

mountain laurel,
  Nurseryman Dick
  Jayne's (*Kalmia
  latifolia*), 59

Muir, John, 159

Musa acuminate var. sumatrana (syn. *M. zebrina*), 226

Muscari 'Pink Sunrise', 27, 27

N

naked gardening, 220, 221

name changes, 69, 89, 91
See also scientific names of plants

Nandina domestica, 51, 140

narcissus plants, 208

Nassella tenuissima, 156

nasturtiums, 198, 208, 238

native plants, 19–20

Nectoscordum tripedale, 15

needles from trees, 115

Nepeta cataria (catnip), 206

Nepeta 'Walker's Low' (catmint), 13, 34, 37, 37, 72, 242

nettle, variegated (*Boehmeria nipononivea* 'Kogane Mushi'), 42, 43

New Jersey, 9, 11, 26, 27, 29, 164, 217

Newton, Sir Isaac, 131

New York asters, 47, 47

New York Botanical Garden, 225

Nickou, Nick, 200

Nicotiana alata, 94, 196

Nicotiana 'Ken's Coffee', 128

Nicotiana langsdorfi, 216

Nicotiana 'Lime Green', 40

Nicotiana mutabilis, 224

Nicotiana x *sanderae* 'Baby Bella', 216

night-blooming cereus (*Epiphyllum oxypetalum*), 8

Ninebark (*Physocarpus opulifolius*), 72

nitrogen fixation, 71

North American lily species, 91

North Carolina, 150, 225, 229

North Hill, VT, 103, 172

Nuphar lutea, 166

Nurseryman Dick Jayne's mountain laurel (*Kalmia latifolia*) varieties, 59

Nymphaea odorata, 166

O

Ocimum basilicum (basil), 21, 198, 206, 216

Oenothera speciosus, 215

O. fragilis, 107

Old Westbury Gardens, NY, 112–13

Olea europaea, 174

Ophiopogon planiscapus 'Nigrescens', 136

opium poppy (breadseed poppy), 86, 104, 127

Opuntia engelmanii, 12

Opuntia fragilis, 186

Opuntia humifusa, 107

orange, trifoliate (*Poncirus trifoliata*), 46, 51

orchids, lady slipper (*Cypripedium* species), 36, 37, 62

oregano (*Origanum vulgare*), 198, 206

Orienpet lily hybrid, 90

Oriental poppy (*Papaver orientalis*), 86

Origanum marjoram (marjoram), 206

Origanum vulgare (oregano), 174, 198, 206

ornamental grasses, 84, 85, 85

Osmunda regalis (royal fern), 34, 46

P

Pachysandra terminalis 'Variegata', 155

Paeonia lactiflora 'Pink Dawn', 15

Panicum virgatum, 84, 160

pansy (*Viola* cv.) "Hearts-ease", 140, 198, 218

Papaveraceae family, 86, 86

Papaver atlanticum, 118

Papaver nudicaule (Icelandic poppies), 86

Papaver orientalis (Oriental poppy), 86

Papaver (poppy genus), 86, 86, 87

Papaver somniferum pod, 126, 127

paperbark maple (*Acer griseum*), 105

Papilio multicaudata (swallowtail butterfly), 195

paradise found, 179, 229

parsley, Italian (*Petroselinum crispum* var. *neapolitanum*), 206, 230

parsnip (*Pastinaca sativa* 'Hollow Crown'), 234

Parthenocissus quinquefolia 'Variegata', 102

Passiflora alatocaerulea, 190

Passiflora 'Lady Margaret', 226

Pastinaca sativa 'Hollow Crown' (parsnip), 234

Pathenocissus tricuspidata 'Lowii', 102

peaceful places, 164

peace lily (*Spathiphyllum*), 66

Peacock maple (*Acer japonicum* 'Aconitifolium'), 46

pea family and relatives, 70, 71

Pelargonium citrosum 'Mint Rose', 190

(*Pelargonium*) red hothouse geraniums, 210, 211

Peltandra virginica, 166

Pennisetum glaucum 'Purple Majesty', 136

Pennisetum massaicum 'Red Bunny Tails', 84

Pennisetum vilosum, 84

Pennisetum x *advena* 'Fireworks', 84

Penstemon digitalis, 138, 215

Pentas lanceolata, 94, 196

peonies, 137, 184, 185

peppermint (*Mentha piperita* 'Variegata'), 198

pepper plants, 231

perennials, 28, 65, 95, 102, 111, 191
herbaceous, 11, 13, 27, 48–49, 50, 72, 73, 95, 124, 237
hybrids, 65

perfumed flowers, 191, 193

Perovskia atriplicifolia, 196

Perovskia atriplicifolia (lavender Russian sage), 111

Petasites japonicus 'Variegatus', 133, 236

Petroselinum crispum var. *neapolitanum* (Italian parsley), 206

pheasant's eye (*Adonis vernalis*), 76

philodendrons, 66

Phlomis fruticosa, 110

Phlomis russeliana (Jerusalem sage), 38, 39

Phlox divaricata, 148

Phlox paniculata, 190, 195, 220

Phormium varieties, 178, 228

Physocarpus opulifolius, 72
'Dart's Gold', 73
'Diablo', 132

Pieris japonica (Japanese Andromeda), 55, 59

pinnate leaves, 71, 117

Pinus mugo, 114

Pinus parviflora 'Glauca', 114

Piper auritum, 190

places, overview, 19–21

Plant Delights Nursery, NC, 150, 225

Platycodon grandiflorus, 220

Ploygonatum odoratum 'Variegatum', 200

Plumbago auriculata, 226

Poaceae (grass family), 84, 85, 85

poisonous plants, 66, 86, 203, 208
See also toxic plants

Polemonium flowers, 38

Polemonium reptans 'Stairway to Heaven' (Jacob's ladder), 38, 39, 236

pollination, 65, 66, 115, 123

polyantha roses, 75

Polygonatum humile, 88

Polygonatum (Solomon's seal) genus, 89

Poncirus trifoliate 'Flying Dragon', 201

ponds, 167, 170–71, 172

Pontederia cordata, 166

poppy genus (*Papaver*), 86, 86, 87

Portland, OR, 120–21

Potentilla genus, 72

potted plants, 229

prairies, 161, *162–63*

prickly flowers, *126, 127*
  See also thistles

primary colors, 131

primroses, *170–71*

Primula 'Francesca', *18, 118*

Primula japonica, *169*

Primula veris, *32*

Primula x bullessiana, *168*

propagation, *12–13*

Prunus mume (apricot tree), *72*

Prunus persica varieties (red-leaved peach), *34*

Prunus 'Shirotae', *183*

psychological effects of colors, *138, 139*

Purple sedum, *104*

Puschkinia scilloides, *27, 27, 146*

pussy willows, *27, 52*

Pycnanthemum muticum, *110, 160*

Pyracantha 'Gold Rush', *46*

Q

Québec, Canada, *142–43*

queen of the prairie (*Filipendula rubra*), *72*

Quercus robur 'Concordia', *155*

quince, Chinese (*Pseudocydonia sinensis*), *47, 47*, 51

quince, Chinese yellow fruit (*Amsonia hubrichtii*), *50*, 51

quince (*Chaenomeles speciosa* varieties), *22, 26, 27*

R

rain gardens, 172

Ramblers (hybrid Wichuraiana roses), 75

Ranunculaceae family, 76, 77, *78–79*

Ranunculus, *76, 77, 236*

red beech (*Fagus sylvatica* 'Dawyck Purple'), *127*

redbud (*Cercis canadensis*), *20, 63, 71*

red hothouse geraniums (*Pelargonium*), *211*

Red-leafed peach tree, *34*

red maple (*Acer rubrum*), 27

repetition, establishing rhythm with, 13

reproduction, 65, 66, 115, 123

retention planting, 172

retinas, and color perceptions, 131

rhodendrons, 56, 59

Rhododendron amagianum, *56*

Rhododendron indicum hybrids, *60–61*

Rhododendron mucronulatum, *183*

Rhododendron viscosum, *166*

rhubarb, 208

Rhus typhina 'Tiger Eyes', *216*

Ribes odorata, *148*

Rice Mill Pond, The, *60–61*

R. kaempferi tachisene (azaleas), *56*

Robin Hill rhododendron hybrid, *56*

Robinia psuedoacacia 'Frisia', *18*

Robinson, William, 211, 217

rock gardens, *185, 186, 187*

Rocky Hills garden, *170–71*

Rosa carolina (Carolina rose), *75*

Rosaceae (rose family), 59, 72, 73, 75

Rosa (rose), *34, 35, 37, 37, 59, 72, 73, 74, 75, 98, 192, 193, 242*
  'Abraham Darby', *34*
  'American Pillar', *151*
  'Ballerina', *37, 37*
  'Dr. Huey', *34*
  genus, 75
  'Pink Knockout', *190, 216*

rose water, *193*

royal fern (*Osmunda regalis*), *34, 46*

R. palustris (the swamp rose), 75

R. rugosa ("wild" beach rose), 75

Rubus thibetanus (ghost bramble), *52*

ruby-throated hummingbird (*Archilochus colubris*), 197

Rudbeckia daisies, *147*

Rudbeckia hirta, *68, 165*

Rudbeckia laciniata var. 'Hortensia Golden Glow', *195*

Rudbeckia maxima, *124, 125*

Rudbeckia triloba, *195*

rue (*Ruta graveolens*), 208

Ruscaceae family, 89

rushes (*Juncaceae*), 85

Russian sage, lavender (*Perovskia atriplicifolia*), 111

Russo, Michael, *16*

Ruta graveolens (rue), 208

S

Sackville-West, Vita, 141

sage, lavender Russian (*Perovskia atriplicifolia*), 111

Salix alba subsp. *vitellina* 'Britzensis', *52*

Salix alba (willow), *52, 53*, 208

(*Salix caprea*) common pussy willow, *52*

Salix chaenomeloides (pussy willow), *27, 52*

Salix integra 'Hakuro Nishiki', *127, 141*

Salix sachalinensis 'Sekka' (fishtail willow), *52*

Salvia coccinea 'Forest Fire', *42*

Salvia farinacea, *125, 137, 196, 210*

Salvia lyrata (ground cover), *42, 43*

Salvia officinalis 'Icterina', *174*

Salvia 'Sensation Rose', *186*

Salvia superba, *125*

Sambucus canadensis, *168*

San Diego, CA, *106*

San Francisco, CA, *182*

Sanguisorba officinalis 'Lemon Splash', *155*

Santolina chamaecyparissus, *174, 210*

Sarracenia purpurea, *173*

Satureja montana (winter savory), *206*

Saxifraga crustata, *186*

Scaevola aemula, *94*

scent. See fragrant gardens

Schizachyrium scoparium, *165*

Schizophragma (genus), 81

scientific names of plants, 39, 57, 59, 62, 65, 69, 89, 91

Scilla bifolia 'Rosea', *27*

Scirpus cyperinus, *165*

Scutellaria prostrata, *186*

seasons, 14, 23
  See also specific seasons by name

secondary colors, 131

Secret Garden, The (Burnett), 200

secret gardens, 189, 200, *201*

sedges (*Cyperaceae*), 85

Sedum album 'Coral Carpet', *54*

sedum genus, 187

Sedum kamtschaticum, *107*

Sedum lineare 'Variegatum', *107*

Sedum makinoi 'Ogon', *107*

Sedum rupestre 'Angelique', *36*

Sedum spectabile, *46, 111*

Sedum spurium, *107*

Sedum telephium, *107*

seedlings, 66, 85, 123

Sempervivum hybrid, *107*

Senecio cineraria, *147*

Senna didymobotrya, *228*

sensory gardens, 189, 191

Sequoiadendron giganteum 'Hazel Smith', *114, 178*

shadblow (*Amelanchier* tree), 72

shade, 44, 45

Shadow, Don, 124

Shakespeare, William, 189, 203, 219

Shakespeare gardens, 202, *203*

Shipman, Ellen Biddle, 225

shrubs, *13–14, 53, 71, 71, 72, 74*
  flood tolerant, 169
  of rose family, 72, 73

sight, color perception and, 131

Silk, Steve, 226

Silphium laciniata, 68

Silphium terebinthinaceum, 160

silver-leafed plants, 110, 111, 112–13, 132, 175, 200

Sinocalycanthus chinensis (Chinese sweetshrub), 65

Sinocalycanthus 'Venus' (*calycalycanthus* x *raulstonii*), 64, 65

Sissinghurst Castle, England, 141

Skimmia japonica, 201

skunk cabbage, Western U.S. (*Lysichiton americanus*), 66

skunk cabbage (*Symplocarpus foetidus*), 66, 66

S. nova-angliae 'Honeysong Pink', 69

snowdrop (*Galanthus nivalis*), 54, 55

S. oblongifolius 'Raydon's Favorite', 69

soft tissue plants, rooting fastest, 13

soil, well-drained, 71, 91, 111, 157, 237

Solanaceae family, 175

Solenostemon scutellarioides, 209, 216, 226

Solidago nemoralis, 165

Solomon's seal (*Polygonatum*) genus, 89

Someiyoshino (Yoshino), 182

South Carolina, 60–61, 100–101

Southern magnolia (*Magnolia grandiflora* 'Edith Bogue'), 50, 51

Spathiphyllum (peace lily), 66

species, 57, 59, 65

spherical plants, 126, 127

spice gardens, 191

Spiraea japonica, 27, 72

Spiraea prunifolia 'Flore Pleno', 72

Spiraea thunbergii, 71, 72, 183

Spiraea x *bumalda*, 26, 27, 215

spires. *See* vertical plants

spirit of place

California, 178, 179, 180–81

Chinese, 185

Japanese, 182, 183

meadows, 164

Mediterranean and Italy, 174, 175, 176–77

overview, 157

paradise found, 179

prairies, 161

rain gardens, 172, 173

wetlands, 167

woodlands, 159

split complementary colors, 150, 151

spring, 34, 35, 54, 55

determining beginnings of, 14, 25

fresh start of, 26, 27, 27

greens and, 33

spring heath (*Erica carnea*) (evergreen), 53

squashes, 231

squill (*Puschkinia scilloides*), 146

Stachys byzantine, 29, 110, 174

Stachys lanata, 111

Stachyuris 'Magpie', 224

Stachyurus praecox 'Dawn' Viburnum (*Viburnum* x *bodnantense* 'Dawn'), 53

Stachyurus praecox 'Rubriflora', 27

Stamm, Lisa, 232–33

star magnolia flower (*Magnolia stellata*), 145

Steele, Fletcher, 222

Stoddard, Helen, 222

'Strawberry Cream' leaves *Syngonium*, 67

Strobi-lanthes attenuata, 45

Stufano, Marco Polo, 43

Stylophorum diphyllum (wood poppy), 87

succulents, 106, 107, 108–09, 110, 111, 179

sugar maple (*Acer saccharum*), 82

Suhr, Henriette, 170–71

summer, 34, 35, 36, 37, 40, 41, 68, 69

summer squash (*Curcubita pepo* cv.), 198

sunflower (*Helianthus*

'Lemon Queen'), 10, 11, 235

Sunset Magazine, 179

S. virens, 174

swallowtail butterfly (*Papilio multicaudata*), 195

swamp rose (*R. palustris*), 75

sweet alyssum (*Lobularia maritima*), 191

sweet peas, 71

Symphyotrichum genus, 69

Symphyotrichum 'Raspberry Swirl', 69

Symphytum x *uplandicum* 'Axminster Gold' (comfrey), 11

'Variegatum', 10

Symplocarpus foetidus (skunk cabbage), 66, 66

Syneilesis aconitifolia, 9

Syngonium podophyllum varieties (arrowhead vines), 66

Syngonium 'Strawberry Cream' leaves, 67

Syringa vulgaris 'Charles Joly' (lilac), 28

T ———————

Tagetes hybrid, 126

Tagetes tenuifolia 'Lemon Gem', 94

tallgrass prairie, 161

Tanacetum parthenium, 68, 133, 174

Tanacetum vulgare, 174, 220

Tanecetum parthenium, 209

tarragon (*Artemisia dracunculus*), 206

Taxodium distichum 'Peve Minaret', 114

taxonomy, 59, 65, 69, 89, 91

Taxus cuspidata 'Aurescens', 18

temperature extremes, 187

Terra Nova Nurseries, 62

tertiary colors, 131

tetradic color schemes, 150

Thalictrum flavum subsp. *glaucum*, 236

Thalictrum kiusianum, 186

Thalictrum rochebrunianum, 124, 125

themes

boxwood, 204, 205

butterfly gardens, 194, 195

for children, 234, 235

cottage gardens, 214, 215, 216, 217

in denial of zones, 224, 225

edible flowers, 198, 199

fashion, 210, 211

floriography, 218, 219

flower arrangements, 217

fragrant gardens, 190, 191, 192, 193

health and beauty, 206, 207

hummingbird gardens, 196, 197

inspired by masters, 222, 223

literary gardens, 202, 203

medicinal plants, 208, 209

naked gardening, 220, 221

overview, 21, 189

potted plants, 228, 229

secret gardens, 200, 201

tropical, 226, 227

vegetable gardens, 230, 231

thermogenic plants, 66

Thermopsis caroliniana, 236

thistles, 69, 126, 127

Thujopsis dolbrata 'Aurea', 114

Thunbergia alata, 94, 150

Tiarella cordifolia, 32, 158

Tibouchina urvilleana, 226

Tithonia rotundifolia, 95

tomatoes, 21, 175, 175

Torreya nucifera 'Snowcap', 114

Tour, Madame Charlotte de la, 219

toxic plants, 76, 208

See also poisonous plants

Trachelospermum asiaticum 'Ogon Nishiki', 154

trademark plant names, 62

transplanting plants, 11

trees, 82, 83, 148, 159, 222

cherry, 182, *182, 183*
children and, 235
erosion control and, 169
evergreen, pine and
dwarf, 115
laburnum, 222, *223*
maple, 82, *82, 83,* 105
in rose family, 72
willow, 53, 208
triadic color schemes, 150,
152–53
Trichosanthes kirilowii
(snake gourd), 99
Tricyrtis hirta, 45
trifoliate orange (*Poncirus
trifoliata*), 46, 51
Trillium decumbens, 55
Trillium grandiflorum, 19
Trillium luteum, 245
Triteleia (syn. *Brodiaea*)
laxa, 88
Trochodendron araliodes, 201
Tropaeolum majus 'Peach
Melba' (nasturtium), *198*
tropical jungle cacti, 106
tropical plants, *226, 227*
True taro (*Colocasia
esculenta*), 66
tulip, 28, *29,* 202, *202, 243*
'Insulinde', 28, *28*
'Orange Emperor', *26, 27*
'Prinses Irene', *26, 27*
Tulipa clusiana, 28, *29*
Turner, J.M.W., 19
Typha angustifolia, 166
Tyson, Brandon, *178*

U
Ulmus glabra 'Camperdownii'
(Weeping Camperdown
elm tree), 148
Umbelliferae (family), 194
USDA Zones, 14, 27, 53, 55,
81, 119, 123, 157, 179,
200, *200,* 224, 225
Uvularia grandiflora, 88
Uvularia perfoliata, 19
uxus sempervirens var.
koreana x *Buxus
sempervirens* 'Green
Mountain', *204*

V
Vaccinium corymbosum, 166

Vaccinium macrocarpon
(cranberry), 119, *173*
Valerian, Greek
(*Polemonium reptans*)
(Jacob's ladder), 39
variegated redbud (*Cercis
canadensis* 'Silver
Cloud'), *63*
Veeder, Mark, 62
vegetables, 33, *175, 175,* 230,
231, 232–33, 234, 235
Veratrum viridis, 118, 168
Verbascum, 17
Verbascum hybrid, *130*
Verbena bonariensis, 94
Verey, Rosemary, *222, 223*
Vermont, 103, 172
Veronica spicata, 125, 215
*Veronicastrum virginicum,
125, 160*
vertical plants, 124, *125*
Viburnum farreri, 52
Viburnum macrocephalum, 28
Viburnum plicatum
'Rosace', *15*
Viburnum x *bodnantense*
'Dawn' (*Stachyurus
praecox* 'Dawn'
Viburnum), 53
Victorian gardens, *210, 211,
212–13*
Vinca major, *211*
vines, 98, *99, 102, 103*
Viola, 32, 198, 241
violets, 202, *202, 243*
Virginia bluebells
(*Mertensia virginica*
'Alba'), 20
Vitex negundo
'Heterophylla', *190*
Vitis vinifera
'Argentea', *36*
'Incana' (grapevines), *37*

W
Washington state, *134–35,*
179
water. *See* rain gardens;
water gardens;
wetlands
water gardens, 167, 169
waterlillies, *166,* 167
Wave Hill, Bronx, NY, *43,
229*

Wayne, PA, *176–77*
weather extremes, 179, 187
weeds, 20–21
Weeping Camperdown
elm tree (*Ulmus glabra*
'Camperdownii'), 148
weeping Higon cherry
(*Prunus subhirtella*
'Pendula Plena Rosea'),
183
Weigela florida 'Fine Wine',
136
Weigela subsessilis 'Canary'
flowers, *29*
Weigela 'Wine and Roses',
132
wetlands, 167
wheatstraw celosia, *210*
white (color), 137, 140, *141*
Wichuraiana roses, 75
wide-open spaces, 161,
162–63
"wild" beach rose (*R.
rugosa*), 75
wild plants. *See* local
species
willow tree (*Salix alba*), 53,
208
Willowwood Arboretum,
NJ, *164*
Wilson, Ernest Henry, 185
winter, 50, 51, 52, 53, 54, 55
winter aconite (*Eranthis*
spp.), 76
winterberry holly, 47
winter honeysuckle
(*Lonicera fragrantissima*)
(evergreen), 53
winter jasmine (*Jasminum
nudiflorum*) (evergreen),
53
winter savory (*Satureja
montana*), 206
wintersweet (*Chimonanthus
praecox*) (evergreen), 53
Wirtz, Jacques, 222
Wisteria, 208
Wisteria floribunda
'Longissima Alba', *92*
Wisteria frutescens, 100–101
Wisteria sinensis, 100–101
Wisteria venusta (syn. *W.
brachybotrys*) 'Alba', *102,*
103

witch hazel varieties
(*Hamamelis* x
intermedia), 53, *53, 53,*
140
*Wolfgang von Goethe,
Johann, 139*
woodlands, 20, *158, 159*
wood poppy (*Stylophorum
diphyllum*), 87
woody plants, 95, 169, 207
World's Columbian
Exposition (Chicago
Worlds Fair of 1893), 85
wormwood (*Artemisia
genus*), 111
Wrinkle, Louise, 12, *22,* 25,
140

X
Xanthorhiza simplicissima
(yellowroot), 47, *47*

Y
yarrow, 35
yellow angel's trumpet
(*Brugmansia* sp.),
180–81
yellowroot (*Xanthorhiza
simplicissima*), 47, *47,* 76
yellow twig dogwood
(*Cornus sericea* 'Silver
and Gold'), 52
Yoshino (*Someiyoshino*), 182
ypripedium reginae var.
albolabium (lady's
slipper orchid), 62
Yucca filamentosa 'Color
Guard' (variegated
evergreen), 52, *53, 154*

Z
Zantedeschia 'Crystal Blush'
(Calla lily), *67, 209*
Zen gardens, *186,* 187
Zenobia (genera), 59
Zinnia hybrids, *220*
zinnias, 41, *144,* 147
Zone denial, 224, 225
Zones. *See* USDA Zones